FOOD FOR THE GODS
New Light on the Ancient Incense Trade

Claude Lorrain (1648) 'Seaport with the embarkation of the Queen of Sheba'

'When the Queen of Sheba heard about the fame of Solomon, and his relation to the name of the Lord, she came to test him with hard questions. Arriving at Jerusalem with a very great caravan – with camels carrying spices, large quantities of gold, and precious stones – she came to Solomon and talked with him about all that she had on her mind. Solomon answered all her questions; ... And she gave the king one hundred and twenty talents of gold, large quantities of spices, and precious stones. Never again were so many spices brought in as those the Queen of Sheba gave to King Solomon. King Solomon gave the Queen of Sheba all she desired, whatsoever she asked, besides what he had given her out of his royal bounty; then she left and returned with all her retinue to her own country'

(I Kings 10)

FOOD FOR THE GODS
New Light on the Ancient Incense Trade

edited by

David Peacock and David Williams

Illustrations edited by Penny Copeland

With contributions by Joanna Bird, Lucy Blue, Sunil Gupta, Sarah James, Alexander Sedov, Myra Shackley and Caroline Singer

Published by
Oxbow Books, Park End Place, Oxford OX1 1HN

© Oxbow Books and the authors, 2007

ISBN 978 1 84217 225 4   1 84217 225 5

A CIP record for this book is available from the British Library

This book is available direct from

Oxbow Books, Park End Place, Oxford OX1 1HN
(Phone: 01865-241249; Fax: 01865-794449)

and

The David Brown Books Company
PO Box 511, Oakville, CT 06779, USA
(Phone: 860-945-9329; Fax: 860-945-9468)

or from our website

www.oxbowbooks.com

Cover design by Andy Hague: a frankincense tree in Dhofar, southern Oman.

Printed by
Short Run Press, Exeter

Contents

List of Illustrations   vii

Contributors   x

Preface   xiii

Chapter 1: Introduction   1
          David Peacock and David Williams

Chapter 2: The Incense Kingdoms of Yemen: an Outline History   4
          of the South Arabian Incense Trade
          Caroline Singer

Chapter 3: Basalt as Ships' Ballast and the Roman Incense Trade   28
          David Peacock, David Williams and Sarah James

Chapter 4: The Port of Qana' and the Incense Trade   71
          Alexander Sedov

Chapter 5: Frankincense in the 'Triangular' Indo-Arabian-Roman   112
          Aromatics Trade
          Sunil Gupta

Chapter 6: Incense in Mithraic Ritual: the Evidence of the Finds   122
          Joanna Bird

Chapter 7: Incense and the Port of Adulis   135
          David Peacock and Lucy Blue

Chapter 8: Frankincense and Myrrh today   141
          Myra Shackley

List of Illustrations

Fig. 2.1   The southern sluice-gate of the Mārib Dam. An irrigation system at Mārib is thought to have been in operation from *c*. 3000 BC.
Fig. 2.2   A frankincense tree growing in the Nejd region of Dhofar, southern Oman.
Fig. 2.3   A woman from the Hawjeri region of eastern Dhofar harvesting frankincense in the traditional manner.
Fig. 2.4   Frankincense trees flourish in the rocky limestone terrain of Wadi Do'an, Ḥaḍramawt.
Fig. 2.5   The ruins of the Shaqir palace at Shabwa.
Fig. 2.6   Map of main places mentioned in the text.
Fig. 2.7   Remains of the temple of Syn at Shabwa.
Fig. 2.8   The south gate at Timna', with a lengthy inscription in Qatabanian.
Fig. 2.9   A stele in the marketplace at Timna'. The rules of the market were inscribed on all four sides.
Fig. 2.10 Pillars of the so called Mahram Bilqis in Mārib.
Fig. 2.11 Ottoman and pre-Islamic ruins at the site of the Minaean city of Yathil, now known as Baraqish.
Fig. 2.12 One of the nine species of *Boswellia* tree growing on the island of Socotra.
Fig. 2.13 A Dragon's blood tree on the island of Socotra.
Fig. 2.14 The Y-shaped harbour and southern walls of Sumhuram.
Fig. 2.15 The settlement of Sumhuram. The square well in the foreground is thought to be part of the Ilum temple.
Fig. 2.16 The flat-topped volcanic rock at Qana', known today as Ḥuṣn al-Ghurāb, was used as a look-out point and landmark.
Fig. 3.1   Distribution of ballast at Quseir al-Qadim.
Fig. 3.2   The Red Sea and northern Indian Ocean showing coastal outcrops of volcanic rocks.
Fig. 3.3   The Red Sea and northern Indian Ocean showing ancient sites mentioned in the text.
Fig. 3.4   The Ḥaḍramawt coast showing volcanic outcrops.
Fig. 3.5   A comparison of ballast samples and rocks from Al Birk, based on published sources. Ba and Ni.
Fig. 3.6   A comparison of ballast and rocks from the Red Sea islands of Zubair, Hanīsh Zukur and Perim, based on published sources. Zr and Sr.
Fig. 3.7   A comparison of ballast and rocks from Kharaz, Southern Yemen, based on published sources. Ba and Nb.
Fig. 3.8   A comparison of ballast and rocks from Kharaz, Southern Yemen, based on published sources. Ba and Sr.

viii *List of Illustrations*

Fig. 3.9	A comparison of ballast and rocks from Shuqrā, Southern Yemen, based on published sources. Zr and Rb.
Fig. 3.10	A comparison of ballast and samples purchased in Oman, believed to be from Hormuz. Ce and Sr.
Fig. 3.11	A comparison of selected areas which were potential sources for the ballast. Rb and Zn.
Fig. 3.12	A comparison of the rocks of Aden, Adulis, Edd and Assab. Li and TiO_2.
Fig. 3.13	A comparison of ballast and rocks from Djibouti. Rb and Zn.
Fig. 3.14	A comparison of ballast and rocks from Qana'. Rb and Zn.
Fig. 3.15	A comparison of ballast and rocks from Adulis. Rb and Zn.
Fig. 3.16	A comparison of ballast and rocks from Aden. Rb and Zn.
Fig. 3.17	A comparison of ballast with rocks from Adulis and the Ḥaḍramawt. Zr and Sr.
Fig. 3.18	Intermediate and acid ballast compared with rocks from Adulis, Kharaz, Aden, Little Aden and Perim, based partly on published sources. Zn and Sr.
Fig. 3.19	Obsidian from Quseir al-Qadim, Adulis and Dhalak Kebir compared with source rocks from Gela'elo, Bera'esoli, Mersa Fatma and Aliko. Ba and Zr.
Fig. 3.20	Obsidian samples and source rocks as in Fig. 3.19. Nb and Zr.
Fig. 3.21	Routes across the Indian ocean according to Pliny and the Periplus.
Fig. 4.1	1. Ḥuṣn al-Ghurāb, view from the Halaniya island; 2. Bi'r 'Ali Settlement (ancient Qana'), ruins of structures (view from the slope of Ḥuṣn al-Ghurāb).
Fig. 4.2	Bi'r 'Alī Settlement (ancient Qana'). Sketch plan: Areas I-VII ; 1 Burial Structure.
Fig. 4.3	1. Ḥuṣn al-Gurab, ruins of a lighthouse on the summit; 2. Bi'r 'Alī Settlement (ancient Qana'), temple of local deity (Area VII).
Fig. 4.4	Ḥuṣn al-Ghurāb. Structure on the summit (light-house), plan (after S.S.Shirinskiy).
Fig. 4.5	Ḥuṣn al-Ghurāb. Structure on the summit (lighthouse), variant of reconstruction.
Fig. 4.6	Bi'r 'Alī Settlement (ancient Qana'). Area VI, 'lower' (BA-I) period, plan of excavated structures.
Fig. 4.7	Bi'r 'Alī Settlement (ancient Qana'). Area VI, pottery of the 'lower' (BA-I) period.
Fig. 4.8	Bi'r 'Alī Settlement (ancient Qana'). Area VI, pottery of the 'lower' (BA-I) period.
Fig. 4.9	Bi'r 'Alī Settlement (ancient Qana'). Area VI, pottery of the 'lower' (BA-I) period.
Fig. 4.10	Bi'r 'Alī Settlement (ancient Qana'). Area VI, pottery of the 'lower' (BA-I) period.
Fig. 4.11	Bi'r 'Alī Settlement (ancient Qana'). Area VI, pottery of the 'lower' (BA-I) period.
Fig. 4.12	Bi'r 'Alī Settlement (ancient Qana'). Area II, plan of excavated structure.
Fig. 4.13	Bi'r 'Alī Settlement (ancient Qana'). Area IV, plan of excavated structure.
Fig. 4.14	Bi'r 'Alī Settlement (ancient Qana'). Area VI, plan of excavated structures of the 'middle' (BA-II) period.
Fig. 4.15	Bi'r 'Alī Settlement (ancient Qana'). Area III, 'late synagogue', plan of excavated structure.
Fig. 4.16	Bi'r 'Alī Settlement (ancient Qana'). Area VI, pottery of the 'middle' (BA-II) period.
Fig. 4.17	Bi'r 'Alī Settlement (ancient Qana'). Area VI, pottery of the 'middle' (BA-II) period.
Fig. 4.18	Bi'r 'Alī Settlement (ancient Qana'). Area II, pottery of the 'middle' (BA-II) period.
Fig. 4.19	Bi'r 'Alī Settlement (ancient Qana'). Area I, plan of excavated structures.

List of Illustrations

Fig. 4.20 Bi'r 'Alī Settlement (ancient Qana'). Area V, plan of excavated structure.
Fig. 4.21 Bi'r 'Alī Settlement (ancient Qana'). Area I, pottery of the 'upper' (BA-III) period.
Fig. 4.22 Bi'r 'Alī Settlement (ancient Qana'). Areas I and IV, pottery of the 'upper' (BA-III) period.
Fig. 4.23 Bi'r 'Alī Settlement (ancient Qana'). Area I, pottery of the 'upper' (BA-III) period.
Fig. 4.24 Bi'r 'Alī Settlement (ancient Qana'). Area III, 'early synagogue', Greek graffito (tracing).
Fig. 5.1 Map of the Arabian Sea showing the 'triangular' trade.
Fig. 5.2 Indian cooking wares from Kamrej, Khor Rori.
Fig. 5.3 The site of Kamrej.
Fig. 5.4 Rice from Kamrej excavations.
Fig. 5.5 Cloth remains from Kamrej.
Fig. 5.6 Aksumite sherd from Kamrej.
Fig. 5.7 Dressel 2–4 amphorae from Nevasa.
Fig. 6.1 1: handled tazza from Friedberg (after Horn 1994). 2: pierced-rim vessel from Zeughausstrasse, Köln (after Binsfeld 1960–61). 3: pierced-rim vessel from Köln mithraeum I (after Behrens 1952). 4: pierced-rim vessel from Mainz (after von Pfeffer 1960 and Huld-Zetsche 1984). 5: pierced-rim vessel from Stockstadt mithraeum II (after Schleiermacher 1928 and a photograph courtesy of M. Marquart, Museen der Stadt Aschaffenburg).
Fig. 6.2 Detail of the vessel shown on Fig. 1:2, with Sol-Mithras offering incense; the altar is largely missing (after Ristow 1974).
Fig. 6.3 A: snake and crater with what may be a member of the Lion grade placing an offering on an altar, from the Ladenburg / Mannheim tauroctony (after Schwertheim 1974). B: lion, snake and crater from the Heddernheim III tauroctony (after Huld-Zetsche 1986; 1994). C: lion, snake and crater from the Heidelberg-Neuenheim, tauroctony (after Schwertheim 1974). D: lion, snake and crater from a samian beaker, Mühlthal (after Garbsch 1985). 1:2.
Fig. 6.4 A: Cautes holding a pine-cone, from the Tîrgșor tauroctony (after Vermaseren 1960). B: masked Lion with pine-cones, from Rusicade (after Vermaseren 1956).
Fig. 7.1 Adulis: location map.
Fig. 7.2 Cosmas Indicopleustes' map of the Adulis area. From Wolska-Conus 1968.
Fig. 8.1 Ancient frankincense routes.
Fig. 8.2 Modern frankincense tourist routes.

Contributors

Joanna Bird

Joanna Bird is a freelance archaeologist specialising in ceramic archaeology. She is best known for her extensive work on Roman fine wares, but here discusses pottery types which have a bearing on the use of incense in Mithraism.

Dr Lucy Blue

Dr Blue is lecturer in maritime archaeology in the University of Southampton. She specialises in ancient ports and is currently co-director of the Eritro-British project at Adulis.

Dr Sunil Gupta

Dr Gupta is Assistant Keeper (Education and Research) at the Allahabad Museum, India and co-editor of the Journal of Indian Ocean Archaeology. He is a widely published expert on the archaeology of Early Historic India and the early Indian Ocean world. He is currently writing a book on Indo-Roman sea trade, the subject of his doctoral thesis.

Dr Sarah James

Dr James is an analytical geochemist from the Department of Mineralogy, Natural History Museum, London and has a long experience of the analysis of geological materials. She specialises in Inductively Couple Plasma Spectrometry, and is here concerned with the whole rock analysis of basalt. Here she explains her methods in terms comprehensible to the layman.

Professor David Peacock

Professor Emeritus, Department of Archaeology, University of Southampton. He is a specialist on Roman Egypt, and has excavated at Mons Claudianus, Mons Porphyrities and more recently at the Roman port of Myos Hormos (Quseir al-Qadim). He is also interested in the application of geology to archaeology.

Professor Alexander Sedov

Professor Sedov was formerly head of the Department of Ancient Near Eastern Studies in Moscow. He is now Director of the Oriental Museum and has worked for many years at Qana' and Khor Rori.

The Revd Professor Myra Shackley

Myra Shackley is Professor of Culture Resource Management at Nottingham Trent University and Priest-Vicar at the cathedral of Southwell Minster. She has a particular interest in the management of visitors to World Heritage sites, and in issues related to tourism and cultural heritage. Her most recent books include *Visitor Management; Case studies from World Heritage Sites* (1998) and *Managing Sacred Sites; service provision and visitor experience* (2001). Her interest in frankincense stems partly from fieldwork on frankincense tourism in the Middle East and partly from a fondness for its use in liturgy as part of her role as an Anglican priest.

Caroline Singer

Caroline Singer is a freelance writer with an Islamic art historical background, specialising in Yemen and Oman. A recent book is *Yemen: The land of the Queen of Sheba*, an historical account of Yemen published in conjunction with the British Museum Queen of Sheba exhibition.

Dr David Williams

Senior Research Fellow in ceramics and lithics, Department of Archaeology, University of Southampton. Dr Williams has wide interests in ceramic petrology and lithic identification. He has analysed pottery from Qana' and has made a special study of Roman amphorae. Here he is principally concerned with basalt ballast.

Preface

It is now a quarter of a century since Nigel Groom wrote his seminal work on the ancient incense trade. Since then there has been growing interest in the subject and much new research, particularly in the producing lands. Incense was a luxury, but one which was consumed in prodigious quantities by the ancient world, in temples and funerals, but also in private homes. In particular, it was the stuff of emperors.

It was once thought, on the evidence of classical sources, that incense, particularly frankincense and myrrh, grown along the southern Arabian coast, was collected in the port of Qana' in Yemen and then transported northwards by caravan across Arabia to Gaza, whence it would be shipped to the Mediterranean consumers. Recent scientific work on basalt ships' ballast from the coastal sites of Roman Egypt has shown that the bulk originated in Qana'. It is postulated that this was a result of ships from Qana' laden with the relatively light incense, dumping their ballast when they arrived in Egypt to take on heavier commodities for the return leg. It is suggested that this work emphasises an alternative route for the movement of incense. It may have been as important (or more so) than the overland route noted by Pliny (possibly because of its curiosity value).

This work from an unconventional angle, led the editors to investigate the current state of research into incense and it was at once apparent that there is so much new evidence, an overview would be timely. It seemed that a book reviewing the state of the art would meet a very real need. It would now be imprudent to cover the entire chronological field as was possible 25 years ago and we therefore proposed to concentrate, although not exclusively, on the Roman period, which has until now been least studied. Certain key specialists were approached and all agreed willingly to contribute. Due to their enthusiasm and efficiency it has been possible to create this book relatively quickly. The contributors cover a truly international spectrum with papers from workers in Britain, Russia, and India. We believe that these papers blend happily together to produce a coherent and interesting volume. The work is intended to complement Nigel Groom's book *Frankincense and Myrrh: A Study of Arabian Incense Trade* recently reprinted after 25 years. Mention should also be made of the Italian conference proceedings *Profumi d'Arabia*, published by L'Erma di Bretschneider in 1997 and edited by Alessandra Avanzini. We try to build on the firm foundation laid in these works, at the same time exploring new directions and methodology.

In this work, a number of authors look at the same material from different angles. We believe there is a great benefit in this and thus we have not tried to eliminate reiteration of the same themes in different papers. They stand as they were intended – the views of the individual authors. On the other hand Arabic transliterations are a problem. Where possible we have tried to make these accord with the usage in the second edition of the

Encyclopedia of Islam as usually adopted by British Arabists. An exception is Mecca for Makka, and sometimes local colloquial usages have been preferred. We are grateful to Dr A.C.S. Peacock for his advice.

We are greatly indebted to Professor Valerie Maxfield for refereeing this work and for her helpful comments which have enabled us to make improvements. We are also indebted to Carl Phillips for drawing our attention to the Claude painting used as frontispiece and to the National Gallery, London for permission to reproduce it.

David Peacock and David Williams
Southampton, January 2006

Chapter 1: Introduction

David Peacock and David Williams

The story of incense is one of the most intriguing in both eastern and western culture. From the first millennium BC to the present day it has been sought after and valued on a par with precious metals or gems. While there was undoubtedly symbolism in the choice of the three Sages' gifts to the infant Christ, it is interesting to note that frankincense and myrrh, as well as gold, were thought worthy markers of this epoch making event. The history of the exploitation of the resins of *Boswellia* and *Commiphora* trees is outlined by Caroline Singer who relates how these unprepossessing plants produced a substance sought by emperors, priests, apothecaries and the common man alike. Throughout its long history it was a luxury associated with prestige and religion: the story is almost stranger than fiction. She gives a comprehensive account of the history of incense discussing the demand, the production and the growing areas as well as the means of distribution. As Myra Shackley shows, in the final chapter, its importance in religion persists to this day and it is used by perfumers, aromatherapists and in the production of medicines. Finally she assesses the potential for incense driven tourism. Its production is a significant element in the economy of the southern Arabian peninsular and modern frankincense routes bear an uncanny resemblance to the ancient.

Thus, while some of the papers in this volume attempt to paint a broad picture, emulating and updating Nigel Groom's seminal work *Frankincense and Myrrh: A Study of the Arabian Incense Trade,* our main, but not sole, focus is on the Roman period and the archaeology of incense. While the texts are informative they tell but part of the story and if the study is to progress we need the supplementary information that only archaeology can furnish. Here there is a problem because, unlike many luxury items – fine pottery, metals or even textiles, it is seldom preserved in the archaeological record. A small fragment of frankincense, probably Islamic rather than Roman in date, was found in the recent excavations at Quseir al-Qadim, but it is in any case a single small fragment from an extensive excavation conducted over 5 years. Incense can be preserved in archaeological quantities, but it was so valuable that it was conserved and consumed rather than being discarded as rubbish. The chances of finding incense are considerably less than those of finding gold. Gold is a stable enduring material, incense requires suitable conditions of aridity or wetness to ensure its survival. If we are to study the use and distribution of incense this must usually be done indirectly, by looking for clues in more durable media. Fortunately, incense requires special apparatus for burning and the dissemination of aroma so that incense burners are without doubt a major means of getting to grips with the problem. Unfortunately, there have been few studies, partly because it is hard to be certain

Sea, across the desert to the Nile thence to Alexandria from where it would travel to the major cities of the Mediterranean. The seaways would have been considerably easier and more ecomomic than the overland caravan route along the length of the Arabian peninsular to Gaza discussed by Pliny (*Natural History*, 12, 32). The question now remains which was the more important. And this is something only archaeology can attempt to answer, which must be a subject for future research.

Of course the incense trade cannot be studied in isolation. Sunil Gupta argues partly from the little known ancient Indian economic treatise, the *Arthasastra*, and from his own work at Kamrej, that frankincense exports from the Ḥaḍramawt stimulated need for reciprocal supplies in a burgeoning economy. Noting significant quantities of Indian wares found on sites such as Khor Rori, Qana' and, to some extent, Egypt, he concludes that the balance of payment problem may have been partly met by an increased export to Arabia of Indian goods such as cereals, sesame oil, cloth and iron. He sees the situation as analogous to the British substitution of opium for gold, in the purchase of China tea during the 19th Century. The ports of southern Yemen were pivotal in this economic activity. At the centre of the incense trade lies Qana' and we are privileged to include a chapter by Alexander Sedov contributing an important new synthesis of the trading activities of the port based largely on his own analysis of the ceramic finds from recent excavations. He gives a fully documented account of the site: structures, stratigraphy, pottery and coins followed by an evaluation of their significance in the study of incense. Particularly striking is the discovery of incense warehouses at Qana', some with the precious commodity still in them. He also gives a valuable account of the Yemeni island of Socotra which was a source of aloe, frankincense and cinnabar. Finally he discusses the role of Khor Rori in Oman. In each case the starting point is his own original research, giving a valuable resumé of the findings of the most recent archaeological research in these regions. Incense is not seen in isolation but as part of a far reaching trade network evidenced by pottery and particularly amphorae from Italy, Rhodes and later Aqaba in Jordan. The incense trade can now be seen in its broader perspective.

Somaliland was also an important production area as Caroline Singer emphasises. In Chapter 7 we examine this in relation to Aksumite Adulis, now in Eritrea. It is suggested on the basis of literary sources backed by some tentative archaeological evidence, that Adulis could have been an intermediary, shipping aromatics northwards to Alexandria and Ayla (Aqaba). Recent fieldwork has resolved the question of the whereabouts of the Aksumite harbour of Adulis and of Adulis of the *Periplus of the Erythrean Sea*. We include a brief resumé of the main findings of this recent Eritro-British project.

One point to emerge forcibly from this collection of papers is the importance of southern Yemen in Rome's connection with India and the east. Salles (1993) has already claimed *it is unlikely that a cargo of western products shipped at Myos Hormos would have reached Muziris on the same boat at the end of a straight voyage, and vice-versa – direct shipments did certainly exist, but the argument here is that they were not a rule*. In his reading of the *Periplus* he sees a clear segmentation of the journey. The *Periplus* (26:.31–2) clearly states before the sack of Aden (soon before the book was written in the mid first century AD) vessels from India and Egypt met at this port as neither dared to make the full voyage. The new evidence in this book supports the view that Yemen was the trade hub, but it appears that after the demise of Aden this role was assumed by Qana'.

We do not deny that the direct route from Egypt to India would have been feasible, albeit with watering and provision stops, but there is no evidence from archaeology, or from the literature, to suggest it was the norm.

This book answers some questions but raises many more. If it stimulates more research in this important, but neglected, area of social and economic archaeology, it will have served a useful purpose.

Bibliography

Hallet, J., 1990. *The early Islamic soft stone industry*. Unpublished M.Phil. University of Oxford.

Harrell, J.A. and Max Brown, V., 2000. *Discovery of a steatite baram industry of the medieval Islamic period in Egypt's Eastern desert*. Abstract of paper delivered to American Research Center Egypt, Berkeley.

Salles, J.-F., 1993. The Periplus of the Erythrean Sea and the Arab-Persian Gulf. *Topoi*, 3 (2), 493–523.

Chapter 2: The Incense Kingdoms of Yemen:
An Outline History of the South Arabian Incense Trade

Caroline Singer

The overland trade in aromatics between South Arabia – that is, principally, the kingdoms of pre-Islamic Yemen – and the civilizations of Mesopotamia, Assyria, the Levant, the Mediterranean and Egypt, began in earnest at the start of the 1st millennium BC, and had an incalculable effect on the economic, cultural and linguistic life of the Middle East. However, even a cursory search among the sacred literature of ancient Egypt and Sumeria, Old Testament texts or the cuneiform records of Mesopotamia, reveals the importance of incense for religious and royal ceremonies long before the frankincense merchants started to arrive with their camel-trains from southern Arabia, in *c.* 10th to 8th century BC. The very early use of incense in Egypt, Greece, Mesopotamia and the Fertile Crescent, at least from the third millennium onwards, relied on sources much closer to home. The 'incense' mentioned so often in the Pentateuch[1] for example, was likely to have consisted of balsams, scented woods and herbs from the Levant, rather than frankincense from South Arabia. In Mycenaean Greece during the 14th and 13th centuries BC, scented oils, fragrant gums and incenses were used in funerals and worship, and were either procured from Phoenician traders, or manufactured from locally-produced oils and aromatic plants in palaces such as Knossos, Pylos and Zakro.

In ancient Egypt, the elaborate rituals prescribed in the *Book of the Dead* frequently stipulated the use of incense.[2] The Egyptians at this early stage obtained their supplies of frankincense and myrrh from the 'Land of Punt', a mysterious region in the Horn of Africa, which has still not been satisfactorily identified: scholars have located it anywhere from Uganda to Ethiopia.[3] From approximately 2500 to 1150 BC the Pharaohs imported gold, aromatics and other luxuries from Punt, sailing ships along the Red Sea coast down to Eritrea and Somalia. The most fruitful area seems to have been in northern Somalia, where frankincense and myrrh trees still grow abundantly. In the funerary temple of Queen Hatshepsut, *c.*1480 BC at Deir el-Bahari in Luxor, texts and wall paintings tell of an expedition to the Land of Punt to fetch 'fresh incense' and 'living incense trees' from the 'incense terraces of Punt'. The aim of this undertaking was to transport live frankincense and myrrh trees, and re-plant them in Egypt, thus securing a local supply of fragrant resin for religious rituals, without having to pay the high prices charged by the African merchants. The mission ultimately failed, because frankincense and myrrh trees require specific conditions in order to grow (see p. 8), none of which Egypt could provide.

The trade between Egypt and Punt seems to have gone into decline from *c.* 12th

Fig. 2.1. The southern sluice-gate of the Mārib Dam. An irrigation system at Mārib is thought to have been in operation from c. 3000 BC.

century BC. The rise of controlled, regular commercial exchange between South Arabia and the civilisations of the north, including Egypt, began between the 10th and 8th centuries BC. This was made possible by several converging factors – social, technological and economic – which together created the right conditions for an organised system of long-distance trade.

By the first millennium BC, the settled people of inland South Arabia had established a successful way of life based on the skilful management of highly specialised irrigation systems, and the prosperity and growth of these agricultural settlements gave rise to political, economic and social integration (Fig. 2.1). It was only when the South Arabians had the economic and social structures in place to provide a secure system of maintained roads, with well-stocked oases and shelters along the route, plus a regular supply of pack-animals, that they turned to commerce as a means of further enrichment. Donkeys had long been used to transport goods from one settlement to another, but the large-scale, highly organised exchange of commercial quantities of goods over long distances would not have been possible without one of the greatest technological advances in history: the domestication of the camel. Opinions differ as to the exact date of the camel's domestication, but it has been suggested that it began in southern Arabia during the second millennium BC.[4] This process, by which the camel became harnessed first as a pack animal and then as a riding animal, allowed the inhabitants of settlements and civilisations that had previously been separated by deserts and long distances, to meet, exchange goods, and develop a rich cultural and commercial interchange.

The two most important and most valuable commodities that the South Arabians carried to the cities of the north, came from the genera of balsam trees belonging to the *Burseraceae* family, known as *Boswellia* (frankincense) and *Commiphora* (myrrh). Both trees produce fragrant resin, which oozes from ducts beneath the bark. This was gathered annually by harvesters during the late spring and summer months, when the resin was most abundant. Once dried, the lumps of frankincense burned slowly on hot coals to release a pure white smoke and heady, astringent aroma that was greatly prized throughout the ancient world. Myrrh, a darker, oilier resin with a bitter-sweet aroma, was also valued, although it was used for different purposes, mainly medicinal, and was never purchased in such quantities as frankincense.

The South Arabian merchants also traded goods from abroad, such as cinnamon and pepper, silk, cardamom and turmeric, sandalwood, Dragon's blood resin and aloeswood. These goods arrived in trading ships which landed at South Arabian ports from Socotra, India, Sri Lanka and south-east Asia. South Arabian merchants purchased these exotic, highly prized goods and loaded them onto their camels in order to sell them in the distant markets of the Mediterranean, together with their supplies of frankincense and myrrh. The merchants passed all these luxury goods off as their own produce and, having transported them at great cost, priced them at a premium in the markets of the north.

From around the 8th century BC onwards, frankincense and myrrh became available to all who could afford it, and the fashion for burning fragrant resin spread throughout the civilized world. By 500 BC, Pythagoras had declared that Greek worshippers should burn frankincense instead of sacrificing animals to their deities. Sack-loads were burned on the golden altar of the temple of Bel in Babylon, and a thousand Babylonian talents (almost 25 tons) were given as a tribute payment by the Arabs of Gaza to the Persian king Darius in *c.* 496 BC, in exchange for autonomy within the Achaemenid empire. As the Mediterranean terminus for the incense trade routes, Gaza was strategically very important, and was one of only three provinces in the empire to be granted independent status. When Alexander the Great captured Gaza, he sent his old tutor Leonidas five hundred talents of frankincense and a hundred talents of myrrh. Plutarch[5] recounted that as a young boy, Alexander had heaped frankincense onto the fire as a sacrifice to the gods, and Leonidas had admonished him; 'when thou hast conquered the country where these sweet things grow, then be liberal of thy perfume; but now, spare that little thou hast at this present.' Alexander reportedly sent a message accompanying his gift to Leonidas: 'We do send thee plenty of frankincense and myrrh, because thou shouldest no more be a niggard unto the gods.'[6]

Frankincense and myrrh were highly sought-after throughout Egypt, Greece, Persia, Assyria, Babylon and Rome, to be burned opulently for guests in the home; as sacrificial gifts most pleasing to the gods, and as a way of honouring both the dead and the living. Herodotus, writing in the 5th century BC, described the habits of wealthy Babylonians, who would sit over incense to fumigate themselves before making love, and of Scythian women, who crushed cypress, cedar and frankincense into an aromatic paste and coated their skin with it as a beauty treatment.[7] Frankincense and myrrh are also found in countless recipes for medication: ground up, burned or melted down to treat everything from depression to infertility, from mouth-ulcers to haemorrhoids.

From the beginning of the 2nd century BC, the Romans began to use frankincense and myrrh in ever-greater quantities, and the four hundred-year period from the 2nd century BC to the 2nd century AD can be regarded as the zenith of the aromatics trade, with the territories ruled by Rome as the centre of consumption. Frankincense was considered by the Romans to be the finest, purest and most effective incense for propitiating the gods, and was burned in temples, at funerals, and on domestic altars throughout the empire. Its increased price during this time reflected its high demand, and its limited supply. Although myrrh was more expensive in Roman markets, demand was substantially less. It was used in perfumes and unguents, and to flavour wine, and, like frankincense, as an ingredient in medicine.

South Arabian merchants and their exotic, expensive cargoes excited great interest among scholars in the civilizations of Greece, Persia, Egypt and Rome. Greek geographers were particularly interested in the region they named *Eudaimôn Arabia*, or 'Arabia the Blessed' (in Latin, 'Arabia Felix'), and began to compile historical and geographical information about the distant land. The earliest account we have of southern Arabia comes from Herodotus, who wrote that the whole country 'exhales an odour marvellously sweet', and gave a vivid account of the flying snakes that circled around the frankincense trees.[8] Theophrastus, writing in around 295 BC, devotes a whole section of his *Enquiry into Plants* to frankincense and myrrh, and for the first time mentions, albeit inaccurately, the names of the South Arabian tribes who cultivated and traded in the aromatics: 'the trees of frankincense and myrrh grow partly in the mountains, partly on private estates at the foot of the mountains… the whole range, they said, belongs to the portion of the Sabaeans.'[9] Further information about the incense lands was supplied by Agatharchides of Cnidus in the 2nd century BC, and by Diodorus Siculus in the 1st century BC. Strabo of Pontus (*c.*64 BC – *c.* AD 25) added to the sum of knowledge about the South Arabians, quoting in large part from a study made by Eratosthenes of Cyrene (276–196 BC). He mentions the four largest tribes; the Minaeans, the Sabaeans, the Qatabanians and the Ḥaḍramites, and their capital cities, and wrote: 'all these cities are ruled by monarchs and are prosperous, being beautifully adorned with both temples and royal palaces.'[10] However, by far the most important source of information about the incense trade at its height, comes from Pliny the Elder (AD 23–79). His *Natural History*,[11] a vast compendium of geographical, ethnographical, botanical, agricultural and medical information, contains comments on the land in which the frankincense and myrrh trees grew; the harvesting techniques; the customs, languages and cities of the South Arabians; the incense trade itself – the length and route of the journey, the amount of taxes the merchants paid at each station, and a detailed description of the price, uses and popularity of frankincense and myrrh once the merchants had reached the Mediterranean.

* * * *

There are over 25 different species of frankincense trees. They grow in the Dhofar region of southern Oman; the Ḥaḍramawt and Mahra regions of Yemen; the island of Socotra; Ethiopia and Somalia, and in parts of Rajasthan and Madhya Pradesh in India. Every species produces a different quality of resin, from dark brown lumps yielding a bitter smoke, to pale tears which melt slowly and emit a fine, clean scent. The physical attributes of the trees differ according to the species, but a description of the *Boswellia* tree written

Fig. 2.2. A frankincense tree growing in the Nejd region of Dhofar, southern Oman.

by the traveller and political officer Bertram Thomas during his journey through Dhofar in 1930 gives a good impression: 'In appearance it is like a young sapling, having almost no central trunk, but from near to the ground there springs out a clump of branches which grow to a camel's height and more, with ash-coloured bark and tiny crumpled leaves.'[12] The very purest frankincense, both during the height of the ancient trade and today, comes from *Boswellia sacra* trees that flourish in the limestone hills, plains and valleys of Dhofar (Fig. 2.2). Myrrh trees grow in southern Oman and Yemen, in the 'Asir region and in Ethiopia and Somalia: myrrh comes from a number of different species of the genus *Commiphora*, but principally from *Commiphora myrrha*.

In southern Arabia, the harvesting of frankincense and myrrh was concentrated primarily in the Ḥaḍramawt region and latterly in Dhofar, although myrrh was also found in abundance in the area around Beihan. The *Boswellia* species is extremely sensitive to location and environment, and frankincense trees flourish in these areas because of several vital factors. Firstly, the trees require a limestone soil, which both Dhofar and the Ḥaḍramawt region provide in abundance. Secondly, they require moisture rather than rain. This is one of the main reasons why the climates of Ethiopia, Somalia, southern Yemen and particularly Dhofar, are so well suited to the growth of frankincense. From the end of May to the beginning of September, the region is visited by the *khareef*, the monsoon wind that blows across East Africa from the south-west, clipping the south of

Fig. 2.3. A woman from the hawjeri region of eastern Dhofar harvesting frankincense in the traditional manner.

Fig. 2.4. Frankincense trees flourish in the rocky limestone terrain of Wadi Do'an, Ḥaḍramawt.

Yemen and the island of Socotra. It brings dampness and drizzle, and in many areas, torrential rain and flash floods, for close to four months. A fine mist hovers over the coastal plain and central mountain range of Dhofar all summer long, turning the land a rich emerald green. The frankincense trees that grow in the Nejd region of Dhofar – a limestone escarpment beyond the mountains, at a height of 2,000 to 2,500 feet – have the advantage of being beyond the reach of the monsoon. Cool winds laden with water vapour sweep up from the coast to the mountains, creating dense clouds which, when evaporated, provide the trees of the Nejd plateau with enough moisture to flourish, without being drenched with rain. Those trees that grow along the coastal plain, where drizzly rain falls almost constantly for three or four months, produce a far inferior type of frankincense; the trees are known in the local Jibbali dialect as *irhiz*, or 'washed' and their dark, lumpy resin is the cheapest grade sold in the souq. Nejdi frankincense, from the Nejd plateau in central Dhofar, is of a much finer quality, golden in colour and with a good, clean smoke. The finest quality of all is known as *hawjeri*, and comes from the east of Dhofar. The trees here seem to enjoy optimum conditions for growth, and the resin they produce comes in perfect tear formations with a pale green tinge, and burns with a single white column of smoke, producing a potent fragrance.

Frankincense and myrrh trees cannot be cultivated in great numbers; they grow wild in gullies, on limestone plains and along wadis. Clumps of trees growing close together, or in a particular wadi, are known as a *manzilah* or 'grove'. For centuries, and until very recently, every *manzilah* was owned by a certain family, who had the right to harvest the trees. According to Pliny, 'there are not more than 3,000 families who retain the right of trading frankincense as a hereditary property, and consequently the members of these families are called sacred.' Pliny goes on to describe the method of harvesting; a technique that had changed little, it seems, from the days of Theophrastus writing in the 3rd century BC, and which remains remarkably similar to the harvesting techniques still in use today (Fig. 2.3). Pliny writes: 'They make an incision where the bark appears to be fullest of juice and distended to its thinnest; and the bark is loosened with a blow but not removed. From the incision, a greasy foam spurts out, which coagulates and thickens, being received on a mat of palm leaves... the residue adhering to the tree is scraped off with an iron tool, and consequently contains fragments of bark.'[13]

* * * *

There were four main kingdoms in the territory of South Arabia, known by the Greeks and Romans as *Eudaimôn Arabia* or *Arabia Felix*. They were concentrated around the desert region of pre-Islamic Yemen, an area known in the Middle Ages as the Sayhad, and nowadays as Ramlat al-Sab'atayn. Each kingdom had its own language, its own style of art and architecture, its own deities, rulers and laws. The principal Sayhadic kingdoms were the Kingdom of Ḥaḍramawt, with its capital at Shabwa; the Kingdom of Saba', with its capital at Mārib; the Kingdom of Qataban, whose capital was Timna', and the small Kingdom of Ma'in in the north, whose capital was Qarnaw. Myrrh trees flourished along the wadis of the Qatabanian empire, while frankincense grew and was harvested within the boundaries of the Ḥaḍramawt kingdom. Wadi Ḥaḍramawt itself is a vast dried-up river-bed approximately 160 km long and 300 meters deep, in the south-east of Yemen. Frankincense trees flourished in the limestone plateau of the Jol, in the gullies and river-beds off the main tributaries of the Ḥaḍramawt, such as Wadi Hagr, Wadi al-Masilah, Wadi Amaqin and Wadi Do'an, and in the Mahra region to the east. All of these areas were part of the Ḥaḍramawt kingdom, and came under the control of the ruler at Shabwa (Fig. 2.4).

Although only two of these four Sayhadic kingdoms actually produced fragrant resin, all were, to a greater or lesser extent, involved in the overland trade in aromatics. Each of the four capital cities acted as an important stopping-off point for the merchants, who were charged high taxes on entry, and who paid substantial fees for services such as food, shelter, water, fresh camels and local guides. The lucrative taxes and healthy profits of international commerce enriched pre-Islamic Yemen, and it was during the height of the aromatics trade that Sayhadic culture – its art, architecture, script and language – reached its apogee.

As has been indicated above, international commerce alone could not sustain an entire population, and the basis of life for all four South Arabian kingdoms was agriculture. Each kingdom was established in a great alluvial valley, in what has been described as an 'ecological pocket'; sheltered from the sea by mountains; protected from overland invasions by the desert, and each close to its own large wadi, which channelled floodwater during the biannual monsoons. These agricultural settlements relied for survival on complex

Fig. 2.5. The ruins of the Shaqir palace at Shabwa.

and well-maintained systems of irrigation. A network of dams and sluice-gates, channels, tunnels, canals and reservoirs, carried floodwater across vast stretches of land which was carefully planted with crops such as millet and barley, grapes, flax and sesame.

Consequently, the political structure of life in the Sayhadic kingdoms was based largely upon the organisation of the land. Unlike the nomadic pastoralism of the northern part of the Peninsula, theirs was a sedentary life centred upon towns and cities, fields and crops. The majority of people were farmers. Society was divided into village communities which were made up of one or more family groups, known as *bayts*. Several village communities, made up of *bayts* and clans, formed a *sha'b*. The *sha'b* was a tribal group, bound by genealogical ties, and could be anything from a small group to an entire nation. The ruler of each kingdom was responsible for military operations and the expansion of territory, for building towers, temples and defensive walls, and crucially, for the maintenance of the irrigation systems. In the kingdom of Saba', which was for centuries the strongest and most powerful of the Sayhadic kingdoms, the system of irrigation reached its zenith with the great Mārib Dam, whose extensive network of channels, canals and tunnels carried floodwater across 9,600 hectares of farmland. In the territory around Shabwa, the capital of the Ḥaḍramawt kingdom, some 12,000 acres were under cultivation, with a similar amount in the land surrounding the Qatabanian city of Timna'. Reports of verdant gardens, lush fields of crops, trees yielding shade and abundant fruit seem hard to believe when one stands amongst the desiccated ruins of the cities today (Fig. 2.5).

A network of trade routes had been established between the kingdoms for many centuries, carrying goods such as salt and wheat, wine, weapons, dates and animal skins from one fortified settlement to the next. These paths were the basis of the frankincense trade routes between the kingdoms of southern Arabia, and formed the starting-point of the route north (Fig. 2.6). Although Pliny talked about 'the high road' leading north, there was never simply one great 'Frankincense Route' as is popularly imagined, but rather a complex system of paths, with subsidiary tracks leading from the main roads to various stopping-off points, where goods could be bought and sold, and shelter and food obtained.

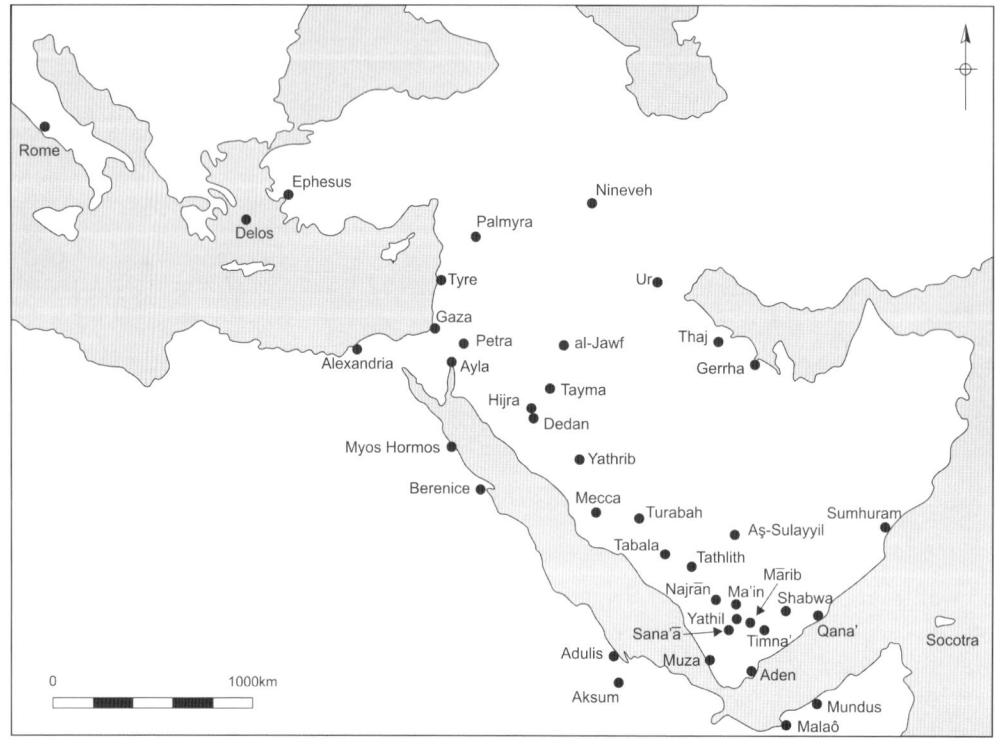

Fig. 2.6. Map of main places mentioned in the text.

* * * *

As has been noted, the Ḥaḍramawt kingdom was the epicentre of the South Arabian frankincense trade for many centuries. The territory ruled by the Ḥaḍramite kings contained an abundance of frankincense trees, while its capital city, Shabwa, was the mandatory point of taxation for all the caravans taking aromatics up to the civilisations of the north; a place which every merchant would have had to enter by law, and on pain of death, during his journey. Crucially, the ruler of Ḥaḍramawt controlled a network of wadis and fortified staging-posts which linked Shabwa to the port of Qana' on the Arabian sea. From *c.* 1st century AD, Qana' was one of the key points for the ancient aromatics trade, both on the overland and the maritime routes.

At the end of the harvest, in June or July each year, frankincense was carried down from the wadis where it had been gathered and dried; a journey which, according to Pliny, took eight days. It was taken through the vast limestone gates that marked the entrance to Shabwa, and up the main road that led from the palace of Shaqir to the great temple, home of the Ḥaḍramites' principal deity, Syn (Fig. 2.7). The basket-loads of resin went first to the priests in the temple, who weighed the goods and extracted their share in taxes.[14] Then the merchants purchased their supplies, and the overland journey north could begin.

The merchants themselves would probably not have been natives of Shabwa: there is no evidence for either Ḥaḍramites or Sabaeans acting as incense dealers. It appears instead that there was a very specific group of South Arabians who acted as long-distance traders, and who came from the kingdom of Ma'in. According to Pliny, the Minaeans were the best-known South Arabians in the Roman world. They took consignments of incense to Syria, Egypt and Assyria, as well as to the Greek and Roman world, and they established a dynamic network of traders, each under the supervision of a magistrate, in various key points along the route. There was a settlement of Minaean traders in the Qatabanian capital of Timna'; in the Ḥadramite capital Shabwa; in the oasis of Dedan, and in various cities in Egypt, including Alexandria.

The Minaeans supplied frankincense and myrrh to the holy temples of a city. The coffin of a Minaean frankincense merchant named Zayd'il, for example, dating to the 3rd century BC, was discovered at Memphis in Egypt.[15] Inscriptions on the side of the coffin make it clear that he supplied aromatics to the temples of Egypt and was afforded a dignified and costly Egyptian-style burial.

As professional long-distance merchants, the Minaeans would be well acquainted with all the preparations for the arduous journey north. The caravan leader would have an intimate knowledge of every water stop, settlement and taxation point along the way, and his job was to oversee the preparation and safe transportation of all the trade goods, and to ensure that there was enough food and water for the camels and merchants, especially along the most difficult stretches where there were no shelters or wells for miles around. A loaded baggage camel could travel around 2.5 miles per hour over level ground, and an average day's journey lasted for 10 hours, so the merchants could calculate quite

Fig. 2.7. Remains of the temple of Syn at Shabwa.

Fig. 2.8. The south gate at Timna', with a lengthy inscription in Qatabanian.

accurately how long the entire journey would take and where the caravan would stop at the end of each day.

The main caravan routes were usually maintained and secured by officials and soldiers of the kingdom through which they passed, and there would have been military settlements as well as taxation points along the way. From around the 5th century BC, most caravans consisted of at least 200 camels, together with the merchants and their servants. There was also usually an armed guard of local nomads who would travel ahead of the group to deflect attack from bandits, plus a local guide, to lead the merchants through difficult terrain. The purpose of travelling in such a large convoy was to ensure mutual security and protection. A lone trader leading a handful of camels across a vast inhospitable desert would not fare well.[16]

From Shabwa, the merchants may have travelled west through Wadi Markha, which was the main artery that linked Shabwa to the city of Timna', the capital of the Qatabanian kingdom (Fig. 2.8).[17] Myrrh trees grew throughout the region, as did indigo, one of the world's oldest dyes. Timna' was also the inland terminus for the Indian and far-eastern luxuries that were transported from the coast at Aden. Aden was the principal port of the Qatabanian kingdom, and one of the most important harbours on the international trade network. Ships from the east – mainly from India, Sri Lanka and south-east Asia – arrived at ports all along the South Arabian coast, but Aden, which the Greeks called *Arabia Emporion*, or 'Arabia's emporium', was for several centuries the most important port for the trade in luxury goods between Arabia, Africa and the east.

Fig. 2.9. A stele in the marketplace at Timna'. The rules of the market were inscribed on all four sides.

From Aden, the aromatics and luxuries were carried overland to Timna' in the north, where they were taxed, sorted and displayed in the market (Fig. 2.9). Timna' was an important city within the great eastern trade network, and fragments of pottery and glassware unearthed by archaeologists in the ruins of the city match finds in the sites of Arikamedu, an Indo-Roman trading station on the west coast of India, and in Seleucia on the River Tigris.

From Timna', the merchants travelled north towards Mārib. Pliny estimated that the journey from here to the Mediterranean spice entrepôt of Gaza was 2,437,500 steps – approximately 65 days' travelling. The direct route from Timna' to Mārib is a journey of about ninety miles across the desert. It is likely however, that most of the caravans would have avoided the high dunes and waterless conditions of this route, and opted for the longer journey, which led through a range of mountains separating Timna' from the kingdom of

Fig. 2.10. Pillars of the so called Mahram Bilqis in Mārib.

Fig. 2.11. Ottoman and pre-Islamic ruins at the site of the Minaean city of Yathil, now known as Baraqish.

Saba'. At the height of the incense trade there were several specially-constructed passes, including the Mablaqah pass and Nagd Marqad, built and maintained by the Qatabanian authorities, with level pavements, religious shrines and taxation points along the way, which channelled the merchants single-file through the mountains.

After a journey of ten days, the merchants arrived in Mārib, the capital of the Sabaean kingdom. Although the connection between the principal city of Saba' and the legendary Queen of Sheba is unproved, Mārib was certainly one of the largest of all the pre-Islamic Yemeni cities. It was surrounded by an oasis of green fields and trees, which were irrigated by the vast Mārib Dam (Fig. 2.1) and inhabited by grazing cattle and other livestock. The farmers who lived here produced an abundance of agricultural produce including fruit, vegetables, dates, grain, flax and sesame oil, which Sabaean merchants traded throughout the region. Mārib was a centre of power, and the heart of a great warrior nation. Many inscriptions recount battles fought and won by the Sabaean army; cities razed to the ground, entire tribes taken captive. It was also a religious centre, with many temples and shrines, including the vast oval temple to the Sabaeans' principal deity Almaqah, which stood outside the city gates (Fig. 2.10).

The merchants would have spent several days in Mārib, exchanging their goods and resting their camels. Then they would have headed north through Mārib's outlying fields and orchards, before entering the arid desert stretch of Kharibat Sa'ud, which led to the small state of Ma'in – the home of the frankincense merchants.

The kingdom of Ma'in lay on the outer fringes of the Sayhad, and was the final stop for the caravans before they left Arabia Felix and entered what the Romans called Arabia Deserta, or 'desert Arabia', in present-day Saudi Arabia and Jordan. The city of Yathil, now known as Baraqish, was a three-day journey from Mārib. It was not the Minaean capital, but was the region's most important frankincense-trading centre, a small, prosperous city ringed by high, strong walls and surrounded by fields and palm groves. From around the 1st century BC, Yathil was under the control of the Sabaeans, the kingdom of Ma'in having effectively been taken over by Saba'. However, it still continued to operate as an important stop on the route north (Fig. 2.11).

After leaving Yathil, the merchants would have travelled north to the Minaean capital, Qarnaw, and onwards into Arabia Deserta. For the first six or seven days, there was one single route leading north, taking the merchants to the oasis of Najrān, the first main stop, where they would find food, shelter and water.

After Najrān, some of the merchants would branch north-east to Qaryat al-Faw, heading for the port-town of Gerrha on the Persian Gulf. There is still a good deal of debate as to the exact location of Gerrha;[18] Strabo notes that it was inhabited by Chaldaean exiles from Babylon. The Gerrhaeans were a wealthy people, and made great profits from their position as middlemen, buying frankincense, myrrh and other aromatics from the South Arabian merchants, and the Seleucid kingdom to the north-east, to which they sold frankincense, myrrh and other aromatics. In turn the South Arabian merchants bought goods such as purple-dyed wools from Phoenicia, multicoloured textiles from Persia and embroideries from southern Anatolia from the Gerrhaeans.

The next stop on the route north was Yathrib, a key trading town and a thriving oasis famous for its dates. In Islamic times it became known as al-Medina – short for *madinat an-nabi'*, 'the Prophet's city'. It was here that the Prophet Mohammed found sanctuary in AD 622, fleeing persecution in Mecca. Even before the days of the Prophet, Yathrib was an important stop for the incense caravans, and for pilgrims, who flocked to the holy city of Mecca several days' journey to the south-west.

After Yathrib, some of the merchants would have split off from the main route and headed either north-east to southern Mesopotamia, or due north to Taymā' on the south-western edge of the great Nafud Desert, and then on to western Babylonia or Assyria, where they exchanged their aromatics for silver, precious stones and purple-dyed cloaks. The route to the Mediterranean, Damascus and Egypt, however, continued north-west to the next oasis called Dedan, now known as al-'Ula, seven days' journey from Yathrib, where a permanent colony of Minaean merchants lived until probably some time in the 1st century BC. Dedan was the seat of the North Arabian Lihyanite kingdom, and a commercial hub where several trade routes met. From here, a road led west to the Red Sea coast.

It appears that the importance of Lihyanite Dedan as a political and economic centre suffered a decline from *c.* 1st century BC, while the settlement of Hegra – known today as Mada'in Salih – which is less than 20 km north of Dedan, became the main centre in the Dedan valley during the latter half of the same century. Hegra lay in a sandy plain surrounded by rugged mountains. From the 1st century BC until AD 106, this area was under the control of the Nabataeans, a formerly nomadic people of obscure origin, who settled in southern Jordan and expanded north to the Hawran and south to the Hejaz. The Nabataeans established a kingdom and a series of settlements whose survival was based upon a successful system of irrigation, and whose economy was enriched through control of this important section of the overland trade routes. At its height, the Nabataean kingdom stretched from the southern oasis of Hegra, north to the southern Negev and for a short while included Damascus. The Nabataeans were a literate people – Aramaic was the official written language – and were involved in the asphalt trade of the Dead Sea. According to Strabo (*Geog.* 16, 4, 26), they imported goods such as brass and iron, purple cloth, saffron and works of art.

After Hegra the main route carried on northwards to Tabuk, which was another important hub of trade, and thence to Ma'an. Merchants travelling north to Syria, Phoenicia and Anatolia would have travelled through Petra, the seat of the Nabataean kings. The Nabataean port of Leukê Kômê, the 'white village' lay on the Red Sea coast, to the south of Petra. Up until the late 1st century BC it seems that Leukê Kômê mainly dealt with goods travelling to and from Egypt. With the rise of the maritime trade routes linking the Roman-controlled Red Sea ports of Egypt with southern Arabia and the coast of India in the 1st century AD, (a process described in more detail below), cargoes from East Africa and South Arabia would also have arrived here. All goods arriving at this port were subject to a 25 per cent tax by Nabataean customs officials, before being transported north to Petra.

For many merchants, the final stop on this northward journey was Gaza, the main spice entrepôt of the ancient Graeco-Roman world. It lay at the southern edge of the Mediterranean, midway between Jerusalem and Alexandria, and acted as the terminus for the overland incense routes, and a springboard for the onward journeys to Egypt, Palestine and Mesopotamia. From Gaza, frankincense was shipped to Alexandria, which from the 1st century AD was an important sorting and processing centre for frankincense destined for the Roman Empire. All goods arriving at the harbour were charged with the standard 'Alexandrian tariff', an import tax of 25 per cent. Once it had been sorted and packaged, the frankincense left Alexandria in great cargo-ships which plied the Mediterranean and deposited supplies of incense at all the main ports along the coast.

* * * *

To this deeply-entrenched pattern of overland trade was added, in the 1st century BC, a new set of routes, and a new pattern of Indian-Arabian-Mediterranean trade. In his *Geography*,[19] Strabo writes that, in around 120 BC, a half-drowned Indian sailor was found washed up on the Red Sea coast of Egypt and taken to Alexandria, where he was looked after and taught Greek. Once he could communicate he explained that he was a Tamil from southern India, and had been shipwrecked in a vessel which had sailed across the Indian Ocean to Arabia, and thence north up the Red Sea to Egypt. The Indian promised his hosts that he would teach them how to navigate the Red Sea south from the Egyptian coast and across to India, something they had previously been unable to do.

From at least the 2nd millennium BC, ships had been sailing between Mesopotamia, Arabia and India in order to conduct trade. The Arabs and Indians learned to exploit the seasonal monsoon winds that blow from the south-west during the summer and from the north-east in winter, speeding their journey across the Indian Ocean. However, for centuries, Greek and Egyptian sailors had been unable to make the journey down the Red Sea and across to India, because the Red Sea has its own strong wind patterns which do not always correspond to the monsoon seasons. Traditionally, goods from Indian and Arabian ships had been carried to Aden, while ships from the Red Sea ports of Egypt sailed the *c.* 100 nautical miles south to Aden to pick them up.

A Greek helmsman named Hippalos had recorded the secret of the monsoon winds in the early 1st century BC, realising that they started up and died down at certain predictable moments each season. In the spring of 116 BC, a diplomat and geographer named Eudoxus of Cyzicus, following the shipwrecked Tamil sailor's directions, reportedly made the pioneering journey, sailing from the Egyptian shores of the Red Sea to India, and returning the following year 'with a cargo of perfumes and precious stones.'[20]

At first only a few ships made the annual journey from Egypt to India each summer, at the start of the monsoon season. However, in 30 BC, the Roman Emperor Augustus brought Egypt under Roman administration, ushering in a period of great prosperity and peace. With Egypt and its Red Sea ports now part of the Roman empire, the volume of sea-traffic increased at an incredible rate. Vessels laden down with Roman goods such as textiles, grain, oil, wine, copper and tin, cosmetics, fragrant ointments, horses, pack mules, silver and gold artefacts, expensive clothing and – most importantly – sacks of coins, departed from the ports of Myos Hormos and Berenike on the Red Sea coast of Egypt. They stopped off at ports along the coast of southern Arabia, principally Aden, the Ḥadramite port of Qana', and the great headland of Syagros (Ra's Fartak) in Mahra, before crossing the ocean to the Malabar coast. Strabo noted that in his day 120 vessels sailed regularly from Egypt to India, whereas previously very few made the journey.[21]

There were two main trade routes that opened up with the discovery of the monsoon passage. Both departed from the Red Sea ports of Egypt every July, and both journeys spanned approximately 3,000 nautical miles. The first, the African route, travelled down the Red Sea coast, through the Bab al Mandab Strait and along the eastern coast of Africa to the port of Rhapta, near present-day Dar es-Salaam. Ships on this route did not venture over to the Arabian coast. Their journey took around two years – twice as long as the route to India – but it was safe, cheap, and involved only short coastal hauls, so it was generally favoured by the owners of smaller crafts.

The second journey was altogether a larger-scale operation, and far more risky. It required a ship of 500 tonnes or more, strong enough to withstand ocean storms and currents. Merchants would set off on this journey to the east from one of the Egyptian ports on the Red Sea coast, passing through the Bab al-Mandab Strait to the southern coast of Arabia, where they would dock at the ports of Aden and Qana'. From there they would set sail for the open waters of the Indian Ocean, reaching the coast of south-west India by September. On their return they would stop at a string of ports along the Red Sea coasts of Africa and Arabia, where they could exchange their eastern goods for local produce. Then they would head back to the Egyptian ports of Myos Hormos and Berenike. There, consignments of African, Indian and Arabian treasures such as animals and spices, ivories, gold, frankincense and myrrh, were sent overland on camel caravans, via a chain of fortified watering-stations, to Coptos, on the banks of the Nile. From Coptos, the goods were shipped up-river to the commercial hub of the Egyptian Roman empire, the city of Alexandria, where frankincense was sorted,[22] and goods were distributed throughout the Mediterranean world.

At every harbour on both these routes, there were different commodities for sale, and local traders demanded a variety of goods in exchange. Some ports preferred gold and coins, others were content to use barter. Some wanted cloth and silver statues, others required cereals and olive oil. The journey from the Red Sea to India involved stopping at many ports along the way, and so planning a voyage was a difficult task, requiring many years' experience. A handbook for sailors, written in the middle years of the 1st century AD, affords invaluable insights into the maritime trade at this time. The *Periplus Maris Erythraei*, or 'Periplus of the Erythraean [Red] Sea',[23] was written by an anonymous Greek sea captain living in Egypt. It was intended as a practical manual for seafarers trading between Roman Egypt, East Africa, southern Arabia and India. The *Periplus* described the people and geography of the various lands along the way, the languages spoken, the food eaten and the likes and dislikes of the local rulers. It provided information about the tides and anchorages along the route, and listed in meticulous detail the commodities to be bought and sold at each port. The Roman traders, for example, loaded their ships with supplies of gold and silver bullion, Alexandrian glass, barley, wheat, sesame oil, wine from Italy and Syria, cloth, tin and iron. At the 'far-side' port of Malaô – modern Berbera in Somalia – the local traders wanted sour grape juice, glass vessels, cloth, wheat, wine, tin, drinking cups, copper, iron, and gold and silver coins. In return, traders could buy myrrh, frankincense, the harder cinnamon, Indian copal, and macir, a type of fragrant bark. In the Red Sea port of Muza, on the other hand, the locals wanted purple cloth, saffron, cloaks, blankets, sashes and horses in exchange for frankincense, myrrh and alabaster.

It is clear from the *Periplus* that, while most of the goods bartered by the Roman traders were brought from the Mediterranean, the sailors could also pick up goods *en route* and exchange them at ports further along the journey. Frankincense from South Arabia found a ready market in India, for example, and Indian merchants who dealt with Chinese traders travelling down through Bactria could trade East African ivories and South Arabian aromatics for Chinese silks and pelts, which they sold on to the Egyptians and Romans.

* * * *

The information contained in the *Periplus* reflects the aromatics trade at its very height. The years from the reign of the Emperor Augustus to the death of Marcus Aurelius in AD 180, the so-called *Pax Romana*, was a time of great peace and prosperity throughout the Roman Empire. The opening up of the maritime route between the Roman Empire and Arabia and India, combined with a flourishing overland trade, and Trajan's annexation of 'Provincia Arabia'– the Nabataean kingdom that had controlled much of the northern incense route – and his establishment of a Roman fleet in the Red Sea to protect ships from piracy, meant that the supply of luxury goods reached new heights, and Roman ships plied the waters of the Red Sea and Indian Ocean in ever-greater numbers.

Wealthy Romans looked to the east for their fashions. Clothes were brighter, dyed with a range of costly pigments and stitched from Chinese brocades and textiles imported via India. Houses were filled with ornamental furniture made from teak, tortoiseshell, ivory and ebony. Menageries of unusual pets became popular; monkeys, tigers and leopards were regularly shipped from Africa, and played an important role in public games and festivals. Precious gems like turquoise and lapis lazuli regularly hung from Roman wrists. Cosmetics and perfumes were concocted from ever-more exotic ingredients: Pliny described many such perfumes, including the 'royal unguent', originally invented for the kings of Parthia, which became popular among the wealthiest Romans. It was made from some of the most expensive ingredients money could buy, including cinnamon, myrrh, rosewood, saffron and spikenard. Even Roman cuisine became infused with exotic flavours. Recipes for sauces and meat glazes routinely listed at least ten foreign ingredients: the Roman cookbook *Apicius*[24] for example, recommended making a salad dressing by mixing vinegar and fish sauce with cumin from Ethiopia or Libya, an ounce of ginger, some fresh rue, 12 dates, pepper and honey. Indian pepper was particularly popular, and extremely expensive. It was used in fish and meat sauces, in medicines and in stimulating tonics which were believed to cure impotence. Romans also mixed pepper and other aromatics into their wine: ingredients such as frankincense, myrrh, cinnamon flowers, ginger and cardamom were added, and the wine was heated over a slow fire.

Many of the ingredients used in perfumes and wines, including cinnamon, cassia,

Fig. 2.12. One of the nine species of Boswellia tree growing on the island of Socotra.

Fig. 2.13. A Dragon's blood tree on the island of Socotra.

myrrh and nard, were more expensive than frankincense. According to Pliny (*Natural History* 12, 32), writing at the start of the 1st century AD, there were three commercial grades of frankincense sold in the Roman markets, costing six, five and three denarii a pound. This can be compared with the cost of myrrh at 16 denarii for a pound; 15 denarii for a pound of long pepper, and an astonishing 1,500 denarii for a pound of cinnamon.

Although frankincense was, relatively speaking, cheaper, demand for it was far greater, and it formed the bulk of the trade between Arabia and the Roman world. More money was spent on buying frankincense than on any of the other foreign resins and spices. Unlike myrrh, which was mainly used by apothecaries and perfumers, frankincense was widely used by all sections of society. Throughout the Roman world, statues of emperors adorned the streets, and lanterns and incense burners were placed before them, emitting a constant stream of fragrant smoke. Since the reek of sewage, dung, rubbish and rotting meat plagued even the finest cities in antiquity, the scent of frankincense in crowded public places was a necessary disguise. Frankincense was purchased as an offering at the temples and burned in order to gain favour from Roman deities. It was burned before household gods in domestic shrines, and vast quantities were burned during public games and victories, at banquets, weddings and cremations. At funeral ceremonies, frankincense was heaped onto the pyres to honour the dead and disguise the stench of burning flesh; at the funeral of the general and dictator Sulla in 78 BC, a life-size statue of the dead man, fashioned from frankincense and other aromatics, emitted fragrant smoke throughout the ceremony.

The annual harvest of South Arabian frankincense was approximately 3,000 tons. According to Pliny, the Emperor Nero burned an entire year's supply of frankincense to mourn the death of his beloved consort Poppaea, and it was clear that supply from Arabia could not meet the extravagant demand in Rome. In the late 1st century BC or early years of the 1st century AD, several developments took place under the rule of the king of Ḥaḍramawt, to try and increase the supply. A second harvest was introduced, so that the frankincense trees were tapped in the winter months for collection in early spring, as well as at the main summer harvest.[25] Secondly, the Ḥaḍramites began to strengthen their control over the other frankincense-producing lands of southern Arabia. They turned their attention to two places in particular – the island of Socotra, and the region of Dhofar.

The island of Socotra, known by the Romans as Dioscorida, lies off the south-east coast of Yemen. It has nine unique species of *Boswellia* tree, and there are frankincense trees growing everywhere from the coast right up to the central mountains (Fig. 12). For centuries before the Ḥaḍramite occupation, the Socotris had harvested and traded their frankincense, aloes, Dragon's blood resin and tortoiseshell, selling them to passing Indian and Arabian merchants and the occasional pirate or mercenary. But during the 1st century AD, the precious resins and plants that grew wild on the island became international commodities with fixed prices and tariffs, controlled by the Ḥaḍramites and bound into a cycle of seasonal harvests and trading patterns. Socotri frankincense, Dragon's blood resin, aloes and tortoiseshell were all rare items that fetched high prices on the international trade market (Fig. 2.13). Tortoiseshell was popular in almost every port mentioned in the *Periplus*. Dragon's blood resin was widely used in medicines, veneers and dyes throughout the Mediterranean world, and the aloe plant was greatly sought-after; believed by Roman physicians to cure all kinds of diseases and afflictions. All these precious goods left Socotra at the end of each harvest and were shipped to Qana' on small boats and rafts held up with inflated animal skins, according to the *Periplus*. At Qana' they were either sold to passing merchant-ships, or stored for transportation inland to Shabwa.

In Dhofar, which lay 400 miles to the south-east of Shabwa, frankincense trees grew abundantly along the limestone ridge beyond the mountains, from the west of the region to the very furthest east. The Ḥaḍramites established two inland positions in frankincense territory, both with easy access to a natural water supply. One, named Hanoon, lay in the Nejd region, where frankincense was most plentiful. The other, Andhur, lay further east, in *hawjeri* territory, where the quality of frankincense was at its very finest. Most importantly, they secured a position on the coast. This was vital, as the overland journey back to Shabwa was

Fig. 2.14. The Y-shaped harbour and southern walls of Sumhuram.

Fig. 2.15. The settlement of Sumhuram. The square well in the foreground is thought to be part of the Ilum temple.

a punishing thirty days or more, whereas the sea route was relatively easy.

The site the Ḥaḍramites settled on the coast, which they named Sumhuram,[26] and which today is known as Khor Rori, was perfectly located (Fig. 2.14). To the south, east and west, steep escarpments led down to the waters of the lagoon and the ocean beyond. The harbour itself was a Y-shaped channel flanked by two flat-topped cliffs – which provided distinctive landmarks for passing merchant ships. To the north of the site lay an expanse of flat plain, which was at the time cultivated farmland, and in the distance was Wadi Darbat, which provided a constant source of fresh water. Approximately 200 Ḥaḍramites settled here, and the settlement contained a temple, houses, shops, paved streets, at least one marketplace and frankincense warehouses, all protected by heavily-fortified walls and a prominent gate-tower (Fig. 2.15).

From Sumhuram, the frankincense was sold to passing ships: most of the sailors who docked here would have been Greeks and Egyptians on their way back from India, over-wintering before returning to Egypt. From around the 1st century BC however, with the establishment of the port of Qana', much of the Dhofari frankincense harvest was packed onto flotillas of small wooden rafts buoyed up on inflated goatskins, and sailed 500 miles along the south Arabian coast, via Syagros, to Qana' which, by the start of the 1st century AD, was the most important frankincense depot in the ancient world.

Qana' was the main port and shipyard of the Ḥaḍramite kingdom, the place where all sea-going vessels belonging to the Ḥaḍramite ruler were built, and one of the major stops on the Egypt-India maritime trade route. Traders came here from the Roman Empire, from Scythia and Oman, from Persia and from the ports of East Africa. Finds discovered here include *terra sigillata* from Italy, Nabataean bowls, Indian bronzes, artefacts from Persia and the Arabian Gulf, and fragments of amphorae which would have contained wine, oil, fish paste and other perishable luxuries from the Roman Empire. Royal agents regularly travelled down from Shabwa to Qana' in order to buy expensive goods from the passing ships on behalf of the Ḥaḍramite king. Items such as Graeco-Roman statues, gold and silver plates, and finely-woven cloaks were especially popular.

The location of Qana' was important for two main reasons. Firstly, it had excellent inland connections, with good caravan roads leading to the capital, Shabwa. Secondly, its coastline was particularly distinctive. The *Periplus* devotes much attention to describing the particular landmarks of each port, in order to help sailors identify the harbour and avoid wasting valuable time tacking up and down the coast. There are four islands opposite the harbour of Qana', and a large black flat-topped volcanic rock, which Yemenis today call Ḥuṣn al-Ghurāb or 'fortress of the crows', which rises up from the edge of the beach to the south of the settlement. These features would have been important landmarks, helping sailors to find their way to Qana'. Being relatively flat on top, the volcanic rock also provided an excellent vantage point, and there was a settlement on the summit for guards to keep watch over the entire area (Fig. 2.16).

At the end of each harvest, consignments of fresh frankincense were shipped to Qana' from the island of Socotra and from Dhofar, and stored in large warehouses. The frankincense was either transported onto larger ships and sold to passing traders, or packed up for the start of the overland journey to Shabwa, where all goods had to pass in order to be taxed.

Fig. 2.16. The flat-topped volcanic rock at Qana', known today as Ḥuṣn al-Ghurāb, was used as a look-out point and landmark.

There were two main overland routes from Qana' to Shabwa. Both were similar distances – around 170 miles, but one was considerably easier for a caravan to negotiate than the other. The first route followed the course of Wadi Mayfa'a, a wide, sandy highway that snaked through the mountains to the west of Qana', passing water stops, small fertile settlements and an important walled oasis-city named Mayfa'at along the way. The route crossed a narrow pass through the mountain range, led into Wadi Jirdan and skirted round the northern edge of the mountains that circled the desert. From there, the merchants would cross the sandy tracts that led to Shabwa. The second route, along Wadi Hajr, was more difficult. It bypassed the flat fertile valley and headed straight for the mountains. This route led the camels single-file through narrow mountain passes, directly down to Wadi Irmah and into the city of Shabwa. Either way, the Socotri and Dhofari frankincense joined the consignments of Ḥaḍramite frankincense, to be taxed in the temple. Here, as described above, the overland route from Shabwa to the Mediterranean began.

The network of the aromatics trade was complicated and many-stranded, particularly after the discovery of the maritime routes from the Red Sea to the Indian Ocean from the late 1st century BC onwards. The international trade in aromatics flourished in this way for at least another 200 years. From the beginning of the 3rd century AD onwards however, the economic crisis within the Roman Empire meant that demand for frankincense and other eastern luxuries went into steep decline. This in part resulted in the fragmentation and weakening of the incense kingdoms of southern Arabia, although there were other internal factors at play, including the rise in the 1st and 2nd centuries AD of a powerful new tribal group, the Himyarites, who shifted the centre of power away from the Sayhadic kingdoms. The introduction of Christianity as the state religion of the Roman Empire in AD 323 dealt another blow to the incense trade, since the earliest Christians rejected the pagan rituals of the past, outlawing the use of frankincense in religious ceremonies and abandoning cremation rites in favour of simple burials without the accompaniment of incense. Although merchants from South Arabia continued to travel north in a feeble trickle for centuries, and the Himyarites took control of the maritime trade along the southern stretch of the Red Sea, without the former insatiable demand for frankincense from the pagan Roman world, the Arabian aromatics trade never again reached the heights of profitability and complexity that it had achieved during the time of Pliny, the *Periplus* and the *Pax Romana*.

Notes

I am immensely grateful to M.C.A. Macdonald for reading this chapter prior to publication, and for providing so many invaluable corrections and comments. Any remaining faults are, of course, entirely my own.

1. See for example the Lord's instructions to Aaron in Exodus and Leviticus, which contain numerous prescriptions for the use of incense, including: Exodus 30 v 7: 'Aaron must burn fragrant incense on the altar every morning when he tends the lamps', and Leviticus 16 v 12–13, instructions to Aaron on the Day of Atonement: 'He is to take a censer full of burning coals from the altar before the Lord and two handfuls of finely ground fragrant incense and take them behind the curtain. He is to put the incense on the fire before the Lord, and the smoke of the incense will conceal the atonement cover above the Testimony, so that he will not die.'

2. For example Chapter 19, the Chapter of the 'Chaplet of Victory' of the *Egyptian Book of the Dead* concludes with the words: 'thou shalt cast incense into the fire on behalf of Osiris'. Wallis Budge (1967).
3. The location of Punt is the topic of an ongoing scholarly debate: see for example Kitchen (1997).
4. See for example Bulliet (1990) chapters 2 and 3 for an outline of the debate.
5. Plutarch, 'Life of Alexander the Great' in *The Lives of the Noble Grecians and Romans*, trans. T. North, Wordsworth Editions, Herts, 1998, pp. 385–465.
6. *Ibid*, chapter 25 pp. 411–412.
7. Herodotus, *Histories* trans. George Rawlinson, Wordsworth Classics 1996, see Book one, chapter 198.
8. *Ibid*, Book three, chapter 113.
9. Theophrastus, *Enquiry into Plants*, trans A. Hort, Loeb Classical Library, Heinemann and Harvard University Press, 1916, book 9 chapter 4, section 4. According to A.F.L. Beeston, quoting Jacques Ryckmans, Theophrastus and other Greek writers may have been referring to people from Shabwa rather than Saba', since "it would be virtually impossible for a Greek speaker to make a clear distinction between 'Sabaean' and 'men of Shabwa'". Beeston (2005).
10. Strabo, *Geography* 16, 4., trans. H.L. Jones, Loeb Classical Library.
11. Pliny, *Natural History*, trans H. Rackham, Loeb Classical Library.
12. Thomas (1932), 122.
13. Pliny *Natural History*, 12, 30.
14. Pliny writes: 'Frankincense after being collected is conveyed to Sabota [Shabwa] on camels, one of the gates of the city being opened for its admission; the kings have made it a capital offence for camels so laden to turn aside from the high road. At Sabota a thithe estimated by measure and not by weight is taken by the priests for the god they call Sabin, and the incense is not allowed to be put on the market until this has been done.' *Natural History*, 12, 32.
15. See for example, Swiggers (1995).
16. See Maraqten (1996).
17. This section of the route is still open to debate. A.F.L. Beeston for example, suggests that the merchants bypassed Timna' altogether, and instead headed west-north-west from Shabwa, through a gravel corridor in the Sayhad desert, which passed a rocky outcrop named Thaniyyah, directly to the Wadi Jawf in the kingdom of Ma'in. See Beeston (2005).
18. See for example Groom (1982).
19. Strabo, *Geography*, 2, 98–99.
20. Strabo, *Geography*, 17, 1.
21. Strabo wrote: 'These regions have become far better known to us of today than to our predecessors. As many as 120 vessels are sailing from Myos Hormos to India whereas formerly, under the Ptolemies, only a very few ventured to undertake the voyage and to carry on traffic in Indian merchandise.' *Geography*, 16, 4.
22. Pliny wrote that at Alexandria, 'frankincense is worked up for sale', and described the security arrangements at the processing plants. Workers were dressed in special aprons and masks, and were stripped before leaving the premises, to ensure they could not steal any of the precious resin. *Natural History*, 12, 32.
23. See Schoff (1912), and Casson (1989).
24. Flower and Rosenbaum (1961). Chapter 3, section 18.
25. Pliny writes that: 'It used to be the custom, when there were fewer opportunities of selling frankincense, to gather it only once a year, but at the present day trade introduces a second harvesting'. *Natural History*, 12, 32, 58.
26. The most recent excavations at Sumhuram have posited important new information about the

dating of this settlement. Whereas previously its foundation was thought to have dated to *c.* 1st century BC, it is now believed to have been settled as early as the 3rd century BC, which pre-dates the establishment of Qana' by as much as 200 years. This seems to indicate that from the 3rd to the 1st century BC, Sumhuram was the most important coastal settlement of the Ḥaḍramawt kingdom. See Avanzini and Sedov (2005).

Select Bibliography

Avanzini, A., and Sedov A.V., 2005. The stratigraphy of Sumhuram: new evidence. *Proceedings of the Seminar for Arabian Studies* 35.

Casson, L., 1989. *The Periplus Maris Erythraei*, text with introduction, translation and commentary. Princeton.

Beeston, A.L.F., 2005. The Arabian aromatics trade in antiquity. In M.C.A. Macdonald and C.S, Phillips (eds), *A.F.L. Beeston at the Arabian Seminar and other papers*. Oxford

Bulliet R.W., 1990. *The Camel and the Wheel.* New York.

Flower, B., and Rosenbaum, E., (trans) 1961. *Apicius*. London.

Groom, N., 1982. Gerrha – A 'Lost' Arabian City. *ATAL, Journal of Saudi Arabian Archaeology*, 6.

Kitchen, K.A., 1997. Punt, Egypt and the Quest for Aromatic Resins. In *Yemen au Pays de la Reine de Saba'*, Institut du Monde Arabe.

Maraqten, M., 1996. Dangerous trade routes: on the plundering of caravans in the pre-Islamic Near East, *Aram*, 8.

Schoff, W.H., 1912. *The Periplus of the Erythraean Sea.* New York.

Swiggers, P., 1995. A Minaean Sarcophagus inscription from Egypt. In *Immigration and Emigration within the Ancient Near East*, Festschrift E. Lipinski, Leuven.

Thomas B., 1932. *Arabia Felix*. London.

Chapter 3: Basalt as Ships' Ballast and the Roman Incense Trade

David Peacock, David Williams and Sarah James

During the period when all imports of cod into England from Iceland came through the town [Kingston upon Hull], the ships used to bring back with them as ballast from Iceland large cobble stones, because their cargo of fish was too light, and as a result these cobbles were used to pave the whole of Kingston from one end to the other.

John Leyland *Itinerary* 1546, ed. J. Chandler (1993)

Summary

This paper is an attempt to characterise basalt ships' ballast from Quseir al-Qadim and Berenike on the Egyptian Red Sea coast. Samples were examined petrographically and analysed chemically for trace and major elements. Fifteen samples were dated by the Argon – Argon method. Comparative rocks from Eritrea, Djibouti and Yemen were analysed, in other cases limited published data were available. The resulting data were processed using bivariate plots and Principal Component Analysis.

The results suggest that the ballast originated in an area of recent volcanism rather than the much older Deccan traps of India as originally suspected. The source or sources must lie in the southern Red Sea or Gulf of Aden. It is suggested that about 70 % of the ballast came from Qana' in Yemen, and about 30 % or less from Aden.

In the light of the *Periplus of the Erythrean Sea*, it is suggested that Aden was the meeting place for Indian and Egyptian ships and that this role was later transferred to Qana'. Heavy cargoes such as wheat or wine would be exchanged for lighter ones such as frankincense necessitating the use of ballast to balance the ships.

Two pieces of obsidian found in Roman contexts at Quseir are probably of Eritrean origin and may have been acquired through trade with Adulis, whence ivory and tortoise shell would have been exported.

Introduction

Before water ballasting was introduced in the nineteenth century, lightly laden or empty ships would need to take on ballast to balance them. This usually consisted of a locally available rock, which would be dumped when a heavy payload was taken on. The provenance of ballast stones can often be determined by geological means, thus affording a means of assessing ancient trade: they provide direct evidence of empty or lightly laden ships loading with a heavier cargo. However, the potential of this material has been little exploited to date and one of us has already surveyed the meagre evidence from Britain (Peacock 1998). The importance of this material is emphasised by, for example, eighteenth and nineteenth century La Rochelle on the Atlantic seaboard of France which was virtually built of Canadian granite or by the streets of Hull, which in Leyland's time, were paved with cobbles of Icelandic lava as the above quotation indicates. Elsewhere, the topic has been virtually ignored: Keith and Simmons (1985) regard ballast as 'the most thoroughly ignored object category of shipwreck archaeology'. The same applies to land archaeology, but now with the notable exception of work done on the re-used ballast incorporated in the town wall of medieval Kings Lynn (Hoare *et al.* 2002). This demonstrated an origin in the Baltoscandian area or more precisely, western Estonia, apart from one piece from Scotland. Generally, there is a marked *lacuna* in our knowledge of ships' ballast and this paper is attempt to address the problem.

Keith and Simmons (1985, 416) list the problems in ballast study:

- Determining the origins of the stones depends on the investigator's ability to discern geographical signatures from the rocks.
- If the stones represent loading episodes in different regions, the investigator must be able to unravel a complex pattern of rocks.
- If the suite of stones result from random human collection or mixture rather than collection from one particular region, no clear geographical signature will emerge.

These are very real constraints on the study, but they are by no means insuperable and can be addressed by:

- Restricting the study to a well-defined region and undertaking field-work in relevant parts of the coast, predetermined by study of existing geological maps.
- Restricting the study to rock types which can be readily characterised by scientific means and which have been the subject of extensive geological study.
- Examining the stones carefully to ascertain whether they have been used previously, in a building, for example.

In this case, the area selected is the Roman Red Sea, where a common ballast material was beach boulders of basalt, a rock which can be examined petrographically and chemically and dated by isotopic methods. For these reasons it is ideal for testing the potential of ballast study. Here an attempt is made to characterise basalt using petrographic examination in thin section and geochemical study, particularly of the trace element distribution using Inductively Coupled Plasma Spectroscopy (ICPS). In addition, fifteen samples were dated using the ^{39}Ar–^{40}Ar method.

The Red Sea, which in Roman times would have incorporated parts of the Indian Ocean, is an excellent study area, because many of the major ports have now been investigated by modern techniques and they are described in the *Periplus Maris Erythraei* (Casson 1989). This is, in essence, a mid 1st century AD sailors' log book describing the harbours and sailing conditions between Egypt, Arabia, Africa and India. It discusses the best anchorages and what can be bought in the local ports, but with a strong emphasis on luxuries. The Periplus is an essential tool in the understanding of ballast.

The Material

In recent years there has been renewed interest in the ports on the Red Sea coast of Egypt, which were pivotal in articulating Rome's trade with the east. Since 1994, the port of Berenike has been excavated by a Dutch-American team and from 1999–2003 new excavations were undertaken at Quseir al-Qadim (Myos Hormos) by the University of Southampton, supported by the Peder Sager Wallenberg Charitable Trust and the AHRB. Berenike is a Ptolemaic foundation which persisted to the end of the Roman Period. Quseir al-Qadim may have been founded at the same time, but was only occupied until the 3rd century AD and then again in the Ayyubid-Mamluk period.

Both sites have revealed heaps of Roman ballast, comprising fresh basaltic lava which does not occur in the Quseir region and only as small inland outcrops in the area of Berenike. They must have been imported by human agency. Fig. 3.1 shows the concentrations of basalt at Quseir al-Qadim. While they are scattered across the site, there are marked concentrations in the area of the sabkha (which would have been the ancient harbour), reminiscent of the Medieval and later ballast dumps identified on the banks of the Tyne (Ellison *et al.* 1993; Goodrick *et al.* 1994). Many of the stones are rounded and some have shells adhering, suggesting that were collected as beach boulders. The main concentrations are in the Roman

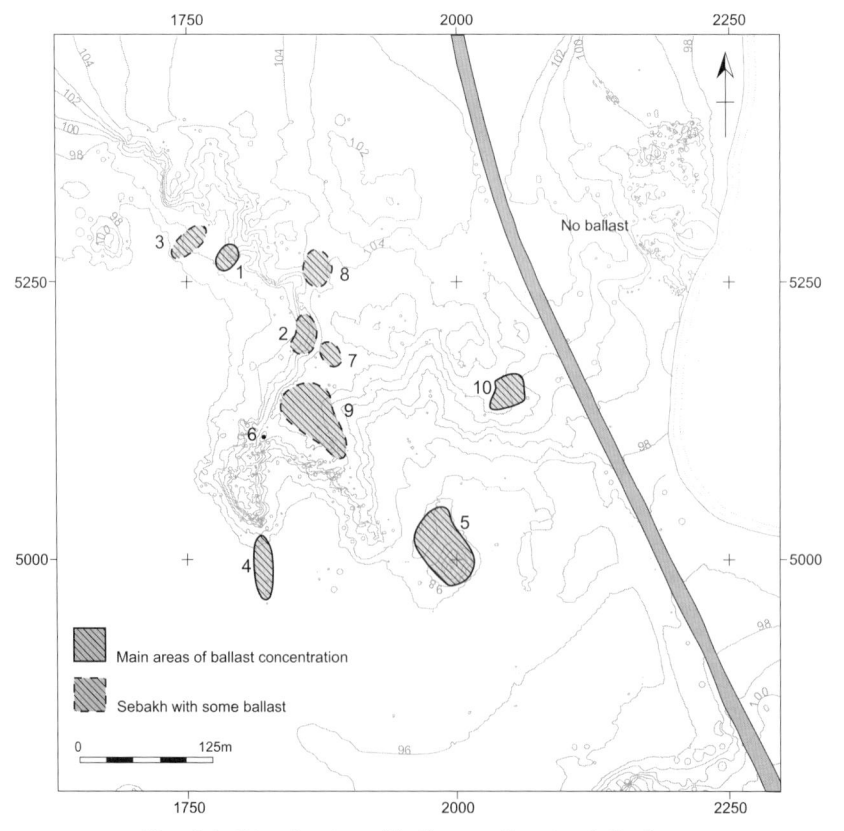

Fig. 3.1. Distribution of ballast at Quseir al-Qadim.

part of the site suggesting that they date from this period. Certainly basalt ballast was being imported during the Roman period because boulders are built into the 'pond' discovered in 2001–2 (Peacock and Blue 2006) and appear in the walls of the 'Roman Villa' excavated by the American team in 1980 (Whitcomb and Johnson 1982). They are found less frequently on the Islamic parts of the site where they may derive from Roman contexts. They abound on the island thought by Whitcomb and Johnson to be a result of dredging of the Roman harbour. Most of the ballast is thought to be of Roman rather than Islamic date because:

1. It occurs in Roman contexts
2. It is common at Berenike where later occupation is absent
3. Islamic ships did not generally use ballast, relying on the careful distribution of the pay load for balance (information Prof. D. Agius)
4. As will be shown later in this study the bulk of the material comes from Qana'in the Yemen where the latest occupation seems to be in the 5th or 6th centuries AD, with no known Islamic occupation (Sedov 1992 and below chapter 4).

Despite this, there is a small possibility that some of the samples may be of Islamic rather than Roman date.

The ballast heaps of Quseir were carefully examined for their petrography and all appeared to be fresh volcanic rocks, mainly basalt, but with a few intermediate varieties. No material other than volcanics could be positively identified in the heaps. At Berenike, Harrell (1996) recorded the presence of basalt which he suggested could emanate from the Saudi Arabian coast, or the Red Sea Islands if not 'Sudan and Ethiopia'. He does not consider the alkali basalts from nearby Shalatein (Moghazi 2003), but as these are inland they are unlikely to be a source of stones at Berenike, which like those from Quseir show evidence of a marine origin. Harrell also noted large numbers of carbonate cobbles with *Pholad* borings, which he suggested could have originated in the Gebel Duwi and washed down to the coast in the region of Quseir. Less probably they originated in the Esh-Mellaha Range about 20 km north-west of the fort of Abu Sha'ar. These carbonate cobbles comprise a problem: in both areas the geology is complicated and the beaches would reflect this complexity: if they are to be regarded as ballast picked up on northern beaches, they should be accompanied by other rock types, which does not appear to be the case. Equally, despite careful examination, they were not seen in the ballast heaps of Quseir al-Qadim.

The only material which can, with some certainty, be regarded as imported as ballast is basalt or kindred rocks. Both Quseir al-Qadim (Myos Hormos) and Berenike were concerned with Rome's eastern trade and ultimately with India. Basalts abound in India, where much of the north-western part of the country comprises the massive outpourings of the Deccan traps. It was thought therefore that this was a probable source. However, some preliminary dates, later supported by a larger sample, demonstrated that this could not be the case as the ballast was geologically very young, of recent or Tertiary age, whereas the Deccan traps are around 65+ ma old. It seems therefore that the source must lie in the recent volcanics of the Red Sea and the Gulf of Aden. The task of discerning origins can be further limited. The rounded nature of the boulders and cobbles, the presence of adhering sea shells suggest a beach deposit. As the assemblages are purely volcanic, the source should be close to a coastal volcano or else the basalt would be intermingled with sedimentary or metamorphic rocks.

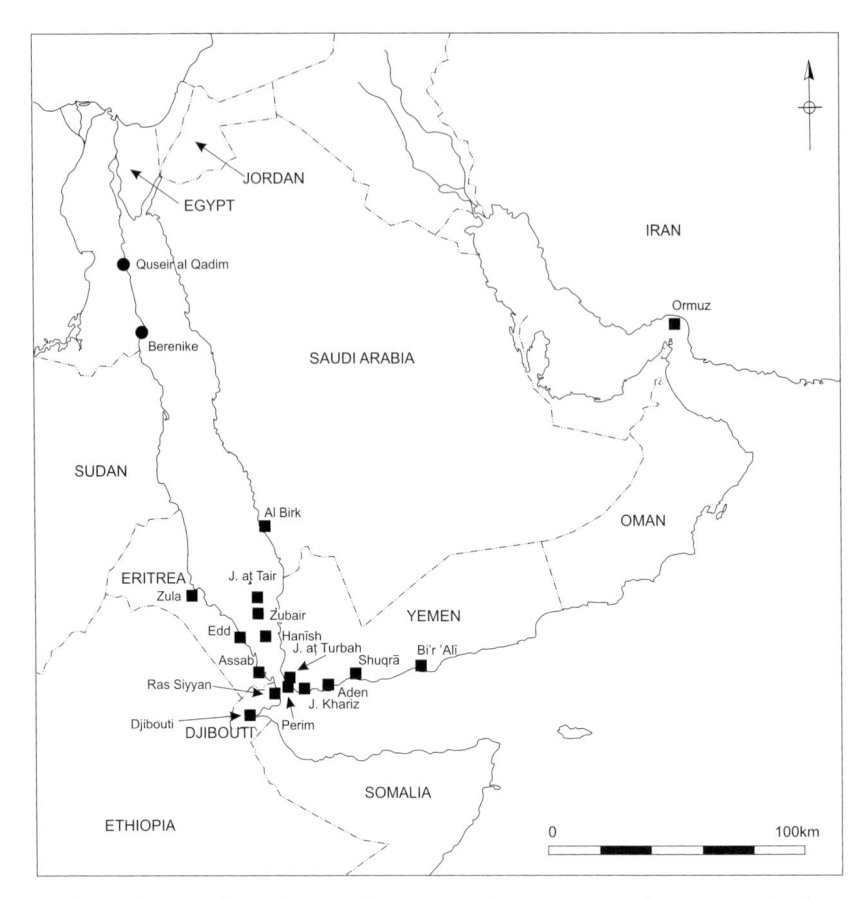

Fig. 3.2. The Red Sea and northern Indian Ocean showing coastal outcrops of volcanic rocks.

Potential Sources

Volcanic rocks occur widely in the countries of the southern part of the Red Sea and the Gulf of Aden, but there are relatively few places where these rocks are found in coastal localities and these are shown in Fig. 3.2, together with the sites of Quseir al-Qadim (Myos Hormos) and Berenike. We were able to collect material from some of these localities which were incorporated in our programme of analysis. The samples were obtained in the field or from collections housed in the University of Leeds and the Natural History Museum. In other cases, because of political constraints we were unable to make our own collection and have had to rely on published data. This is much better than nothing, but is less satisfactory as the range of elements quoted is more limited, in turn limiting the scope for detailed comparison. Where possible we have restricted our comparanda to data obtained by X Ray Fluorescence analysis (XRF) rather than rapid methods such as optical emission spectroscopy. The situation is as follows:

Saudi Arabia
Black volcanic rocks abound in Saudi Arabia forming the so-called Harrats or volcanic

massifs. However, they all lie inland and are separated from the coast by a wide band of Quaternary sediments, comprising gravels, sands etc, where any basalt blocks would undoubtedly be diluted with other materials. The sole exception is the Harrat Al Birk, which lies in the Tihāmat between Al Qunfudhah and Jīzān on the Saudi coast. The petrography has been described by Arno *et al.* (1980) who date the rocks between 0 and 1.9 ma. They do not give trace element data, but the same eruption appears about 100 km further south in the area of Jabal aṭ Tirf where Coleman *et al.* (1977) quote major and some trace elements. Ghent *et al.* (1980) quote semi-quantitative data for Gebel al Haylah, only 30 km west of the main outcrop. These results are in line with those of Coleman *et al.*, giving reason to believe that extrapolation is reasonable and justified.

No samples were available from this outcrop, but this is not considered a major problem. The Periplus (20:7.11–12) suggests that the southern parts of the coast of Arabia were considered altogether too risky because of hostile inhabitants and a dangerous rocky shore-line. Inspection of a new satellite image (http://landsat.usgs.gov/gallery/detail/392/) suggest that the coast around Al Birk is very dangerous with numerous reefs and offshore shoals. It is unlikely to be a major source of ballast material.

The Red Sea Islands
The Periplus (20:7.15–16) indicates that the Roman sailor would set a central course down the Red Sea making for Katakekaumenê (burnt) island (Fig. 3.3). This can hardly be other than Jabal aṭ Tair which still displays fumarolic activity, although there is no unequivocal historical record of an eruption (Gass *et al.* 1973). However, the lava which caps the island is tholeitic rather than alkali basalt so characteristic of the ballast and it can be dismissed as a potential source.

The other Red Sea islands further south, Zubair, the Hanīsh-Zukur group, and Perim in the Bab al Mandab, do have alkali basalts and both petrography and geochemistry have been described by Gass *et al.* (1973) and Mallick *et al.* (1990). Significantly only Perim is mentioned in the Periplus (28:8.17), as the landmark of Diodôrus island. All of these islands are currently out of bounds to foreigners and we were unable to obtain new specimens, but again this is not considered a serious deficiency.

Jabal aṭ Turbah, Yemen
There is a small lava flow dating to about 10.5 ma forming part of the Ra's Bab al Mandab adjacent to Perim island. We were unable to find published information or to obtain samples, but the lavas are almost certainly the same as those on Perim.

Kharaz, Yemen
The recent volcano of Kharaz, dating to about 9 ma, is not directly on the coast, but it is sufficiently close to be worthy of consideration. It lies to the west of Aden in Lahij province, not far from Dar Mujabhar. The rocks have been described by Vencl and Zamarský (2002) and by Gass and Mallick (1968) who include data on the major minor and trace elements as well as the petrography. Dr Vencl and Professor Zamarský kindly provided their data on disc, thus greatly facilitating the analysis of this outcrop. However, its location away from the coast, the lack of a mention in the Periplus and the absence of any archaeological remains on this part of the coast suggested that it was unlikely to be a source.

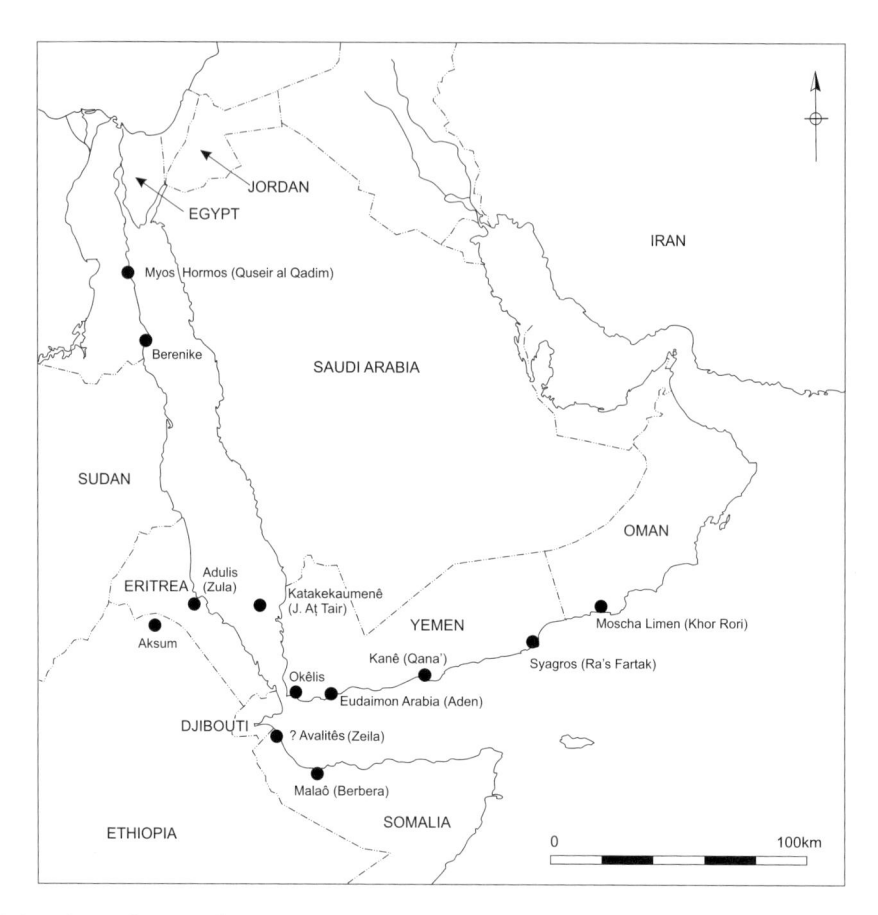

Fig. 3.3. The Red Sea and northern Indian Ocean showing ancient sites mentioned in the text.

To the east is the small volcanic area of Al Birka. We were unable to obtain data or samples, but as it is small and not directly on the coast, it is not thought to be important. Presumably Jebel Kharaz would equate with the Cabubathra Mons of Ptolemy's *Geography*, to the east and west of which were the minor ports of Mardecha and Sanina (Stevenson 1932). However, these almost certainly lay on either side of the volcanic outcrop rather than on it.

Aden (including Little Aden and Ra's 'Imram)
Aden is of volcanic origin and it is certainly the most intensively studied volcano in the present study area, largely because it was easily accessible from Europe. The literature on Aden is extensive and it would be superfluous to review it all here, but indicative papers are those of Cox *et al.* (1969), Vencl and Zamarský (2002) and Bletcher (1997). We were able to obtain 14 samples from Aden and a further 18 thought to be from that source. As they closely match the known samples they have been included in the study. All the known material comes from six different localities on or near the Aden peninsula dominated by Jabal Shamsam, rather than the western peninsula known as Little Aden ('Adan aş Şughra)

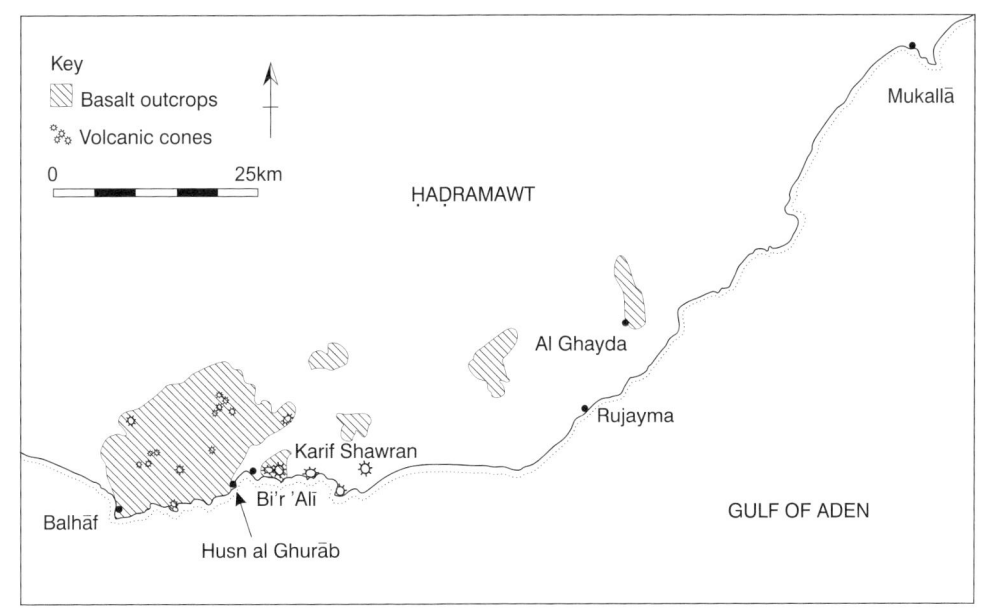

Fig. 3.4. The Ḥaḍramawt coast showing volcanic outcrops.

or Ra's Imrām to the west. Limited geochemical data has been published for Little Aden and Ra's Imrām (Cox *et al.* 1968; 1970).

Aden was known in Antiquity as *Eudaimôn Arabia* (Fig. 3.3). The Periplus (26:8.22–32) describes it as the meeting place for ships coming from India and those coming from Egypt as neither dare make the full journey. The author adds the remark that 'not long before our time, Caesar sacked it' implying that it was no longer used for this purpose or that it now played a much reduced role (see p. 62).

Shuqrā
The Shuqrā volcanic field occupies some 4000 km² on the coast about 120 km east of Aden in Ayban province. The petrography and geochemistry have been described by Cox *et al.* (1977) and Cox *et al.* (1993). We were not able to obtain samples, but the absence of archaeological remains on this part of the southern Yemen coast, suggests that it would not have been an important source of ballast. Presumably the Shuqrā volcanic field would equate with Niger Mons of Ptolemy's *Geography* (Stevenson 1932). The only place on the outcrop would be Agamanispha (presumably modern Shuqrā), but this is only classed as a village.

Bi'r 'Alī and Ḥaḍramawt, Yemen
Extensive recent volcanics outcrop on the Yemen coast between Balḥāf and Mukallā (Fig.3.4). The main concentration is between Balḥāf and Bi'r 'Alī in the heart of which lies the ancient port of Kanê (Qana') at the foot of the volcanic vent of Ḥuṣn al Ghurāb. We were unable to find any published accounts of these rocks but they are clearly crucial to this study. Kanê is mentioned in the Periplus (27:9.3–4, 8) as the point for setting out for India and the major port for frankincense. It was clearly a key port of call.

We were unable to visit this locality because of the political situation, but obtained a good collection of material, principally from Ḥuṣn al Ghurāb and Qana' at its foot, about 5 km west of Bi'r 'Alī. We are indebted to Dr Anne-Marie Lezine, Professor Alexander Sedov and Dr Abdu Ghaleb for assisting us. In addition, we were able to locate further material in the Natural History Museum. These included four samples from the Shawran volcano, 5 km east of Bi'r 'Alī, two from Wadi Hajar 35 km east, one from Wadi Ghiadat (Al Ghayda on Fig. 3.4) 60 km east, and three from Wadi Raima, (almost certainly Rujayma) 40 km to the east. One sample simply labelled 'Ḥaḍramawt' could come from this general area, but it might come from a minor volcanic field beginning at Quṣay'ar about 125 km east of Mukallā. This may be of less importance from our point of view as there are no archaeological remains in the area and the volcanic field is separated from the coast by a belt of sediments. Ptolemy records two ports, Pretos and Trulla, on this stretch of the coast, and two villages, Embolium and Thialemath, but no metropoli or emporia (Stevenson 1932).

Djibouti
The small republic of Djibouti (Fig. 3.2) on the western side of the Gulf of Aden is composed solely of volcanic rocks, most of recent date, but some of Miocene age. In a collecting visit during April 2003, we were able to obtain samples of all the volcanics outcropping around the Gulf of Tadjoura. These included recent lavas and sub aqueous flows from west of the Ghoubbat al Kharâb, Plio-Pleistocene basaltic fissure flows from east of Tadjoura and west of Djibouti town, the Afar Stratoid Series (4–1 ma), and the Miocene Dalha basalts (8–6 ma). These rocks have been briefly described by Mohr (1961).

Further north, on the approaches to the Bab al Mandab is the small scoriacious hill forming Ra's Siyyan, with lavas forming the diminutive offshore Sawabi' islands. Ms Antonia Willis kindly donated scoria samples from Ra's Siyyan.

As far as can be seen, Djibouti is not mentioned in the Periplus and it is archaeologically barren. The single amphora discovered in Djibouti (off the Sawabi' islands) has been published by Empereur (1993), who correctly identifies it as a type appearing in 18th century AD. It is a common and widely spread variety, which we believe originated in North Africa, possibly Tunisia. One of us (DP) has seen two more in Eritrea. One is used for water storage on the island of Dese, the other from Afta is in the Massawa museum. The form is almost identical to the *sefrî* jars still produced on the island of Djerba (Combès and Louis 1967, Ph.IV.8), and furthermore the paste is of a type characteristic of North Africa (Peacock 1984). This seems a more likely source than the eastern origin suggested by Empereur, and equally the date range can be extended from 18th century to the present.

Desanges and Reddé (1993) conducted an archaeological reconnaissance on the Djibouti side of the Bab al Mandab. They recovered some sherds from around Ra's Siyyan and a little supplementary material from the same site has been shown us by Ms Antonia Willis. It is very difficult to date, but could be late Roman. However, the scarcity of the material makes it unlikely that this was a major port of call in any period.

Somaliland
The southern coast of the Gulf of Aden is dominated by Precambrian metamorphics blanketed partly by Mesozoic and Tertiary sediments. The only recent volcanics are small

outcrops around Qandala and 50 km east of Las Qoray, but they are all a little inland rather than coastal. This area is therefore unlikely to be a source.

East of Yemen

There are no coastal volcanic rocks in Oman or Iran with the exception of small island volcanoes in the Strait of Hormuz. The Ormus Islands in the Gulf of Oman between the Persian Gulf and the Arabian Sea are of volcanic origin. According to Hantke (1951, 204) these islands still have well-shaped craters and lava flows (Neumann van Padang 1963, xii). We purchased some pieces of scoria, used as scourers, in the souq at Mutrah, Muscat. They almost certainly come from this source, although the vendor knew nothing of their origin. They were analysed, but because of their uncertain origin the data must be used with caution. Eastwards the only volcanics are the massive outpourings of the Deccan traps, which are more than 65 ma old. Otherwise recent volcanic activity occurs to the east of India in the Bay of Bengal, or to the south in the islands of Comoro and Réunion on the latitude of Madagascar.

In 2003, we were able visit Khor Rori in southern Oman, which was almost certainly Mosca Limên of the Periplus. No basalt is recorded from this site, either as building material or as portable artefacts (Avanzini 2002) and we saw none. Equally it was absent from the Medieval site of Al Balid on the outskirts of Salalah. It seems that basalt ballast is found west of Qana'and there is nothing to the east.

Eritrea

Recent volcanic rocks are common on the southern Eritrean coast and they have been briefly discussed by Mohr (1961, 210) who quotes some older major element analyses. They occur on the Bay of Zula and are a major building material at Adulis, further extensive flows occur in the Danakil to the south of Edd and there is a range of volcanic hills at Assab. We were able to collect extensive comparative material from all these localities in 2002.

Adulis features in the Periplus (4:1.19–2.15) where it is described as a 'legally limited port'. It seems to have been a major source of ivory and tortoise shell. There has been some debate about the whereabouts of Adulis of the Periplus as all the material from the site dates to the Aksumite period or to the Prehistoric period. Until recently no Roman material had yet come to light. Casson (1981) has suggested that it originally lay at Massawa and later moved to the site on the Bay of Zula. This has always seemed an extravagant theory, but a current field programme by the Universities of Southampton and Asmara and the National Museum of Eritrea has resolved the matter. About 6.5 km south-east of Adulis is a range of hills surrounded to the south by salt marsh which would have been sea in Roman times. Off these hills to the east is a prominent rock which would have been an island. On it was found Dressel 2–4 amphorae and Eastern Sigillata dating to the Augustan period. This is thought to be Diodôrus Island of the Periplus and the Roman harbour of Adulis.

Adulis is a possible source of ballast, but on site metamorphic schists occur in some quantity and random collection of ballast would result in a mixed assemblage. Diodôrus Island is composed of pillow lavas.

No Roman material has been found further south in Eritrea and it is probable that the

Edd area with its rocky coastline would have been avoided. On the other hand Assab has been equated with Avalitês of the Periplus (7:3.13–14) and it has an adequate harbour. The main reason for this is the statement that it lay in the narrowest point between Africa and Arabia of the trading with Okêlis and Muza. The problem is that the distance given from Adulis to Avalitês is 4800 stades.

The problem of the length of a stadium was reviewed by Schoff (1912, 54). It appears that three different measures were in vogue at the time of the Periplus. However, now that it has been established that Myos Hormos equates with Quseir al-Qadim (Peacock and Blue 2006) we can calculate the length of a stadium accurately for we are told that it was 1800 stadia from Myos Hormos to Berenike, a distance of exactly 300 km. This gives the length of a stadium as 166.67 m. This in turn means that the distance between Adulis and Avalitês was 800 km. It is possible that the Periplus is in error, but testing the above formula on other known points of reference suggests that generally it is incredibly accurate. As Assab is only about 400 km from Adulis, any error would be of the order of 100%, which seems unlikely. An alternative contender is Zeila in Somalia which is exactly 800 km from Adulis. This is supported to some extent by another co-ordinate, because the distance from Avalitês to Malaô is given as 800 stadia. The latter is almost certainly modern Berbera, which is about 200 km from Zeila, more like 1800 stadia. On the other hand the distance from Assab to Berbera is about 400 km or 3,500 stadia. The odds are stacked more favourably in favour of Zeila rather than Assab. Placing Avalitês in Somaliland resolves many problems, not least why it is referred to as the first of the 'far side' ports. If we assume that the author was referring, not to the narrows of the Bab al Mandab, but to the narrowest point crossing of the Gulf of Aden to Arabia everything begins to fit into place. It is worth noting that Claudius Ptolemy (Book 4, Chapter 7), writing in the second century AD quite unequivocally places Avalitês 'after the strait in the Red Sea' (Stevenson 1932, 107).

Analytical Method

The geochemical composition of the samples was determined within the Geology Department of Royal Holloway, University of London (RHUL).

Instrumental Techniques

The geochemical composition of the samples was determined using a combination of Inductively Coupled Plasma-Atomic Emission Spectrometry (ICP-AES) and Inductively Coupled Plasma-Mass Spectrometry (ICP-MS). Both of these techniques require the sample to be in the form of a solution and a combination of two sample dissolution methods were used as described below.

ICP-AES is a robust technique capable of determining major elements and selected trace elements within a range of matrices. The instrument at RHUL is a Perkin Elmer Optima 3300RL ICP-AES which can achieve detection limits in the parts per million range in the original sample. The analytes determined by ICP-AES were: SiO_2, Al_2O_3, Fe_2O_3, MgO, CaO, Na_2O, K_2O, MnO, P_2O_5, TiO_2, Ba, Co, Cr, Cu, Li, Ni, Sc, Sr, V, Y, Zn and Zr.

ICP-AES is not sensitive enough to determine the majority of the remaining trace elements at the concentrations at which they are found in the basalts. These elements were therefore determined by using a Perkin Elmer Sciex Elan 5000 ICP-MS which has far superior detection limits. Cs, Hf, Nb, Rb, Ta, Th, U, La, Ce, Pr, Nd, Sm, Eu, Gd, Dy, Ho, Er, Yb, and Lu were all determined by ICP-MS.

Sample Dissolution Methods

The samples were collected as rock chips for the most part, and these had to be crushed prior to dissolution. If required, the sample chips were first dried at 80°C and then crushed to a fine powder in a Swing Mill grinder, using a toughened steel barrel and puck.
After crushing, the samples were prepared for major and trace element analysis using two preparation methods, a Lithium Metaborate fusion and a Hydrofluoric acid dissolution.

The lithium metaborate fusion involves mixing the sample powder with lithium metaborate flux and heating it to approximately 900°C in a platinum-gold crucible. At this temperature the silicates within the sample fuse with the lithium metaborate and form a molten glass bead. This bead is then allowed to cool and solidify into glass, which is then dissolved in dilute nitric acid. The advantage of this preparation over the Hydrofluoric acid dissolution is that all the mineral phases within the sample are attacked, and the majority of elements are retained quantitatively in the resultant solution. Therefore, this method is ideal for major element determinations, and for those elements that are found in refractory phases within the sample. To produce reliable silica data it is usually necessary to add an internal standard to ensure maximum precision. The internal standard used for this analysis was Gallium.

There are some drawbacks to this method. Firstly, lithium cannot be determined, as it has been added in the flux. Secondly, the resultant solution is very high in dissolved material, containing all of the sample as well as large quantities of lithium metaborate. Sample solutions need to be diluted by a large amount before being analysed because both ICP-AES and ICP-MS required the Total Dissolved Solid (TDS) content of a solution to be below a certain amount. In the case of ICP-MS this large dilution is offset by the very high sensitivity of the technique, meaning that trace elements can be determined successfully. However, in the case of ICP-AES, the large dilution means that trace elements are present at too low a concentration in solution for the instrument to measure.

To measure trace elements by ICP-AES, a Hydrofluoric acid dissolution is needed. In this preparation the sample powder is attacked with a mixture of hot Hydrofluoric (HF) and Perchloric ($HClO_4$) acids. The HF attacks the silicates in the sample and forms silicon tetrafluoride (SiF_4), which is volatile. The SiF_4 evaporates off along with the excess HF and leaves the sample (minus Si) and the perchloric acid. This is then dried and all of the remaining elements in the sample form perchlorates, which can be re-dissolved in dilute nitric acid. The advantage of this preparation is that the solutions do not need to be diluted to the same extent as with the fusion, because the most abundant element (Si) has been removed and the TDS are consequently much lower. This permits the determination of many trace elements by ICP-AES, including many that cannot successfully be done by ICP-MS.

Methodologies

Both methods are based on those described in Thompson and Walsh, 2003.
Unless stated otherwise, all reagents are AnalaR grade, all water is de-ionised, and the acids used are concentrated.

Lithium metaborate fusion

- Weigh 0.5g ± 0.0005g of powdered sample into a Pt/Au crucible, add 1.5g ± 0.001g of Aristar grade $LiBO_2$ and mix well.
- Place the crucible on a Meker burner at around 900°C and put the lid on, leaving an air gap to ensure complete oxidation of the sample during heating. Heat for at least 20 minutes and occasionally swirl the contents to ensure complete mixing.
- Add approximately 150ml of water to a 250ml plastic beaker, add 25ml of HNO_3 and the internal standard.
- Add a PTFE stirring bean to each beaker and place on a magnetic stirrer.
- When the fusion bead is ready, allow to cool and solidify. Then tip out the glass bead into the appropriate beaker. It is essential that the mixture is stirred continuously during the dissolution; otherwise the bead will not dissolve completely, and any material that does initially dissolve may not remain in solution.
- Pour some of the acid mixture from the beaker into the appropriate crucible; add a stirring bean and place on the stirrer.
- When the entire solid from the fusion has dissolved in both the crucible and the beaker recombine them, rinsing the crucible well.
- Make up to 250ml in a volumetric flask, mix well and then transfer to a plastic storage tube, discarding any unnecessary solution.
- The solutions can be analysed without further dilution by ICP-AES, however, they should be diluted further prior to analysis by ICP-MS.

Hydrofluoric acid dissolution

- Weigh 0.2g ± 0.0010g of powdered sample into a PTFE (or Pt) crucible.
- In a $HF/HClO_4$ compatible fume cupboard, add 4ml of HF and 2ml of $HClO_4$ and place crucible on a hotplate set at approximately 100–120°C. Allow to slowly evaporate to dryness.
- Remove from hotplate, allow to cool and then add 2ml of HNO_3. Carefully add approximately 10ml of water and gently warm on the hotplate for 15–20 minutes. Remove crucibles from the hotplate and allow to cool.
- When cool make up to 20ml, mix well and transfer to storage tubes.
- The solutions can be analysed for trace elements by ICP-AES without further dilution.

Rock Characterisation

In order to ascertain the source of the ballast from Quseir and Berenike it is necessary to find features which discriminate and differentiate the various potential sources. This was done by searching for systematic differences in geochemistry that might 'finger-print' sources. The problem was tackled by simple inspection and by using the sort facility on Excel, seeing which sources clustered together when data for individual elements were ordered. This suggested that the most diagnostic elements were few in number, usually, TiO_2, Cu, Li, Ni, Co, Sr, Ba, Zn, Zr, Rb, Nb, U and Y. Other elements tended to vary considerably within regions or showed little differentiation. Geochemists have developed an impressive armoury of techniques for studying relationships within chemical data and these have been reviewed by Rollinson (1993). Our problem is rather different for instead of looking for connections, we are searching for discrimination between data sets. The primary analytical tool was to show significant elements (usually trace elements) on bivariate plots. This enabled sources to be compared with one another and to be compared or contrasted with the ballast. Most sources could be resolved by choosing a sequence of different variables until differentiation had been achieved with the samples occupying their own fields.

The volcanic rocks form a continuum from ultra basic to acidic defined by increasing content of silica. At the most fundamental level a distinction was made between basic rocks and intermediate and acid, the cut off point between the two being an arbitrary 53% silica. Obsidian, or volcanic glass, is highly distinctive and was also separated from the initial data set. Our data are thus considered under three headings, basic, intermediate/acid and obsidian.

A second line of approach was to subject the basic or basalt data to Principal Component Analysis. This is a powerful technique which reduces a large number of variables into a few uncorrelated ones.

As we were unable to obtain comparanda for all potential sources in a number of cases we had to make comparison between published data and with the results of our study of ballast. In order to ensure reasonable reliability we restricted ourselves, with one exception, to measurements obtained by XRF. The problem is that the range of elements was much more restricted and furthermore the elements recorded varied from one field programme to another. Because of this, it was necessary to adopt an outcrop by outcrop approach, in each case comparing published data with the same elements recorded in

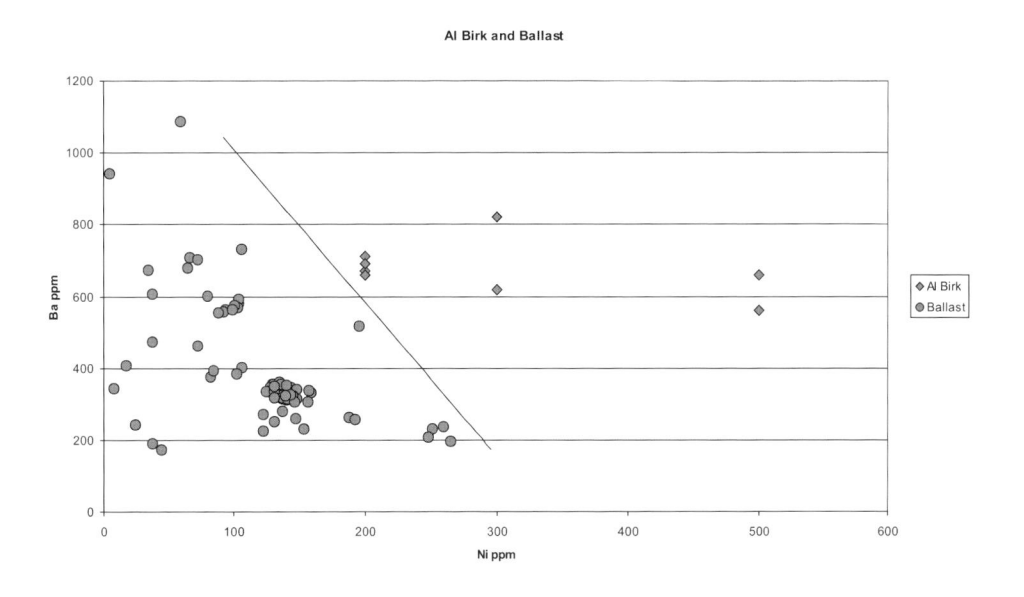

Fig. 3.5. A comparison of ballast samples and rocks from Al Birk, based on published sources. Ba and Ni.

our ballast samples. In order to ensure we were comparing like with like, basic and intermediate/acid rocks were considered separately.

Basic rocks

Al Birk

As mentioned above the data from Al Birk is not as good as that from other published volcanic outcrops, both with respect to sample location and methodology. However, it is only possible to work with what is available and no material could be obtained from this outcrop. It was suggested that this would be an unlikely source, a view confirmed by the trace element distribution. The most telling parameter is the Ni:Ba ratio, for when Al Birk is compared with data from the ballast both occupy discrete fields, with ballast to the left of the line, and Al Birk to the right (Fig. 3.5). There is thus no case for suggesting that any ballast came from this volcano.

Red Sea Islands

The Red Sea Islands are treated together, but comparison with the ballast is less clear-cut, largely because of the limited data and the range of elements available. In general, the ballast has higher Sr and lower Zr than the island basalts and higher Nb and Rb with lower Y (*e.g.* Fig. 3.6). On the data available it seems that Zubair, the Hanīsh-Zukur group and Perim are all different, but there is a little overlap with the ballast, particularly with Hanīsh-Zukur, which cannot be definitively separated.

It was argued above that the islands are an unlikely source for the ballast and the trace element distribution lends its support to this argument. It tips the balance of probability even further away and the islands are best discounted.

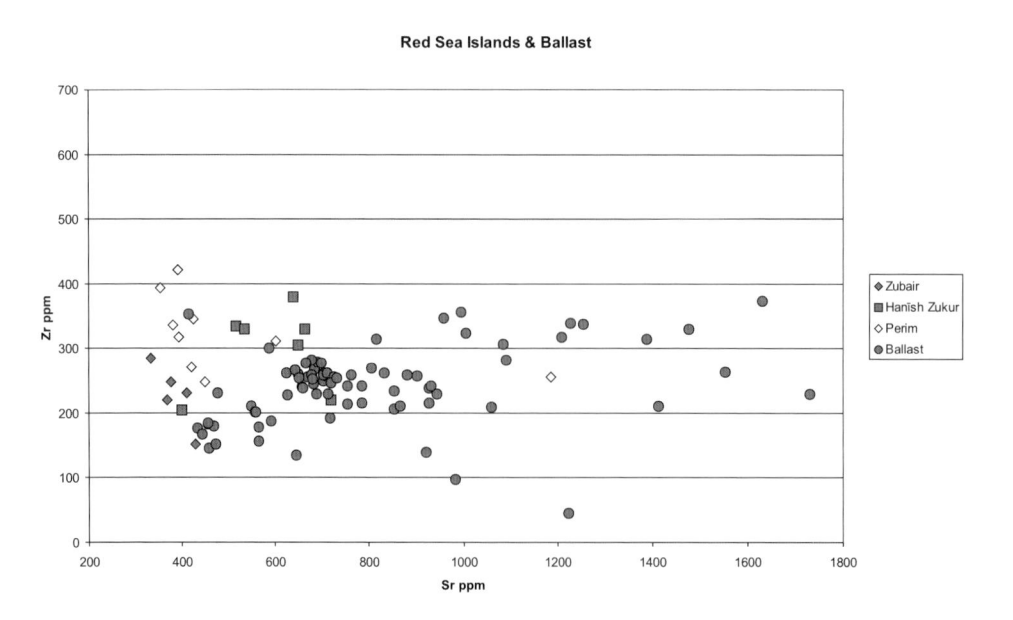

Fig. 3.6. A comparison of ballast and rocks from the Red Sea islands of Zubair, Hanīsh Zukur and Perim, based on published sources. Zr and Sr.

Kharaz

The separation of Kharaz and ballast is again less clear cut but there do seem to be differences in the Ba:Nb and Ba:Sr ratio (Figs 3.7–8). In general Ba is higher at Kharaz than in the ballast with considerable variation. Nb and particularly Sr show more variation in the ballast. The impression is two separate but partly overlapping clusters. The data do not disprove an association, but they certainly do not support the hypothesis that the ballast was derived from this source. It seems probable that the overlap is caused by a similarity in geochemistry between Aden and Kharaz, but the data are not detailed enough to make this distinction. Given the archaeological improbability of Kharaz and its distance from the coast, it can be legitimately eliminated.

Shuqrā

More published data are available for the Shuqrā volcanic field making comparison a little easier. The ratios of Zr:Nb and particularly Zr:Rb are indicative as Shuqrā occupies a field which is distinct from most of the ballast (Fig. 3.9). Most ballast lies above the line, most Shuqrā samples below. It is clear that very little, if any, ballast came from this source which fits well with archaeological expectation.

Oman

The six pieces of scoria purchased in the Mutrah souq are demonstrably very different from the ballast. The most striking difference is the much higher Ce in the Omani samples. The ratio Sr:Ce conveniently separates the two groups making it highly improbable, despite the small sample size, that this is a source (Fig. 3.10).

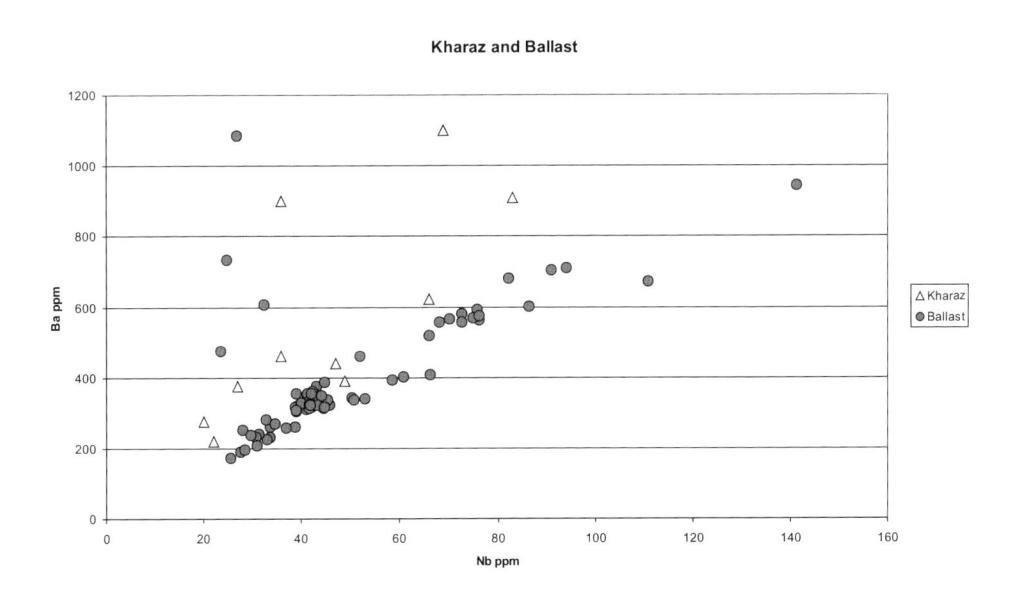

Fig. 3.7. A comparison of ballast and rocks from Kharaz, Southern Yemen, based on published sources. Ba and Nb.

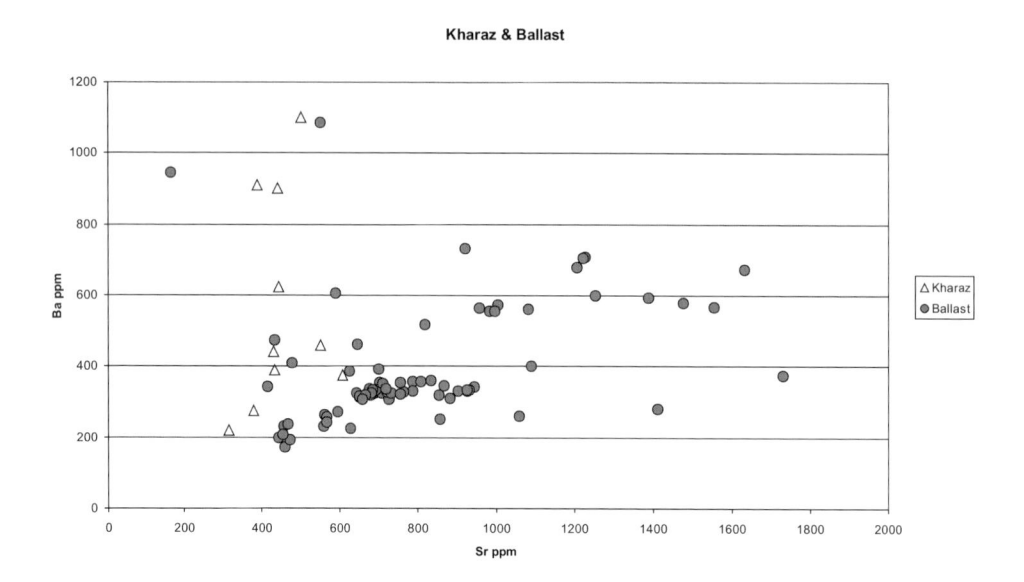

Fig. 3.8. A comparison of ballast and rocks from Kharaz, Southern Yemen, based on published sources. Ba and Sr.

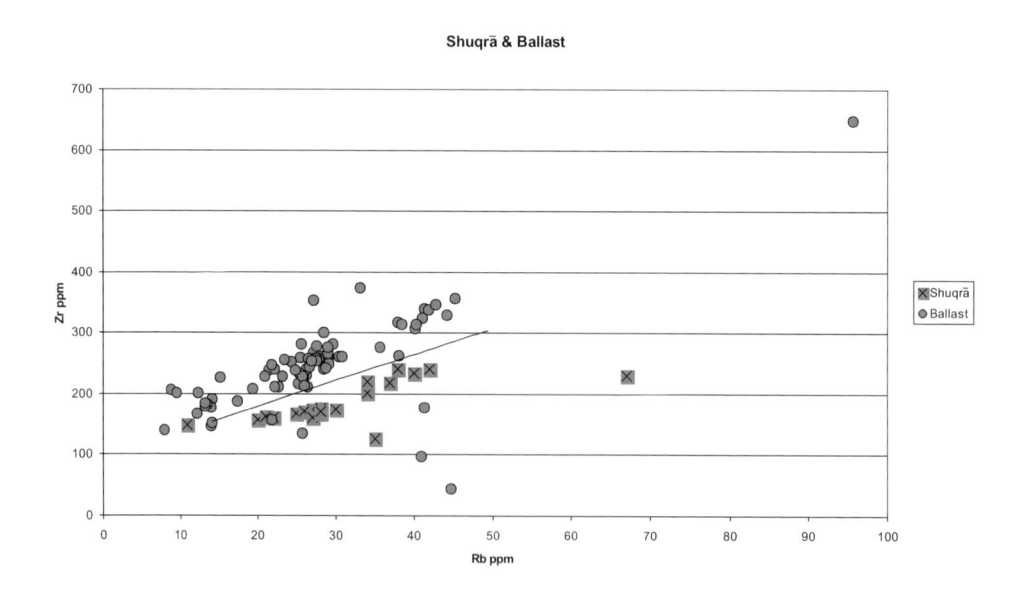

Fig. 3.9. A comparison of ballast and rocks from Shuqrā, Southern Yemen, based on published sources. Zr and Rb.

Djibouti, Eritrea, Aden and Ḥaḍramawt, Yemen

The somewhat slender evidence from published sources gives no geochemical grounds for supposing that any of the above produced significant quantities of ballast. As they are all archaeologically improbable they are best eliminated from consideration and the discussion will now focus on the localities from which we were able to obtain rocks for analysis in this programme. These were perceived, from the outset, as the places most pertinent to this study.

Trial and error on our own data demonstrated that the most satisfactory discrimination between sources was with the ratio of Zn:Rb. The results are shown on Fig. 3.11, where there is a clear distinction between Qana', Adulis, Djibouti and Aden. Djibouti is characterised by a significantly lower Rb level, Qana' has lower Zn which increases in Adulis and Aden. The other samples from the east of Qana' and elsewhere in the Ḥaḍramawt have been omitted from this graph as they have higher Zn values and confuse the picture. This is justified as all these outcrops are somewhat inland and would not have been a source of ballast: only Qana' lies on the coast. In all other respects these samples are indistinguishable from Qana'.

The ratio is less effective in distinguishing Assab and Edd from Aden and here there is considerable overlap. However, other elements can be used to further discriminate, notably TiO_2, which is exceptionally high in the Edd rocks and Li which is generally higher than Aden at both Assab and Edd (Fig. 3.12). It should thus be possible to assign a sample to its source on the basis of Rb, Zn, Li and TiO_2. Further analysis suggests that the ratios Rb:Zr and Ni:Cr are also of considerable value although there is a little more overlap and the clustering is not so crisp. The tools for distinguishing Qana', Aden, Adulis, Assab and Edd are thus established. Comparison with ballast is reserved until other outcrops have been considered.

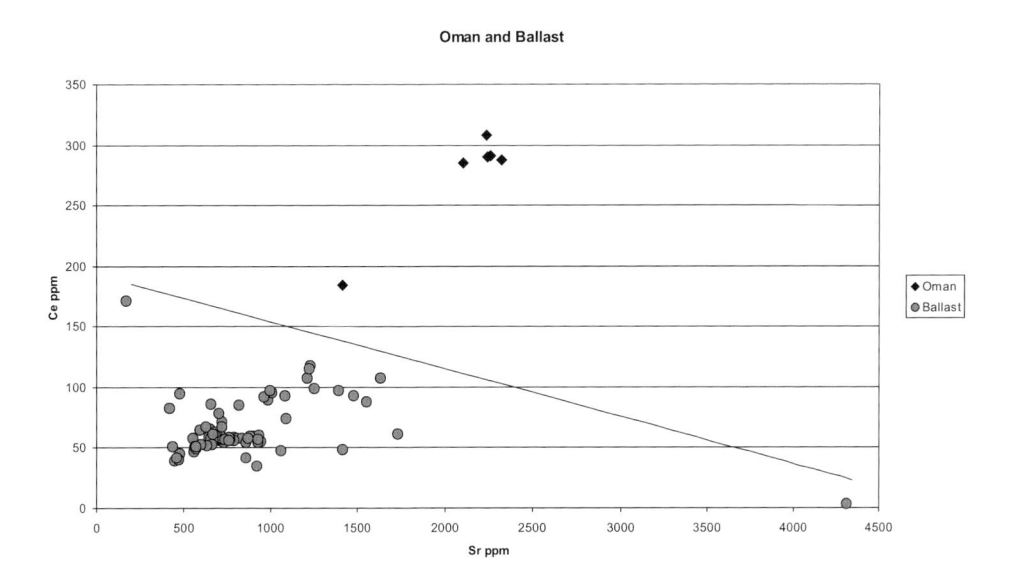

Fig. 3.10. A comparison of ballast and samples purchased in Oman, believed to be from Hormuz. Ce and Sr.

It appears that the Zn:Rb ratio was the best way of discriminating between sources at a preliminary level. The next step is to compare ballast with individual rock sources. Fig. 3.13 shows the relationship between ballast and the rocks of Djibouti using Zn and Rb. There is a clear distinction between the two clusters with no overlap. As the sample is a comparatively large one we may be confident that none of the ballast comes from Djibouti and that potential source can be eliminated. The rocks from Ra's Siyyan were not

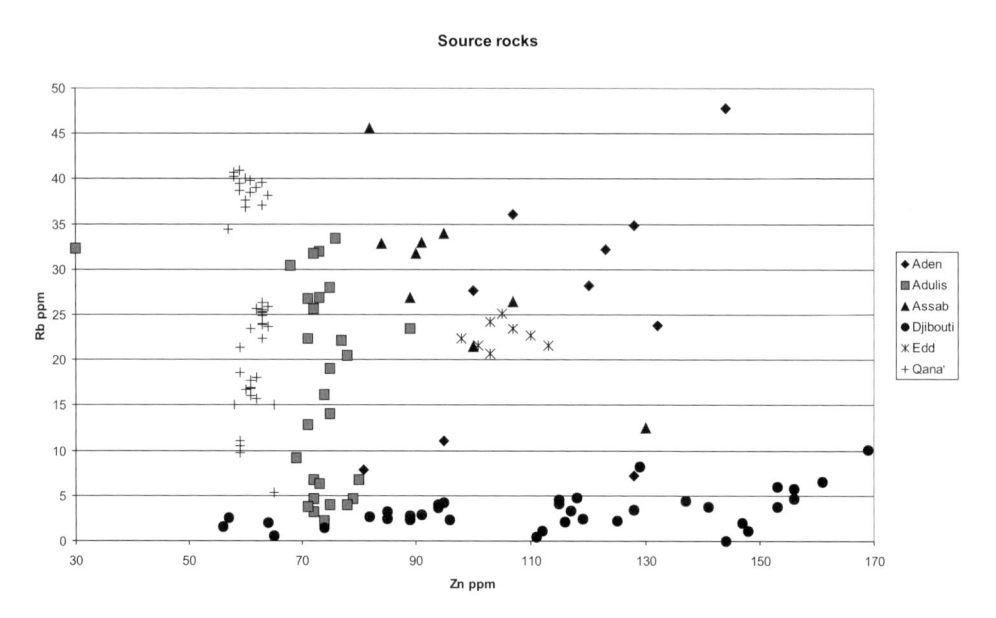

Fig. 3.11. A comparison of selected areas which were potential sources for the ballast. Rb and Zn.

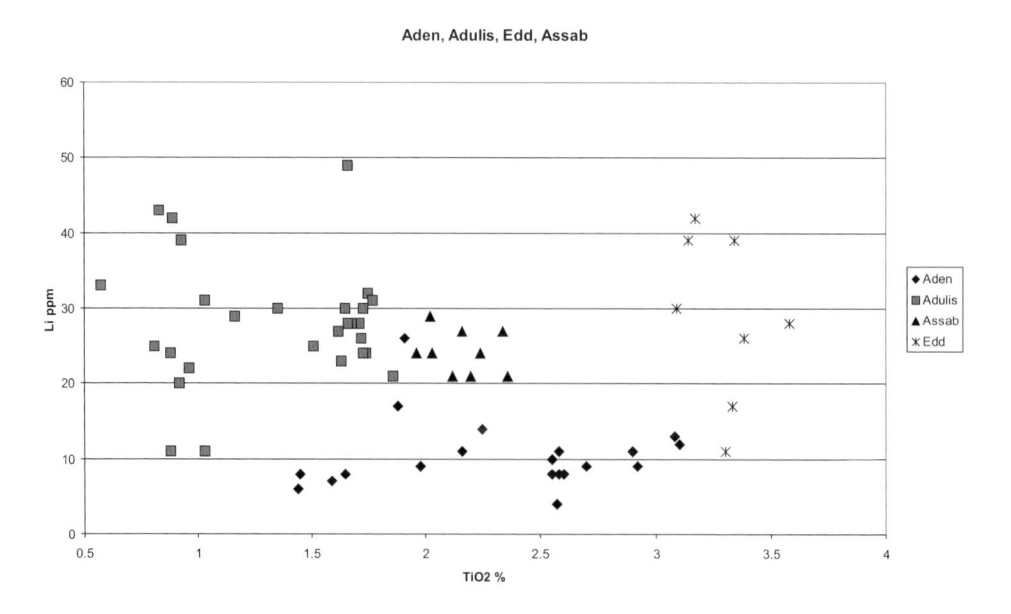

Fig. 3.12. A comparison of the rocks of Aden, Adulis, Edd and Assab. Li and TiO$_2$.

analysed, but thin section study suggests that they are texturally different from the ballast and hence unlikely to be a source rock (see below).

The graph comparing ballast with Ḥaḍramawt rocks is quite different (Fig. 3.14). There is a convincing overlap with the two groups from Ḥaḍramawt particularly at the upper end of the Rb scale where no differentiation can be made. Some of the Ḥaḍramawt samples with lower Rb also show lower Zn than the ballast, but this merely indicates that the range of rocks collected was greater than the range actually used in antiquity.

Similar graphs for comparing Adulis and Aden suggests clear distinctions between

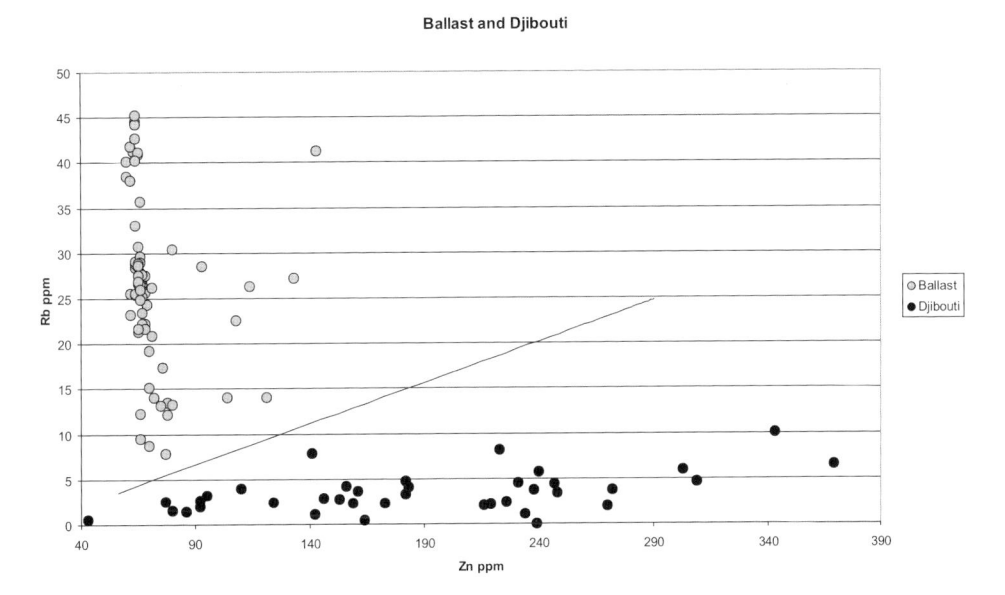

Fig. 3.13. A comparison of ballast and rocks from Djibouti. Rb and Zn.

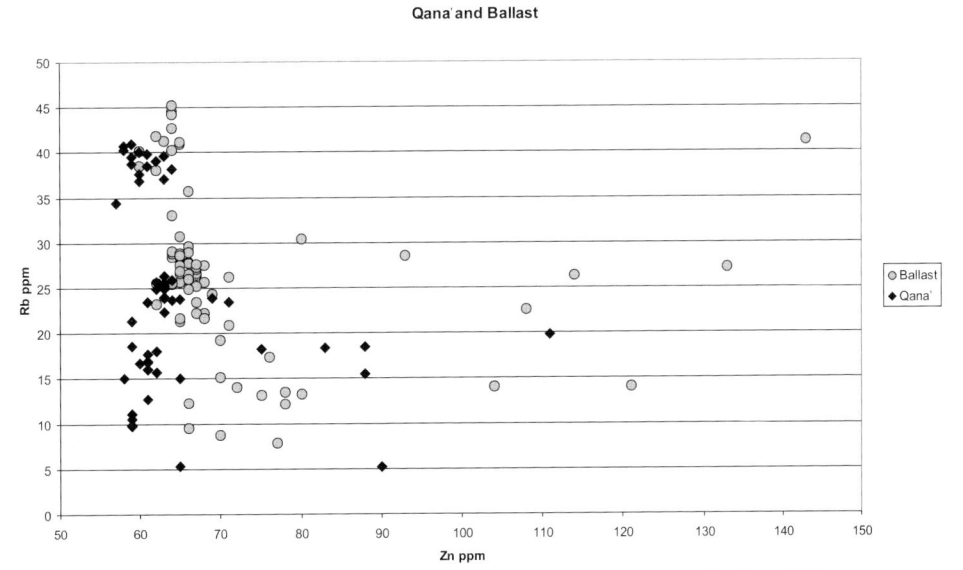

Fig. 3.14. A comparison of ballast and rocks from Qana'. Rb and Zn.

ballast and those areas, i.e. ballast is concentrated to the left of the line in Figs 3.15–16. The matter is not so clear as a number of ballast samples fall into the Aden and Adulis fields. Examination of the Sr:Zr distribution shows a clear distinction between Adulis and the Ḥaḍramawt as Adulis has lower Sr and Zr (Fig. 3.17). When the ballast is plotted on this graph it falls firmly within the field for the Ḥaḍramawt and not a single piece equates with Adulis. This suggests that Adulis was not the source for any of the ballast.

A few samples seem to fall convincingly in the Aden area of Fig. 3.16. There is a good overlap, but the ballast tails to the right with higher Zn values. Eleven samples of

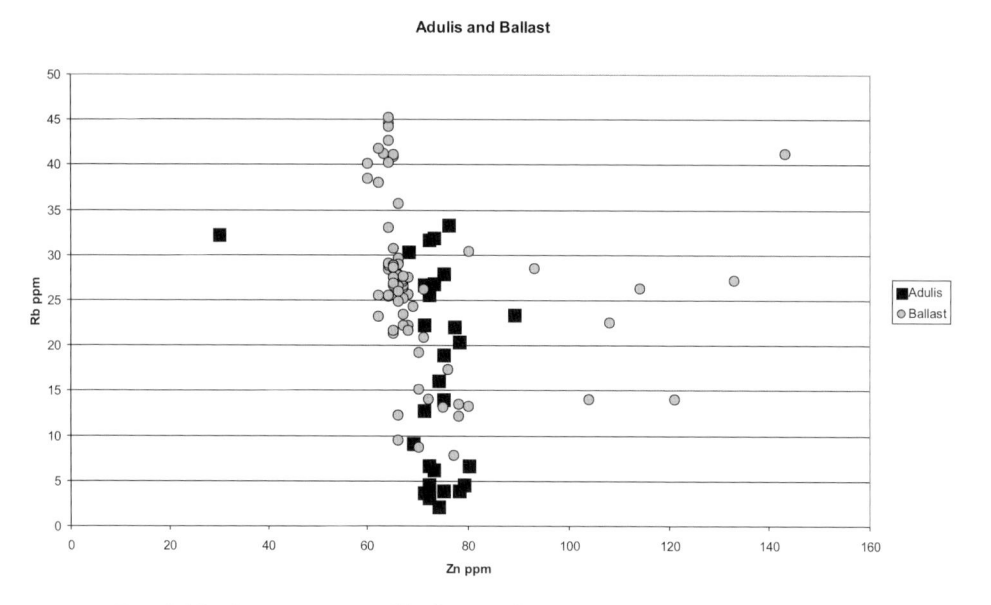

Fig. 3.15. A comparison of ballast and rocks from Adulis. Rb and Zn.

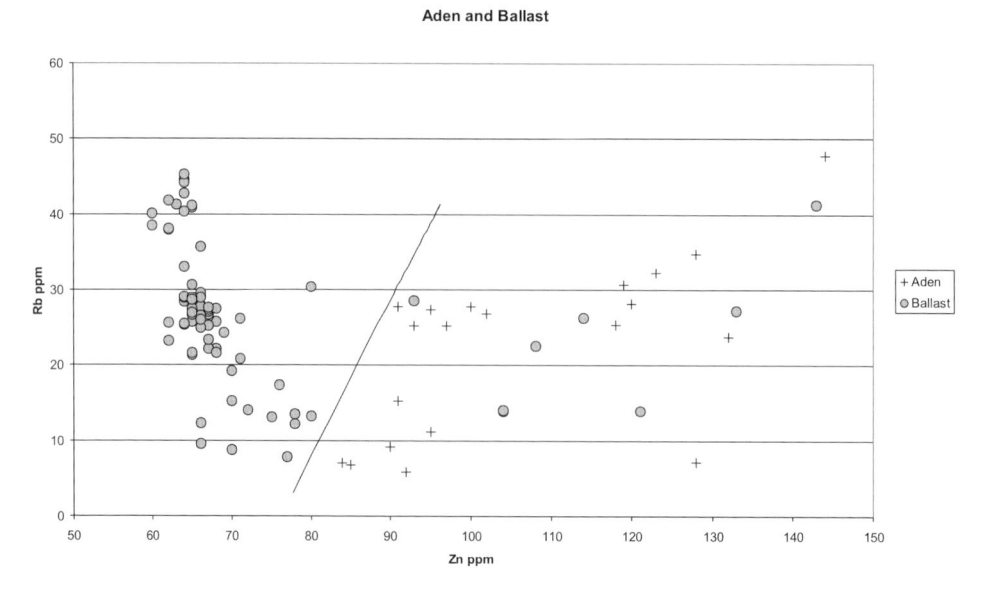

Fig. 3.16. A comparison of ballast and rocks from Aden. Rb and Zn.

ballast with significantly higher Zn values were separated off and plotted on a new graph showing the relationship of Li and TiO$_2$. These samples do not overlap with Adulis and 5 fall firmly within the range for Aden. Two lie on the borders of the Edd/Aden field and two on the Assab Aden field. Principal Component Analysis (below) links the samples with Aden rather than either Edd or Assab. The nine samples involved therefore seem to come from Aden (QAQ/3.1, 8.2, 8.3, 10.3, QAQ/MH5,8,9, BNC2,15).

This study suggests that among the basalt ballast, 68 samples come from Southern Central Yemen, namely Qana', and nine originate in Aden. None come from Adulis, Assab, Edd or Djibouti.

Principal Component Analysis

Principal Component Analysis is a powerful statistical tool which reduces the number of variables to a few uncorrelated ones. The original set of variables is transformed into a new set of 'principal component coordinates' so that if only a few principal coordinates account for the variation the rest may be discarded (Rollinson 1993).

The method is far from a universal panacea and in our case the data is virtually homogeneous, with minor variation serving to differentiate sources. The method can mask these relatively subtle differences which are crucial in characterisation work. Nevertheless it is an alternative approach giving a broad picture of groups of rocks belong together which can be of use when bivariate diagrams fail to give a conclusive result.

The basalt data was subjected to this analysis and grouped into an arbitrary 40 clusters. The results are tabulated below:

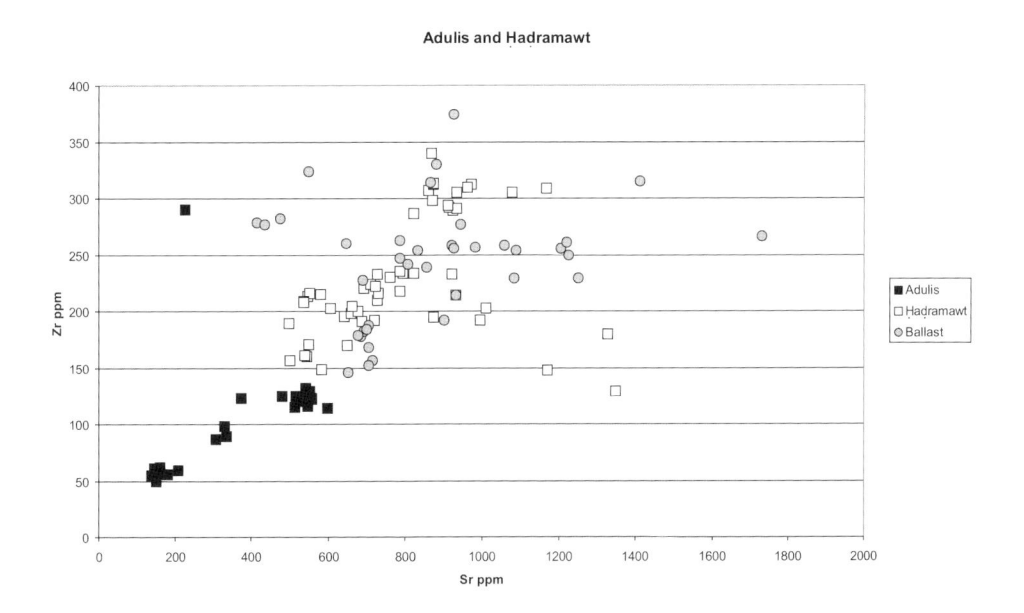

Fig. 3.17. A comparison of ballast with rocks from Adulis and the Ḥaḍramawt. Zr and Sr.

Samples	Cluster	Samples	Cluster
ADEN/85498_2106	1	EDD/5.4	3
DJIB/1	1	EDD/6.4	3
DJIB/6	1	SHAWRAN/1988.P6 [239] 2B 11533	3
DJIB/8	1	SHAWRAN/1988.P6 [230] 11092	3
DJIB/12	1		
DJIB/15	1	SHAWRAN/1988.P6 [276] 273116.6	3
DJIB/32	1	MS/1	3
DJIB/33	1	BA/1	3
DJIB/34	1	BA/2	3
DJIB/35	1	BA/3	3
		BA/7	3
DJIB/22	2	BA/9	3
		BA/14	3
QAQ/1.3	3	BA/18	3
QAQ/1.5	3	BA/36	3
QAQ/2.1	3	BA/37	3
QAQ/2.2	3	BA/39	3
QAQ/3.2	3	BA/40	3
QAQ/4.1	3	BN/1	3
QAQ/5.3	3		
QAQ/5.5	3	DJIB/10	4
QAQ/5.8	3	DJIB/11	4
QAQ/5.9	3	DJIB/13	4
QAQ/6.1	3	DJIB/14	4
QAQ/6.2	3		
QAQ/7.1	3	BNC/18	5
QAQ/7.4	3		
QAQ/8.1	3	BNC/13	6
QAQ/8.4	3	QAQ/MH5	7
QAQ/9.1	3	ASS/8.1	7
QAQ/9.2	3	ASS/8.6	7
QAQ/9.3	3	ASS/8.7	7
QAQ/9.4	3	ASS/10.1	7
QAQ/9.5	3	ADEN/29468	7
QAQ/MH1	3		
QAQ/MH4	3	QAQ/2.3	8
QAQ/MH7	3		
BNC/4	3	QAQ/3.1	9
BNC/7	3	QAQ/8.3	9
BNC/10	3	BNC/2	9
BNC/19	3	ASS/8.4	9
BNC/23	3	ADEN/k.127	9
EDD/5.2	3	ADEN/k.258	9
EDD/5.3	3		

Samples	Cluster	Samples	Cluster
ADEN/k.272	9	QAQ/9.6	15
DJIB/17	9	FS/1	15
		QAQ/11.4	15
ADU/2.12	10	BNC/14	15
ADU/2.13	10	BNC/21	15
ADU/2.16	10	BNC/22	15
		EDD/5.1	15
BNC/1	11	EDD/6.3	15
BNC/6	11	BA/8	15
BNC/11	11	BA/10	15
QAQ/11.6	11	BA/11	15
BA/20	11	BA/12	15
BA/22	11	BA/13	15
		BA/15	15
ASS/8.3	12	BA/38	15
BNC/9	13	ADEN/k.5	16
ADU/2.4	13	ADEN/k.8	16
ADU/2.5	13	ADEN/k.37	16
ADU/2.6	13	ADEN/k.39	16
ADU/2.7	13		
ADU/2.8	13	ADEN/kkcj.3	16
ADU/2.14	13	ADEN/k.7	16
ADU/2.15	13	ADEN/k.11	16
ADU/2.17	13	ADEN/k.336	16
ADU/2.18	13		
ADU/2.20	13	ADEN/29445	17
ADU/2.23	13		
ADU/2.25	13	ADU/2.19	18
ZULA/3.2	13	QAQ/7.2	19
ZULA/3.3	13	BNC/8	19
ADEN/k.124	13	BNC/16	19
ADEN/85498 [2104]	13	WADI HAJAR/1988.P20_32	19
		BA/4	19
QAQ/11.1	14	BA/5	19
BA/17	14	BA/6	19
		BA/16	19
QAQ/1.1	15	BA/19	19
QAQ/1.2	15	BA/31	19
QAQ/1.4	15		
QAQ/4.6	15	QAQ/4.4	20
QAQ/5.1	15	QAQ/11.5	20
QAQ/5.7	15	EDD/6.1	20
QAQ/8.6	15	EDD/6.2	20

Samples	Cluster	Samples	Cluster
BA/27	20	ASS/10.2	28
BA/32	20		
		WADI HAJAR/1988.P6 [67]	29
ASS/8.2	21		
		QAQ/8.2	30
DJIB/19	22	QAQ/MH8	30
DJIB/20	22	QAQ/MH9	30
DJIB/21	22	ADEN/1911.1364 [1]	30
DJIB/23	22		
DJIB/24	22	QAQ/4.2	31
		QAQ/7.5	31
DJIB/27	23	QAQ/8.5	31
		QAQ/11.3	31
QAQ/MH2	24	BA/21	31
BNC/17	24	BA/23	31
ADEN/k.2	24	BA/24	31
ADEN/k.30	24	BA/25	31
SHAWRAN/1988.P6.[218] 11061.4	24	BA/26	31
		BA/28	31
ḤAḌRAMAWT/1988.P7 [154]	24	BA/29	31
WADI RAIMA/1988.P22 [1]	24	BA/33	31
WADI RAIMA/1988.P22 [2]	24	BA/34	31
WADI GHIATAT/1988.P6 [113]	24	BA/35	31
BA/30	24	BA/41	31
		BA/42	31
ADU/2.9	25	BA/43	31
ADU/2.22	25		
DJIB/2	25	BNC/20	32
DJIB/3	25		
DJIB/4	25	DJIB/18	33
DJIB/5	25		
DJIB/9	25	BNC/3	34
DJIB/16	25	BNC/5	34
DJIB/25	25	QAQ/11.2	34
DJIB/26	25	BNC/24	34
DJIB/5a	25		
		BNC/15	35
DJIB/7	26		
DJIB/29	26	ADU/2.2	36
DJIB/31	26	ADU/2.3	36
		ADU/2.11	36
ADU/2.1	27	ZULA/13.1	36
ADU/2.24	27	ZULA/13.2	36
ZULA/3.1	27	DJIB/36	36

Samples	Cluster	Samples	Cluster
QAQ/10.1	37	DJIB/30	37
QAQ/10.2	37		
QAQ/10.3	37	ASS/8.5	38
QAQ/10.5	37		
ADEN/k.3	37	DJIB/37	39
ADEN/k.35	37		
DJIB/28	37	WADI RAIMA/1988.P22 [3]	40

It will be noted that some clusters contain rocks of varying origin and no ballast, while in other cases the ballast remains unassigned. Clusters 3, 15, 19 and 31 are large and suggest that the bulk of the ballast comes from Qana', although some Edd rocks also appear in clusters 3 and 15. In cases such as this where there is a choice, discrimination can be achieved by looking at individual elements as was done above. Edd can be eliminated because of its high TiO_2. Similarly in cases such as cluster 37, where there is a choice between Aden and Djibouti, a decision can be made in favour of Aden.

Overall the results of this analysis accords well with the bivariate diagrams, namely much basalt comes from Qana'with a small quantity from Aden.

Intermediate and acid rocks

All samples with more than 53% silica were separated from the above data to be considered separately. Obsidian is a special case and will be considered in the next section. The table shows the samples and the rock type to which they can be attributed using the system of Le Maitre (1989).

Samples	Rock type	Samples	Rock type
ADEN/1911.1364 [2]	Trachyte	ADU/2.21	Rhyolite
ADEN/1922.111 [2]	Trachyandesite	MN/1	Trachyte
ADEN/1922.111 [5]	Trachyte	QAQ/3.3	Trachyte
ADEN/A.793	Trachyte	QAQ/4.5	Basaltic trachyandesite
ADEN/k.130	Trachyandesite	QAQ/5.6	Basaltic trachyandesite
ADEN/k.133	Trachyte	QAQ/MH3	Dacite
ADEN/k.253	Rhyolite	QAQ/MH6	Trachyte
ADEN/k.4	Trachyte	QAQ/11.9	Trachyandesite
ADEN/L.7210	Trachyte	QAQ/7.3	Basaltic trachyandesite
ADEN/T.627	Trachyandesite	QAQ/10.4	Trachyte
ADEN/86620 [9]	Trachyandesite	QAQ/11.7	Dacite
		QAQ/11.8	Trachyte
ADU/2.10	Rhyolite		

All the ballast samples come from Mersa Nakari or Quseir al-Qadim and all the comparative rocks from Aden, except two rhyolites from Adulis. However, intermediate and acid rocks also occur at Kharaz, Little Aden and Perim for which published data are available. Fig. 3.18 shows a plot of Zn:Zr for the intermediate and acid ballast compared with the above rock data. Extra information has been added from published sources. It is clear that Perim and the Aden samples fall in the same field, but the inclusion of Kharaz, and Little Aden extends the range although they too overlap. In short, the case for suggesting a source other than Aden or Little Aden is not proven, and in view of archaeological probability, this seems the most likely source.

Obsidian

Two samples of obsidian were found in the excavations at Quseir al-Qadim. They both came from trench 7A where they were associated with late Augustan or early 1st century AD amphorae many of which were Italian Dressel 2–4 wine jars. A few pieces of pumice were found in the same deposit (Peacock and Blue 2006).

Obsidian is referred to in the Periplus (5:2.16–18) where there is mention of a source in a very wide bay, almost certainly Howakil Bay to the south-east of Adulis. Henry Salt (1814, 190) landed on the northern shore of the bay at Aréna.

"Near this spot I was delighted with the sight of a great many pieces of a black substance, bearing a very high polish, that lay scattered about on the ground at a short distance from the sea; and I collected nearly a hundred specimens of it, most of which were two three and four inches in diameter. One of the natives told me that a few miles further in the interior,

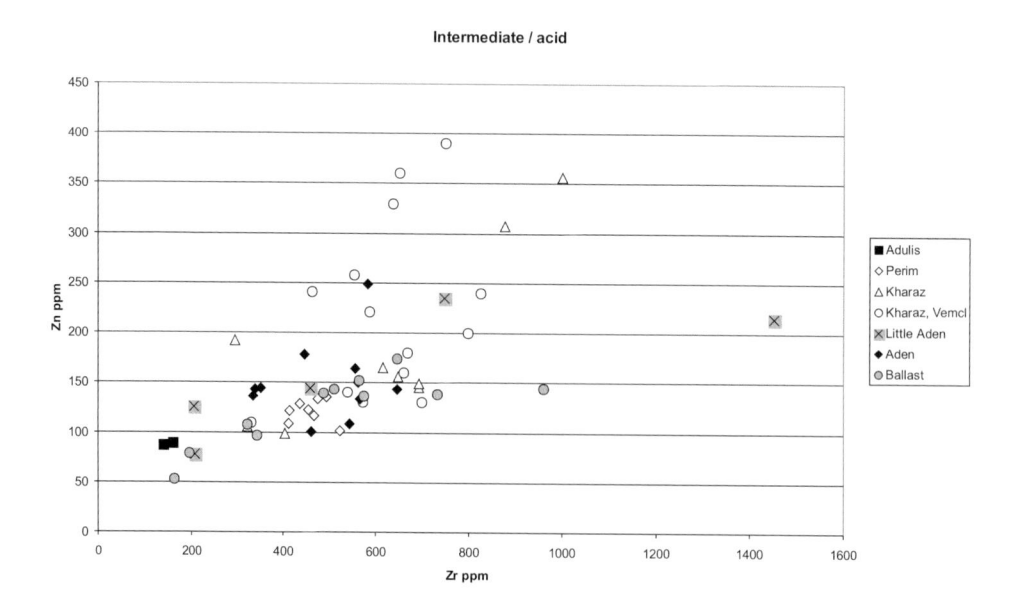

Fig.3.18. Intermediate and acid ballast compared with rocks from Adulis, Kharaz, Aden, Little Aden and Perim, based partly on published sources. Zn and Sr.

pieces are found of much larger dimensions. This substance has been analyzed since my return to England, and proves to be the true opsian, or obsidian, stone, which answers most exactly to the following description given by Pliny: "Among the different sorts of glass may be enumerated the obsidian found by Obsidius in Aethiopia, of a very deep black colour, sometimes a little transparent (on the edges) but opaque in its general appearance, (when in a mass) and reflecting images, like mirrors placed against a wall. Many make gems of it, and we have seen solid images of the divine Augustus cut out of this substance; who ordered four obsidian elephants to be placed, as curiosities, in the Temple of Concord, &c".

It is very tempting to suggest that this was the source of the obsidian from Quseir. However, the association with Mediterranean, specifically southern Italian, amphorae could indicate an alternative source. Within this area, the sources closest to the area of origin of the amphorae would be Pantelleria, Lipari or the Pontine Islands. The obsidian of Pantelleria is very scarce even in the outcrops on the island, but invariably has a distinctive green colour (Peacock 1985). It can be eliminated as a potential source.

Williams-Thorpe (1995) has published a useful review of obsidian characterisation studies and sources in the Mediterranean. Francaviglia (1995) has also attempted to define parameters for discriminating between obsidians of Mediterranean origin. Obsidians are often classified chemically on their content of the oxides of aluminium, calcium and the alkalis, sodium and potassium. On this basis the samples from Quseir would be described as subalkaline, as Al_2O_3 is slightly in excess of Na_2O plus K_2O. The typical compositions given by Williams-Thorpe (1995, Table 1) suggest that the obsidians of the Pontine Islands and Lipari are also subalkaline, but more strongly so, as aluminium is substantially in excess of alkalis. The obsidian from Pantelleria is strongly peralkaline.

The trace element distributions also show marked differences. The Italian sources have markedly lower Zr, higher Y, higher Sr, lower Rb, higher Zn, and lower V. The contrast is complete and convincing, suggesting that these sources are highly improbable.

The eastern sources in the Aegean and Turkey are less probable as there is no evidence of a trade connection between these areas and Quseir. Equally it is possible to detect chemical differences with the Quseir samples (*c.f.* Francaviglia 1995).

As a Mediterranean source is improbable, it seems that the Quseir obsidian should originate further south in the Red Sea. We were able to obtain a small sample from Adulis, but as this is not a source area, it must have been imported from elsewhere presumably in Eritrea. We were able to obtain 15 samples from north of Gela'elo. These took the form of pebbles from a recent gravel deposit which was almost certainly contiguous with the one from which Salt took his samples. Flakes were obtained from Mersa Fatma, Dahlak Khebir and Aliko in the same general region, while from the south of the country we had flakes from the beach at Beylul and near Bera'esoli. All of the samples hover around the subalkaline – peralkaline boundary, a majority just falling into the subalkaline field. This seems to be a regional characteristic.

Amongst the trace elements, Zr:Ba, Zr:Nb and Zr:Rb were adopted by Cann and Renfrew (1964) and more recently by Francaviglia (1995). In this case the Ba:Zr plot is least satisfactory. There seem to be two groups, one with high Ba and generally lower Zr, the other with minimal Ba and high Zr (Fig. 3.19). The former is typical of northerly sources, the latter of southern. One of the Quseir samples, the piece from Mersa Fatma and the Aliko samples fall in the first group, the other Quseir sample, that from Adulis and the piece from Dahlak fall into the second group. However plots of Nb:Zr and Rb:Zr show a clear break between northern and southern sources (Figs 3.19–20), with only one sample from the south falling within the plot for Gela'elo. This is however a waste flake rather than an outcrop sample and may have been imported to Bera'esoli from the north.

The sample is a very small one and it is hard to judge from single analyses, but it is only possible to argue from the data available. The results tentatively suggest the Quseir pieces, that from Adulis, and that from Dahlak originated in the Gela'elo area. It seems entirely probable that Adulis was a distribution centre though which material reached Egypt and the Dahlak Islands.

There is however a chronological problem. The material from Adulis comes from the western edge of the site, where Paribeni (1907) dug and located an early phase of occupation. Most of the site is dominated by Aksumitic material dating between 4th and 7th century AD. However, his trench 1 revealed what he thought was the earliest occupation of Adulis, with hand-made sherds suggesting a prehistoric date. However, he records the presence in the early levels of *una lucernetta di un tipo che è largamente rappresentato in tutto il mondo romano*. This is the only evidence we have of Roman occupation, so clearly attested in the Periplus. It is to be hoped that this lacuna will be filled in the course of the current programme of field work sponsored jointly by the Universities of Southampton and Asmara, and the National Museum of Eritrea. A suggestion that this period must be present comes from recent radiocarbon dates on surface shell fragments from the south-west corner of the site which cluster around 10BC – AD150. It is entirely possible that obsidian would have been a minor object of trade, although whether the material was freshly quarried or recycled from earlier use, is a moot point.

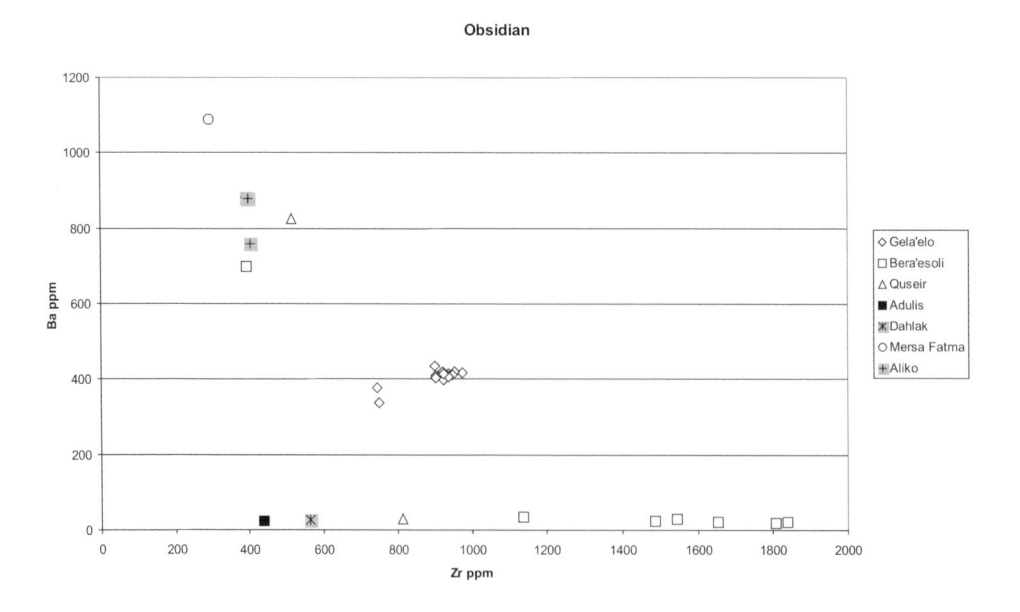

Fig.3.19. Obsidian from Quseir al-Qadim Adulis and Dhalak Kebir compared with source rocks from Gela'elo, Bera'esoli, Mersa Fatma and Aliko. Ba and Zr.

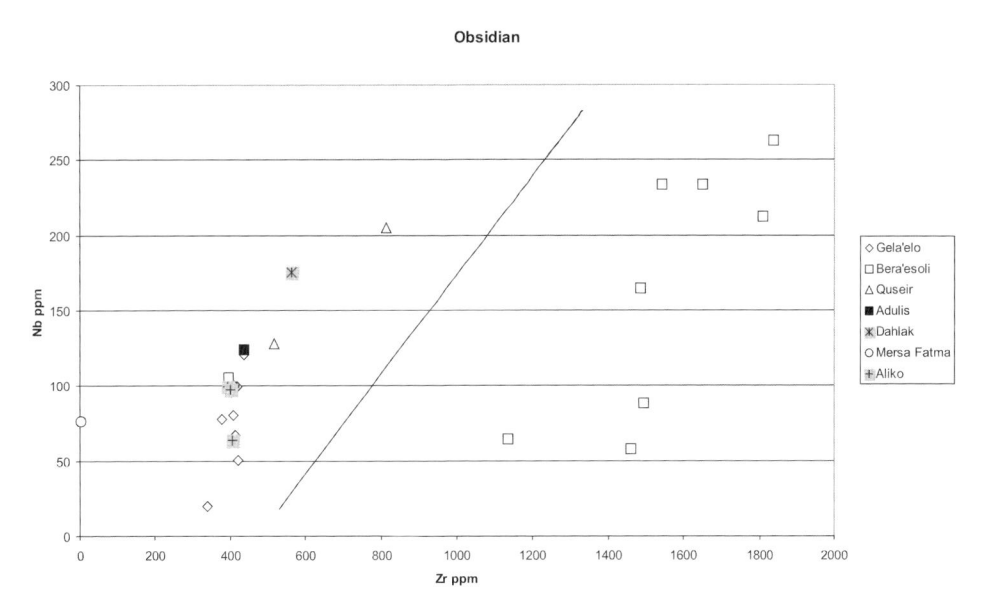

Fig. 3.20. Obsidian samples and source rocks as in Fig. 3.19. Nb and Zr.

Rock Dates

15 samples were dated by Dr Simon Kelley of the Open University using the Argon/Argon method. The results are tabulated below.

Site	*Sample no.*	*Sample Age (ma)*	±
Quseir al-Qadim	QAQ/2.2	0.87	0.47
	QAQ/3.1	No Age (Probably < 0.5 ma)	
	QAQ/5.7	No Age (Probably < 0.5 ma)	
	QAQ/6.1	0.1	0.35
	QAQ/7.3	8.2	1.1
	QAQ/9.1	1.89	1.1
	QAQMH/1	0.5	0.27
	QAQMH/2	Decreasing age release patterns. Youngest *c.* 0.5	
	QAQMH/4	0.87	0.14
	QAQMH/6	5.79	0.05
	QAQMH/8	10.2	2.7
Fury Shoal	FS/1	1	0.5
Berenike	BNC/1	No Age (Probably < 0.5 ma)	
	BNC/3	No Age (Probably < 0.5 ma)	
	BNC/4	2.53	0.64

It will be noted that of the 15 samples, 10 are very recent date, 1 ma or less. The remainder show increasing ages of 1.89, 2.53, 5.79, 8.2, and 10.2 ma. This suggests that most of the ballast comes from an area of very recent volcanism, with a maximum age of Upper Miocene.

Some indicative K/Ar dates are available for the rocks of south-western Yemen:

- Perim Island 10.5 ± 1.0 ma (Mallick *et al.* 1990)
- Jabal aṭ Turbah 10.5 ± 1.0 ma, 10.6 ± 1.0 ma (Vencl and Zamarský 2000)
- Jabal Kharaz 9.6 ± 1.0 ma, 8.8 ± 1.0 ma (Vencl and Zamarský 2000)
- Little Aden 5.3 ± 0.5 ma (Vencl and Zamarský 2000); 5.3 ± 0.5 ma, 6.4 ± 0.6 ma (Cox *et al.* 1968)
- Aden 5.0 ± 0.5 ma, 6.5 ± 0.6 ma (Vencl and Zarmarský 2000); 6.5 ± 0.6 ma, 5.0 ± 0.5 ma (Cox *et al.* 1968)

Two of the ballast samples, QAQ/7.3 and QAQMH/6 could come from Aden (see above) a view confirmed by the matching age. QAQMH/8 is exceptionally old and may originate in outcrops to the west of Aden such as Perim, Jabal aṭ Turbah, or even Jabal Kharaz.

Petrography

A majority of samples chemically analysed were also examined in thin section under the petrological microscope. In general, because of the inherent variation typical of volcanic rocks they add little to the above and it seems pointless to describe each section in detail. However the main characteristics are noted below.

Basalts

All of the basalts considered here are alkali olivine basalts and no tholeitic basalts were found in the sample. There is considerable textural variation, but the commonest type shows a groundmass of small labradorite microlites, often aligned in a flow texture, set in a black or brown glassy matrix. Phenocrysts are commonly of idiomorphic olivine or pyroxene. Two varieties are present, colourless augite or sometimes hypersthene. These minerals occur both in the groundmass and as phenocrysts. Very rarely plagioclase feldspar occurs as phenocrysts, it is usually strongly zoned and of bytownite composition. Brown mica may occur in accessory amounts.

Finer varieties occur more rarely, but apart from their texture, the petrography is the same.

The coarser rock is identical in every way to that forming Ḥuṣn al-Ghurāb above Qana' and provides independent confirmation of this attribution. The samples from Ra's Siyyan in Djibouti arrived too late for inclusion in the chemical programme, but they were examined in thin section. They are olivine basalts, but much finer and more glassy than any of the ballast. The petrography suggests that this was not a source.

Intermediate rocks

The trachytes, trachyandesites and balsaltic trachyandesites are characterised by a much finer groundmass composed of minute feldspar microlites which were difficult to resolve. They have a typical 'trachytic' texture and often show clear flow alignment. Phenocrysts are not abundant, but feldspars include sanidine and oligoclase. Some augite is present and occasionally bright green aegirine is encountered. The same range of minerals and textures is present in the ballast and in the rocks of Aden, but all our rock thin sections, apart from one from Kharaz, are from this source so this conclusion must be treated with caution. Aegirine is a relatively rare mineral, which occurs in the Lower Shamsan series of Aden (Bletcher 1997, 25).

The intermediate rocks are notably less fresh than the basalts and the minerals much more degraded, to the extent that they are often hard to determine. Vesicles are comparatively rare, but when encountered are often filled or lined with zeolites. These rocks appear to be older than most of the basalt, which would accord with an origin in Aden.

Rhyolites

The rhyolites were not examined in thin section and it is not possible to add to the chemical data given above.

Discussion

We must now consider what the above data means in archaeological terms and what light it throws on the mechanism of Roman commerce in the Red Sea area. The salient points to emerge from the above analysis are:

- the obsidian from Quseir comes from the northern shores of Howakil Bay in Eritrea, possibly through the port of Adulis;
- 66 ballast samples (77%) appear to originate at Qana' in the Yemen, 20 (23 %) from Aden (two confirmed by Ar-Ar dates);
- all samples from Berenike and those from Mersa Shuna, Fury Shoal and Bir Nakhil come from Qana';
- at Quseir al-Qadim 45 (70%) can be attributed to Qana' and 19 (30%) to Aden (with one dubious sample dated to 10.2 ma and one from Mersa Nakhari which comes from Aden);
- there is no reason to suppose that any ballast comes from Djibouti, Eritrea, Saudi Arabia or elsewhere in Yemen;
- The ballast does not occur east of Qana', it is known only from Egypt, but sites in Eritrea, Sudan and elsewhere in Yemen have not yet been explored.

The first striking point is the absence of ballast from Aden at Berenike. As the latter is exclusively Roman in date it could suggest that Aden material at Quseir belongs to the Islamic period. Aden was of little importance in the early medieval period, but lying mid way between Cairo and India, with an excellent harbour, it was reinstated after 10th century when trade saw a definitive shift from the Gulf to the Red Sea. (Daum 1987, 168). However, this is not an entirely satisfactory explanation as two stratified pieces from Roman contexts at Quseir can be ascribed to this source (QAQMH/3, QAQMH/6). They date from late Augustan and late 1st to early 2nd centuries respectively (information R. Tomber). In the case of QAQHM/6 source attribution is confirmed by an Ar-Ar rock date. The basalt sample, QAQMH/8, dated to the late 1st or early 2nd century is also ascribed to Aden. However, it has a rock date which accords with an origin either in Aden or more probably in the rocks to the west of the port. It is clear that some of the Aden material is Roman in date, but precisely how much must remain a matter of conjecture until more securely stratified material has been examined.

As Tchernia (1995) has pointed out, there are two ancient sources which bear directly on the mechanism of Roman trade with India. The first is Pliny (*Natural History*, 6, 26), the other is the Periplus. Pliny states that the route from Egypt to India was via Okêlis or Kanê. The quickest way was to set out from Okêlis, from where with the *Hippalus* wind blowing it is possible to reach Muziris in 40 days. Okêlis is believed to lie on the Yemeni side of the Bab al Mandab and Muziris in Southern India. The position of Okêlis is given rather precisely in the Periplus (25–26). It is said to be on the straits, 1200 stades (140 km) west of Aden. Casson (1989, 158) plausibly suggests that the site is located at Shaykh Sa'īd or Khawr Ghurayah, where there is a lagoon, possibly a silted harbour. It is described as not so much a port, but a watering station for those sailing on. Gurukkal and Whittaker (2001) locate Muziris on the coast of Kerala, but Shajan *et al*. (2004) have discovered a site in the same general region which they convincingly claim is Muziris.

Pliny (*Natural History*, 6, 26) also suggests two alternative routes, one running from the Syagros promontory (certainly Ra's Fartak in Yemen) to Patale in India, but a safer route ran from the same cape to Zigerus in India. Ra's Fartak is the most prominent headland on the eastern Yemeni coast (Fig. 3.21). According to the Periplus (30) it had a fortress, a harbour and a storehouse for frankincense. However, as frankincense was exported through Qana' (see below) the harbour may have been of relatively local importance, for collecting rather than distribution and trade. Certainly Ra's Fartak would be a prominent landmark and a navigational aid. It is perhaps best seen as analogous to transatlantic liners from Southampton leaving Lands End on their journey to America. It is extremely unlikely that Syagros was a major port because the Periplus (29, 9.22) informs us that the area was so unhealthy and fatal to those working there that the frankincense was harvested by slaves and convicts.

The two Indian ports are more problematical. Casson (1989, 216) following other commentators, equates Zigerus with Melizeigara, modern Jaigarh, to the south of Bombay. Patale is not mentioned in the Periplus, but Tchernia (1995) locates it in the Indus delta. If that is correct it might equate with Barbarikon which Casson (1989, 188) places in the same area. There is much uncertainty, which will not be resolved until more field work has been done. Interestingly, however, a Chinese document, the *Hou Han shu,* the history of the Han dynasty (AD25–221), mentions Roman trade with *Tianzhu*, usually meaning north-western India, centring on the Indus river (Hill 2003). It appears that it produced elephants, rhinoceroses, turtle shell, gold, silver, copper and iron and that all manner of the precious things of *Da Qin* (Rome) could be found there: fine cotton cloth, excellent wool carpets, perfume of all sorts, sugar loaves, pepper, ginger and black salt. There is no doubt that this was an important trading area, but there is a chronological problem because the *Hou Han shu* was compiled by Fan Ye who died in AD445.

The other document, the Periplus, gives a rather different and more detailed view. One of the most telling comments is the description of *Eudaimôn Arabia* (Aden). It appears (16, 8.31–32) that some years before the Periplus was written in the 1st century AD (Robin 1991), Caesar had sacked the town. This was almost certainly during the campaign of Aelius Gallus in 16–25 BC, the only known Roman attack on South Arabia. Casson (1989, 160) reviews the extensive debate which this statement has generated. The port was little used at the time of the Periplus, but before this time it was a major hub for trade with India. It was here that traders from Egypt and India met, neither daring to make the full journey.

A major question raised by this statement, is did the ships now make the full journey as Casson (1989, 160) suggests, or did another port take over the role as the centre of trade? Our new evidence suggests that while Aden continued to fulfil its original purpose in a relatively small way, Qana'became the new important pivot around which the India trade was articulated. This view is supported by the Periplus which states that it controlled the frankincense trade and carried on commerce with ports to the east as far as India.

'All the frankincense grown in the land is brought to Kanê, as if to a warehouse, by camel as well as by rafts of a local type made of leathern bags, and by boats. It also carries on trade with ports across the water – Barygaza, Skythia, Omana – and with its neighbour, Persis. Its imports from Egypt are wheat, limited quantity, and wine, just as to Muza; also as to Muza, Arab clothing either with common adornment or no adornment or of printed fabric, in rather large quantities; copper; tin; storax; and the rest of the items that go to Muza. Also for the king, embossed silverware and money (?), rather large quantities, plus horses and statuary and fine-quality clothing with no adornment. It exports local wares, namely frankincense and aloe; the rest of its exports are through its connections with other ports of trade.'

(Casson 1989, 67)

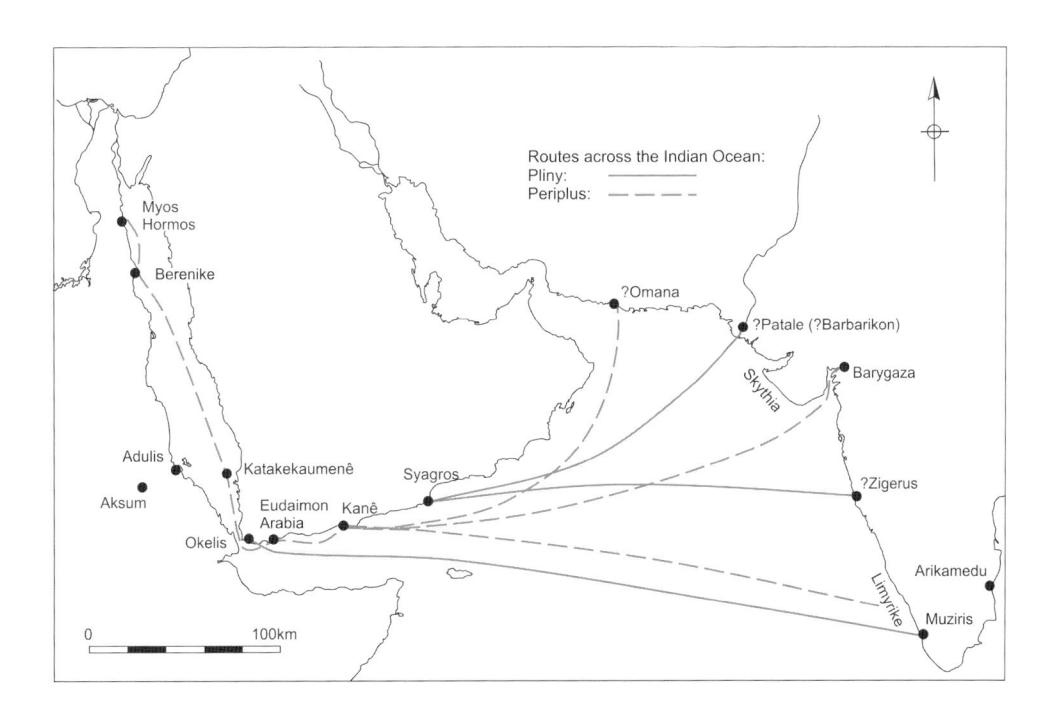

Fig. 3.21. Routes across the Indian ocean according to Pliny and the Periplus.

It is clear that ships from Egypt would have been heavily laden with items such as wine and some wheat as well as copper, tin, storax, horses, statuary and textiles, while for the return journey the commodities would be dominated by frankincense and other rich pickings of the east. The importation of storax, the gum of *Styrax officinalis,* is curious, as it should be a product of Kanê, rather than import. However, in this context we have an explanation of the pre-eminence of Qana' ballast at Berenike and Quseir al-Qadim for in return for heavy goods light ones would be returned and the ships would need balancing. The goods received by Qana' between the 1st and 6th centuries AD have now been illustrated by Davidde *et al.* (2004) and by Sedov (1996; 1997; and chapter 4 below). They include Campanian Dressel 2–4 wine amphorae, Laodician types, Tarraconensian Dressel 2–4, and Gauloise 4 from southern Gaul as well as well as Nubian, Egyptian, and possibly Indian productions. This is a truly remarkable assemblage so far from its Mediterranean homeland which attests the variety and quality of goods arriving at Qana'. Tomber (2004) has shown that the return trade from South Arabia was not restricted to light goods, for she has identified South Arabian storage jars, cooking pots and possibly organically tempered jars from Quseir al-Qadim and Berenike (but not inland sites such as Mons Claudianus and Mons Porphryrites). However, they are comparative rarities and in view of the large quantities of ballast, it seems unlikely that they were a major item of trade.

Equally the absence of basalt at Khor Rori in Oman suggests that the traffic was in one direction only. Khor Rori and Syagros may have had ports but they did not play the same role as Qana'. These were much more concerned with supplying Qana' with frankincense and no doubt it would have been carried on smaller coastal craft, such as the rafts mentioned in the Periplus, which would not have needed ballasting. Pirenne (1975, 95) saw Qana' as the officially appointed port where incense could be brought and exchanged for other commodities, after which it would be transported inland to Shabwah and thence by caravan to the Mediterranean. The route is discussed in more detail by Groom (1981) and more recently by de Maigret (2003), Beeston (2005) and by Singer in chapter 2 above. An Assyrian text suggests that the route may have been used from before 8th century BC and continued until the destruction of the Mārib damm mentioned in the Koran (7th century AD) (de Maigret, 2003). It seems that the road would have led towards Timna', the capital of the Gebbanitae, who according to Pliny (*Natural History*, 12, 32) monopolised the trade. The distances are prodigious. Shabwah was about 270 km from Qana' through a difficult mountain pass. Timna' lay 80 km to the south-west. From there, according to Pliny it was 1487½ miles (about 2250 km) to Gaza, the journey from there (or Shabwah – it is not clear which) being divided into 65 stages. The total overland journey would be 2600 km. Enquiries of Bedouin travelling in the Eastern desert of Egypt suggest that a camel could cover about 30 km a day. If this figure is extrapolated, it would have taken about 90 days to reach the Mediterranean from Qana' by the overland route, an estimate in line with Groom's (1981, 213) suggestion of 69–88 days.

The evidence of the ballast now suggests that the maritime route via Egypt was also important. Unfortunately there is no way of assessing the balance between the two, but travel by sea and across the Egyptian desert must have been much quicker and more efficient. It would also be free from the brigandry which plagued the overland routes through Arabia (Issac 1987).

It is abundantly clear that the importance of aromatics should not be underestimated.

According to Groom (1981) it was the food of the gods and consumed in prodigious quantities in the temples and at funerals and was the stuff of emperors. Perfume, particularly frankincense, was the way in which they symbolised their power (Bowerstock 1997). Bird (2004 and here chapter 6) has recently emphasised its key role in Mithraic ritual to cite an application in but one religious cult. Its importance is further illustrated by the existence of a specialised *collegium* of *thurarii et unguentarii* at Rome and importers at Pozzuoli (Salmeri 1997). Incense is also mentioned in Chinese sources as one of the products of Da Qin (Rome). Both the *Hou Han shu* and the *Weilue,* an account of the peoples of the West written in AD239–245, mention frankincense, myrrh and storax (Hill 2003; 2004). The two accounts are very similar, both concentrating on exotic luxuries. It seems that the writers are listing things that would appeal to a Chinese market. It is clear that Rome and China were anxious to make contact, the Romans wanting to acquire colourful Chinese silks, but access was blocked by the Parthians. The *Hou Han shu* tells us of a breakthrough when in 166 AD the emperor Marcus Aurelius sent an embassy to the East, which met their Chinese counterparts at Rinan (a commandery on the central Vietnamese coast). However, the latter were unimpressed with the offering of elephant tusk, rhinoceros horn and turtle shell.

The extent to which ships sailed directly between Egypt and India or vice versa is a moot point. It is worth noting that no Indian ballast has been found at Quseir or Berenike. One might expect the Deccan traps from the north or metamorphic rocks from the south, both of which seem to be lacking. Equally no ballast has been found in India, although it is doubtful if it has been systematically searched for. On balance it seems that the preferred point was exchange at Qana', with Aden continuing to act in this role to a lesser degree. This accords with the view of Salles (1993, 506), who considered it unlikely that products shipped at Myos Hormos would reach India on the same boat, at the end of a straight voyage, and vice-versa. Such journeys did happen, but were probably a rarity.

The absence of ballast from Adulis is more difficult to understand, and surely cargoes such as tortoise shell or ivory would need ballasting? Equally the presence of obsidian and pre-aksumite pottery at Quseir suggests direct contact between the two ports. If we knew more of the nature of the ships engaged in this traffic we might be able to answer this question.

There is clearly much to be done and many gaps to be filled. More information is needed on the Periplus sites of Sudan and Yemen and more research is needed in India. There are two important points to emerge from the current work. The first is the importance of Qana' in Rome's connection with India, the second is the importance of ballast in understanding the mechanisms of maritime trade. It is a subject unworthy of the neglect it has suffered to date.

Acknowledgements

This work could not have been attempted without the help of numerous colleagues in many different countries. We are grateful to the Leverhulme Trust for a Research Grant without which the programme would not have been possible, and to officers of the Egyptian Supreme Council for Antiquities permission to export rock samples, even though they are not artefacts and hence technically antiquities. ICPS Chemical work was carried out at the NERC facility, Royal Holloway College, London and we are indebted to the steering committee for accepting our project (no. OSS/256/0304). The principal component analysis was conducted at Southampton by Dr Darren Glazier, with the assistance of Dr Graeme Earl. Dr Simon Kelley of the Open University kindly accommodated our samples in the Ar-Ar dating programme.

Many people and organisations helped us with samples. We are grateful to The Natural History Museum and Leeds University, Geology Department, also to Dr Anne-Marie Lezine, CNRS, Paris, Professor Alexander Sedov, of the Oriental Institute, Moscow Academy of Sciences, who collected Qana' material specially for us an Dr Abdu Ghaleb, Ṣanaʿāʾ University who did likewise. In Egypt we were helped by Professor Steven Sidebotham. Our visits to Eritrea were facilitated by Dr Yosief Libsekal of the National Museum and Dr Zemenfes Tsighe, chair of the Asmara University Research Committee. Mr Tedros Kebedde organised the practicalities and took care of our everyday needs. Ms Antonia Willis kindly collected samples from Ra's Siyyan for us.

We also thank Dr Jason Bletcher for information and thin sections from Aden and Dr Jiří Vencl and Professor Vitězslav Zamarský for sharing their data with us. Dr Olwen Williams-Thorpe kindly helped us locate some of the more obscure publications listed below and advised on the obsidian. We are grateful to everyone: without their help our work would not have seen the light of day.

The chemical data on which this chapter is based can be accessed at http://www.arch.soton.ac.uk/data/ballast.

Bibliography

Arno, V., Bakashwin, M.A., Bakor, A.Y., Barberi, F., Basahel, A., Di Paola, G.M., Ferrara, G., Gazzaz, M.A., Guiliani, A., Heikel, M., Marinelli, G., Nassief, A.O., Rosi, M., and Santacroce, R., 1980. Recent basic volcanism along the Red Sea Coast: the Al Birk lava field in Saudi Arabia. In *Geodynamic Evolution of the Afro-Asian rift, Atti dei Convegni Lincei*, 47, 645–54.

Avanzini, A., (ed.) 1997. *Profumi d'Arabia: Atti del convegno*. Rome.

Avanzini, A., 2002. *Khor Rori Report 1*. Pisa.

Beeston, A.F.L., 2005. The Arabian aromatics trade in Antiquity. In M.C.A. Macdonald and C.S, Phillips (eds), *A.F.L. Beeston at the Arabian Seminar and other papers*. Oxford

Bird, J., 2004. Incense in Mithraic ritual: the evidence of the finds. In Martens, M. and De Boe, G., *Roman Mithraism: the evidence of the Small Finds*. Brussels, 191–9.

Bletcher, J.D., 1997. *The Shamsan series of the Aden volcano, Yemen: eruption and inversion of a zoned magma chamber*. Unpublished D.Phil. Thesis, Oxford.

Bowerstock, G.W., 1997. Perfumes and Power. In Avanzini, A., 1997, 543–556.

Cann, J.R. and Renfrew, C., 1964. The characterisation of obsidian and its application to the Mediterranean region. *Proc. Prehist. Soc.*, 8, 111–133.

Casson, L., 1981. The location of Adulis (Periplus maris erythraei 4). In Casson, L. and Price M., (eds.) *Coins, Culture and History in the Ancient World. Numismatic and other studies in honor of Bluma L. Trell*. Detroit, 113–22.

Casson, L., 1989. *The Periplus Maris Erythraei*. Princeton.

Chandler, J., 1993. *John Leyland's Itinerary. Travels in Tudor England*. Stroud.

Coleman, R.G., Fleck, R.J., Hedge, C.E., and Ghent, E.D. 1977. The volcanic rocks of southwest Saudi Arabia and the opening of the Red Sea. *Saudi Arabian Directorate General of Mineral Resources, Bull*. 22, D1–D30.

Combès, J-L., and Louis, A., 1967. *Les Potiers de Djerba*. Tunis.

Cox, K.G., Charnley, N., Gill, R.C.O., and Parish K.A., 1993. Alkali basalts from Shuqra, Yemen: magmas generated in the crust-mantle transition zone? In Prichard, H.M., Alabaster, T., Harris, N.B.W., and Neary C.R. (eds.) *Magmatic Processes and Plate Tectonics.* Geol. Soc. Special Pub., 76, 443–53.

Cox, K.G., Gass, I.G., and Mallick, D.I.J., 1968. The evolution of the volcanoes of Aden and Little Aden, South Arabia. *Quart. Journ. Geol. Soc.*, 124, 283–308.

Cox, K.G., Gass, I.G., and Mallick, D.I.J., 1970. The Peralkaline Volcanic Suite of Aden and Little Aden, South Arabia. *Journ. Petrology*, 11, 433–61.

Cox, K.G., Gass, I.G., and Mallick, D.I.J., 1977. The western part of the Shuqra vocanic field, South Yemen. *Lithos*, 10, 185–91.

Daum, W., 1987. From Aden to India and Cairo: Jewish world trade in the 11th and 12th centuries. In Daum, W., (ed.) *Yemen. 3000 Years of Art and Civilisation in Arabia Felix*. Innsbruck and Frankfurt am Main, 167–73.

Davidde, B., Petriaggi, R., and Williams, D.F., 2004. New data on the commercial trade of the harbour of Kanê through typological and petrographic study of the pottery. *Proc. Seminar Arabian Studies*, 34, 85–100.

de Maigret, A., 2003. La route caravanière de l'encens dans l'Arabie préislamique. Éléments d'information sur son itinéraire et sa chronologie. *Chroniques yéménites*, 11.

Desanges, J., and Reddé, M., 1993. La Côte Africaine du Bab Al Mandab dans l'Antiquité. In *Hommages à Jean Leclant*, 161–90.

Ellison, M., McCombie, G., MacElvaney, M., Newman, A., O'Brien, C., Tavener, N., and Williams, A., 1993. Excavations at Newcastle quayside: waterfront development at Swirle. *Arch. Aeliana*, 21, 155–234.

Empereur, J-Y. 1993. Observations sur l'Amphore "Letaconnoux". In *Hommages à Jean Leclant*, 191–4.

Francaviglia, V.M., 1995 Discriminating between Mediterranean obsidians. *Proc. Geosciences and Archaeology Seminar*, 381–398.

Gass, I.G., and Mallick, D.I.J., 1968. Jebel Kharaz: an Upper Miocene strato-volcano of comenditic affinity on the South Arabian coast. *Bull. Volcan.* 32, 33–88.

Gass, I.G., Mallick, D.I.J., and Cox, K.G., 1973. Volcanic islands of the Red Sea. *Journ. Geol. Soc. London*, 129, 275–310.

Ghent, E.D., Coleman, R.G. and Hadley, D.G., 1980. Ultramafic inclusions and host olivine basalts of the southern coastal plain of the Red Sea, Saudi Arabia. *Amer. Journ. Science*, 280A, 499–527.

Goodrick, G., Williams, A., and O'Brien, C., 1994. Excavations at Newcastle quayside: the evolution of Sandgate. *Arch. Aeliana*, 22, 219–33.

Groom, N., 1981. *Frankincense and Myrrh. A Study of the Arabian Incense Trade*. London.

Gurukkal, R. and Whittaker, C., 2001. In search of Muziris. *Journ. Roman Arch.*, 14, 334–350.

Harrell, J.A., 1996. Geology. In Sidebotham, S.E., and Wendrich, W.Z. *Preliminary Report of the 1995 Excavations at Berenike (Egyptian Red Sea Coast) and Survey of the Eastern Desert*, Leiden, 109–110.

Hill, J.E., 2003. *The Western Regions According to the* Hou Han shu. http://www.depts.washington.edu/uwch/silkroad/index.html.

Hill, J.E., 2004. *The Peoples of the West from the* Weilue *by Yu Huan*. http://www.depts.washington.edu/uwch/silkroad/index.html.

Hoare, P.G., Vinx, R., Stevenson, C.R., and Ehlers, J., 2002. Re-used Bedrock Ballast in King's Lynn's 'Town Wall' and the Norfolk port's Medieval Trading links. *Medieval Arch.*, 46, 91–106.

Issac, B., 1987. Trade Routes to Arabia and the Roman Presence in the Desert. In Fahd, T. (ed.)

L'arabie préislamique et son environment historique et culturel. Travaux du centre de recherche sur le Proche-Orient et la Grèce antiques. 10, 221–5. Strasbourg.

Hantke, G., 1951. Übersicht über die vulcanische Tätigkeit, 1941–1947. *Bulletin volcanologique*, 11, 161–208.

Keith, D.H., and Simmons III, J.J., 1985. Analysis of hull remains, ballast, and artefact distribution of a 16th-century shipwreck, Molasses Reef, British West Indies. *Journ. Field Arch.*, 12, 411–24.

Le Maitre, R.W., 1989. *A classification of igneous rocks and glossary of terms.* Oxford.

Mallick, D.I.J., Gass, I.G., Cox, K.G., De Vries, B.v.W., and Tindle, A.G., 1990. Perim Island, a volcanic remnant in the southern entrance to the Red Sea. *Geol. Mag.*, 127, 309–18.

Moghazi, A-K. M. 2003. Geochemistry of a Tertiary continental basalt suite, Red Sea coastal plain, Egypt: petrogenesis and characteristics of the mantle source region. *Geol. Mag.*, 140, 11–24.

Mohr, P.A., 1961. *The geology of Ethiopia.* Asmara.

Neumann van Padang, M., 1963. *Catalogue of Active Volcanoes of the World including Solfatara Fields. Part XVI Arabia and the Indian Ocean.* International Association Volcanology. Napoli.

Paribeni, R., 1907. Richerche nel luogo dell'antica Adulis. *Monumenti Antichi*, 18.

Peacock, D.P.S., 1984. Petrology and origins. In Fulford, M.G. and Peacock D.P.S. (eds) *Excavations at Carthage: The British Mission, Volume 1.2 The Avenue du President Habib Bourguiba Salammbo. The Pottery and other ceramic objects from the site.* Sheffield, 14–20.

Peacock, D.P.S., 1985. Archaeology of Pantelleria, Italy. *National Geographic Society, Research reports for 1977*, 567–79.

Peacock, D.P.S., 1998. *The Archaeology of Stone: A Report for English Heritage.* London.

Peacock, D., and Blue, L., 2006. *Myos Hormos – Quseir al-Qadim, Roman and Islamic ports on the Red Sea. Volume 1, Survey and excavations 1999–2003.* Oxford.

Pirenne, J., 1975. The Incense Port of Moscha (Khor Rori) in Dhofar. *Journ. Oman Studies*, 1, 81–96.

Robin, C., 1991. L'Arabie du Sud et la date du Périple de la Mer Erythrée. *Journ. Asiatique*, 279, 1–30.

Rollinson, H., 1993. *Using geochemical data: evaluation, presentation, interpretation.* London.

Salles, J-F., 1993. The Periplus of the Erythraean Sea and the Arab-Persian Gulf. *Topoi*, 3, 493–523.

Salmeri, G., 1997. Dell' uso dell' incenso in epoca romana. In Avanzini, A., 1997, 529–540.

Salt, H., 1814. *A Voyage to Abyssinia and Travels into the Interior of that Country.* London.

Schoff, W., 1912. *The Periplus of the Erythraean Sea.* Reprint New Dehli, 2001.

Sedov, A.V., 1992. New archaeological and epigraphical material from Qana'(South Arabia). *Arab. Arch. Epig.*, 3, 110–37.

Sedov, A.V., 1996. Qana'(Yemen) and the Indian Ocean: the archaeological evidence. In Ray, H.P. and Salles, J.-F., (eds) *Tradition and Archaeology. Early Maritime Contacts in the Indian Ocean.* New Delhi. 11–36.

Sedov, A.V., 1997. Sea-trade of the Ḥadramawt Kingdom from the 1st to the 6th centuries A.D. In Avanzini, A., (ed.) *Profumi d'Arabia. Atti del Convegno.* Rome.

Shajan, K.P., Tomber, R., Selvakumar, V., and Cherian, P.J., 2004. Locating the ancient port of Muziris: fresh findings from Pattanam. *Journ. Roman Arch.*, 17, 312–320.

Stevenson, E.L., 1932. *Claudius Ptolemy. The Geography.* Dover reprint, 1991.

Tchernia, A., 1955. Moussons et monnaies: les voies du commerce entre le monde gréco-romain et l'Inde. *Annales, histoire, sciences sociales*, 5, 991–1009.

Thompson, M., and Walsh, J.N., 2003. *A handbook of Inductively Coupled Plasma Atomic Emission Spectrometry.* London.

Tomber, R., 2004. Rome and South Arabia: new artefactual evidence from the Red Sea. *Proc.*

Seminar Arabian Studies, 34, 351–60.

Vencl, J. and Zamarský, V., 2000. Vulcanismus na pobřeží Adenského zálivu: Adenská vulkanická série. *Sbornik vědekých praci Vysoké školy báňské – Technické univerzity Ostrava*, 46, 91–100.

Whitcomb, D.S., and Johnson, J.H., 1982. *Quseir al-Qadim 1980. Preliminary Report.* Malibu.

Williams-Thorpe, O., 1993. Obsidian in the Mediterranean and the Near East: a provenancing success story. *Archaeometry*, 37, 217–248.

Appendix 1
List Of Samples Analysed

Egypt

#	Sample	Code
1.	Quseir Al-Qadim	QAQ/1.1
2.	(Unstratified)	QAQ/1.2
3.		QAQ/1.3
4.		QAQ/1.4
5.		QAQ/1.5
6.		QAQ/2.1
7.		QAQ/2.2
8.		QAQ/2.3
9.		QAQ/3.1
10.		QAQ/3.2
11.		QAQ/3.3
12.		QAQ/4.1
13.		QAQ/4.2
14.		QAQ/4.4
15.		QAQ/4.5
16.		QAQ/4.6
17.		QAQ/5.1
18.		QAQ/5.3
19.		QAQ/5.5
20.		QAQ/5.6
21.		QAQ/5.7
22.		QAQ/5.8
23.		QAQ/5.9
24.		QAQ/6.1
25.		QAQ/6.2
26.		QAQ/7.1
27.		QAQ/7.2
28.		QAQ/7.3
29.		QAQ/7.4
30.		QAQ/7.5
31.		QAQ/8.1
32.		QAQ/8.2
33.		QAQ/8.3
34.		QAQ/8.4
35.		QAQ/8.5
36.		QAQ/8.6
37.		QAQ/9.1
38.		QAQ/9.2
39.		QAQ/9.3
40.		QAQ/9.4
41.		QAQ/9.5
42.		QAQ/9.6
43.		QAQ/10.1
44.		QAQ/10.2
45.		QAQ/10.3
46.		QAQ/10.4
47.		QAQ/10.5
48.		QAQ/11.1
49.		QAQ/11.2
50.		QAQ/11.3
51.		QAQ/11.4
52.		QAQ/11.5
53.		QAQ/11.6
54.		QAQ/11.7
55.		QAQ/11.8
56.	Quseir Al-Qadim Harbour	QAQMH/1
57.	(Stratified Roman) Harbour	QAQMH/2
58.	Harbour	QAQMH/3
59.	Harbour	QAQMH/4
60.	R/Villa	QAQMH/5
61.	R/Villa	QAQMH/6
62.	R/Villa	QAQMH/7
63.	R/Villa	QAQMH/8
64.	R/Villa	QAQMH/9
65.	Quseir Al-Qadim, Trench 7A	QAQ/OB/1 Obsidian
66.		QAQ/OB/2 Obsidian
67.	Fury Shoal, Red Sea wreck site	FS/1
68.	Mersa Nakari	MN/1
69.	Mersa Shuna	MS/1
70.	Bi'r Nakhil	BN/1
71.	Berenike	BNC/1
72.	(Unstratified)	BNC/2
73.		BNC/3
74.		BNC/4

75.	BNC/5	124.	ZULA/3.3
76.	BNC/6	125. North of	GEL/4.1
77.	BNC/7	Gela'elo	Obsidian
78.	BNC/8	126.	GEL/4.2
79.	BNC/9		Obsidian
80.	BNC/10	127.	GEL/4.3
81.	BNC/11		Obsidian
82.	BNC/13	128.	GEL/4.4
83.	BNC/14		Obsidian
84.	BNC/15	129.	GEL/4.5
85.	BNC/16		Obsidian
86.	BNC/17	130.	GEL/4.6
87.	BNC/18		Obsidian
88.	BNC/19	131.	GEL/4.7
89.	BNC/20		Obsidian
90.	BNC/21	132.	GEL/4.8
91.	BNC/22		Obsidian
92.	BNC/23	133.	GEL/4.9
93.	BNC/24		Obsidian
		134.	GEL/4.10
Eritrea			Obsidian
		135.	GEL/4.11
94. Adulis	ADU/2.1		Obsidian
95.	ADU/2.2	136.	GEL/4.12
96.	ADU/2.3		Obsidian
97.	ADU/2.4	137.	GEL/4.13
98.	ADU/2.5		Obsidian
99.	ADU/2.6	138.	GEL/4.14
100.	ADU/2.7		Obsidian
101.	ADU/2.8	139.	GEL/4.15
102.	ADU/2.9		Obsidian
103.	ADU/2.10	140. Mersa Fatma	MF/11.1
104.	ADU/2.11		Obsidian
105.	ADU/2.12	141. Dahlak Island	DAH/12.2
106.	ADU/2.13		Obsidian
107.	ADU/2.14	142. Aliko	ALI/14.1
108.	ADU/2.15		Obsidian
109.	ADU/2.16	143.	ALI/14.2
110.	ADU/2.17		Obsidian
111.	ADU/2.18	144.	ALI/14.3
112.	ADU/2.19		Obsidian
113.	ADU/2.20	145. Bay of Edd	EDD/5.1
114.	ADU/2.21	146.	EDD/5.2
115.	ADU/2.22	147.	EDD/5.3
116.	ADU/2.23	148.	EDD/5.4
117.	ADU/2.24	149. South of Edd	EDD/6.1
118.	ADU/2.25	150.	EDD/6.2
119.	ADU/2.26	151.	EDD/6.3
	Obsidian	152.	EDD/6.4
120. Zula	ZULA/13.1	153. Bera'esoli	BERA/7.2
121.	ZULA/13.2		Obsidian
122. South of Zula	ZULA/3.1	154.	BERA/7.6
123.	ZULA/3.2		Obsidian

155.	BERA/7.7 Obsidian	188.	"	ADEN/k.8
156.	BERA/7.8 Obsidian	189.	"	ADEN/k.37
157.	BERA/7.9 Obsidian	190.	"	ADEN/k.39
		191.	"	ADEN/KKCJ. 3
158.	BERA/7.10 Obsidian	192.	"	ADEN/29445
		193.	"	ADEN/29468
159.	BERA/7.11 Obsidian	194.	"	ADEN/k.7
		195.	"	ADEN/k.11
160 North of Assab	ASS/8.1	196.	"	ADEN/k.30
161.	ASS/8.2	197.	"	ADEN/k.35
162.	ASS/8.3	198.	"	ADEN/k.253
163.	ASS/8.4	199.	"	ADEN/k.336
164.	ASS/8.5	200.	"	ADEN/A.793
165.	ASS/8.6	201.	"	ADEN/L.7210
166.	ASS/8.7	202.	"	ADEN/T.627
167. Assab Port	ASS/10.1			
168.	ASS/10.2			

Ḥaḍramawt (Natural History Museum coll.)

169. Beylul Bay	BEY/9.1 Obsidian
170.	BEY/9.2 Obsidian

Yemen

Leeds University Coll.

171. Aden	ADEN/k.124
172. Aden	ADEN/k.127
173. Aden	ADEN/k.130
174. Aden	ADEN/k.133
175. Aden	ADEN/k.4
176. Aden	ADEN/k.258
177. Aden	ADEN/k.272

Natural History Museum Coll.

178. Aden	ADEN/1911. 1364[1]
179. Aden	ADEN/1911. 1364[2]
180. Ra's Marbut, Aden.	ADEN/1922 111[2]
181. Gold Mohur Valley, Aden	ADEN/1922. 111[5]
182. Sira Island, Aden	ADEN/85498 [2104]
183. Ra's Marshag, Aden	ADEN/85498 [2106]
184. Ra's Tershyne,	ADEN/86620[9]

Leeds University Coll.

185. Probably Aden	ADEN/k.2
186. "	ADEN/k.3
187. "	ADEN/k.5

203. Wadi Hajar,	WADI HAJAR/ 1988.P6[67]
204. Wadi Hajar,	WADI HAJAR/ 1988.P20[32]
205. Shawran volcano,	SHAWRAN/ 1988.P6[218] 11061.4
206. Shawran volcano,	SHAWRAN/ 1988. P6[239] 2B 1153.3
207. Shawran volcano,	SHAWRAN/ 1988.P6 230 1109/2
208. Shawran volcano,	SHAWRAN/ 1988.P6[276] 273116.6
209. Ḥaḍramawt	ḤAḌRAMAWT/ 1988.P7[154]
210. Wadi Raima,	WADI RAIMA/ 1988.P22[1]
211. Wadi Raima,	WADI RAIMA/ 1988.P22[3]
212. Wadi Raima,	WADI RAIMA/ 1988.P22[2]
213. Wadi Ghiadat	WADI GHIADAT/ 1988 P6[113]

A-M. Lezine Coll.

214. Bi'r 'Ali Ḥuṣn al Ghurāb	BA/1

A. Sedov Coll.

215. Qana'	BA/2

216.	"	BA/3	
217.	"	BA/4	
218.	"	BA/5	
219.	"	BA/6	
220.	"	BA/7	

A. Ghaleb coll.

221.	"	BA/8.
222.	"	BA/9
223.	"	BA/10
224.	"	BA/11
225.	"	BA/12
226.	"	BA/13
227.	"	BA/14
228.	"	BA/15
229.	"	BA/16
230.	"	BA/17
231.	"	BA/18
232.	"	BA/19
233.	"	BA/20
234.	"	BA/21
235.	"	BA/22
236.	"	BA/23
237.	"	BA/24
238.	"	BA/25
239.	"	BA/26
240.	"	BA/27
241.	"	BA/28
242.	"	BA/29
243.	"	BA/30
244.	"	BA/31
245.	"	BA/32
246.	"	BA/33
247.	"	BA/34
248.	"	BA/35
249.	"	BA/36
250.	"	BA/37
251.	"	BA/38
252.	"	BA/39
253.	"	BA/40
254.	"	BA/41
255.	"	BA/42
256.	"	BA/43

Oman

Purchased

257. Muscat		MU/01
258.		MU/02
259.		MU/03
260.		MU/04
261.		MU/05
262.		MU/06

Djibouti

263. Arta		DJIB/1 Afar Stratoid series	
264. N1, turn to Arta	a.	DJIB/2 Afar Stratoid series	
265.	b.	DJIB/3	"
266.	c.	DJIB/4	"
267. N1, 25 km W Djibouti	a.	DJIB/5 Basaltic fissure flow	
268.	b.	DJIB/5a Upper part of Stratoid Series	
269.	c.	DJIB/6	"
270.	d.	DJIB/7	"
271. Dorale Beach	a.	DJIB/8	"
272.	b	DJIB/9	"
273.	c.	DJIB/10	"
274.	d.	DJIB/11	"
275.	e.	DJIB/12	"
276. N1, 43 km W Djibouti	a.	DJIB/13 Dalha basalt	"
277.	b.	DJIB/14	"
278.	c.	DJIB/15	"
279.	d.	DJIB/16	"
280. N9, 3 km after N1	a.	DJIB/17 Afar Stratoid series	
281.	b.	DJIB/18	"
282.	c.	DJIB/19	"
283.	d.	DJIB/20	"
284. N9, 20 km after N1	a.	DJIB/21	"
285.	b.	DJIB/22	"
286.	c.	DJIB/23	"
287.	d.	DJIB/24	"
288. N9, 2 km N Guinni Koma bay	a.	DJIB/25 Recent basaltic lava	
289.	b.	DJIB/26	"
290.	c.	DJIB/27	"
291. N9, near Addali	a.	DJIB/28 Basaltic fissure flow	
292.	b.	DJIB/29 Upper part of Stratoid Series	
293.	c.	DJIB/30	"
294.	d.	DJIB/31	"
295. Hill N Tadjoura	a.	DJIB/32	"
296.	b.	DJIB/33	"
297.	c.	DJIB/34	"
298.	d.	DJIB/35	"
299. Plateau du Serpent, sea wall	a.	DJIB/36 Imported block	
300.	b.	DJIB/37	"

Chapter 4: The Port of Qana' and the Incense Trade

Alexander Sedov

Introduction

The ruins of a settlement identified as the ancient Ḥaḍrami city-port of Qana' are situated on the southern coast of the Arabian Peninsula near the modern village of Bi'r 'Alī, on the opposite side of a beautiful bay, at the foot-hill of the black volcanic rock called Ḥuṣn al-Ghurāb, probably one of the best landing places on the southern coast of Yemen (Fig. 4.1 a–b, Fig. 4.2). The rock, with a maximum height of about 140 m, occupies the south-western promontory of the bay. The width of the bay is about 3 km, extending inland about 2 km. There are six islands in front of the Bi'r 'Alī bay: the flat volcanic island of Halaniya is about 800 m south of Ḥuṣn al-Ghurāb, Siha island is about 11 nautical miles south-east of Ḥuṣn al-Ghurāb, three small islands called al-Gaddarayn ('Two Traitors') are about 4 nautical miles east of Ḥuṣn al-Ghurāb, and the large al-Barrāqah island lies on the far south-east of the Bi'r 'Alī bay.

To the west of Ḥuṣn al-Ghurāb there is a rather extensive sandy bay, about 50 km in length, known as Gubbat al-'Ayn. A promontory called Ra's Qusayr (13° 54' N; 47° 47' E) borders the bay to the west. On the north-western side is the mouth of Wadi Mayfa'a, the core of the so-called Western Ḥaḍramawt (al-Mashriq). At the eastern end of Gubbat al-'Ayn is the Wadi 'Arar (al-Huvail) and promontory called Ra's al-'Usaida. The presently abandoned town of Balḥāf, built in the 1930s by the rulers of the al-Vahidi family, is located nearby. The volcanic rock of Ra's al-Ratl lies 6.5 km east of Ra's al-'Usaida, in close vicinity to Ḥuṣn al-Ghurāb. East of Bi'r 'Alī there is another extensive bay called Maqdahā (Majdahā). The ruins of a small village and winter residence of al-Vahidi sultans can be traced in its eastern part. The site of Majdahā was mentioned by Ibn al-Mujāwir (died in AD 1291), who described it as a station on the pilgrim road from Raysut (the present Sultanate of Oman) to Aden (Ibn al- Mujāwir 1954, 270; Sprenger 1864, 145). According to some scholars, the earliest mention of Qana' occurs in the Bible (*Ezekiel* xxvii, 23) and can be dated around the first quarter of the 6th century BC (Doe 1971, 182; Griaznevich 1995, 285) (but *cf.* below). Κανὴ ἐμπόριόν was known to Pliny (*Natural History*, 6, 36, 104) and Ptolemy (*Geography*, V, 7, §10; VIII, 22, §9), and was also mentioned in the *Periplus Maris Erythraei*, the ancient guide written most probably around the middle of the 1st century AD by a Greek-speaking merchant.[1] The site was described as a port of trade, 'belonging to the kingdom of Eleazos, the frankincense-bearing land', and the place where 'all the frankincense grown in the land' was collected (*Periplus*, 27: 9. 4–8).

The toponym Ḥuṣn al-Ghurāb occurs in the works of some Arab geographers of the 13th century, such as Yacut (died AD 1229) and al-Qazwīnī (died AD 1283), probably incorporating earlier reports. Ibn al- Mujāwir describes it as a castle built by al-Sama 'l bin 'Adiyyā al-Yahūdī, the famous Yemeni poet of the first half of the 6th century AD.[2] A geographical name al-Qanā, apparently on the southern coast of the Arabian Peninsula, is mentioned by the Bahraini poet, geographer, historian and anthropologist Ibn al-Muqarrab (AD 1176–1232) (Khulusi 1976, 101). Jaza'ir al-Qanā (Qanā islands), the starting point for sailing to African ports, were known to the famous Arabian pilot Ahmad bin Madjid (second half of the 15th – beginning of the 16th centuries AD) (Madjid 1984, 87) as well as to the recent Yemeni sailors (Ar-Rafik 1966, 82–83; Shihab 1984, 208, 210; Griaznevich 1995, 281). The Portuguese discoverers called them the *Canacani (Canicani) Islands* (Doe 1964, 12, note 3). None of these sources indicate any ruins of an ancient town or city-port.

The first Europeans who visited the site were, in all probability, British naval officers who landed aboard the *Palinurus* on the morning of the 6th of May 1834. In a book published in London in 1838 one of the explorers, Lt. J.R.Wellsted, described the ruins of a vast settlement at the foot-hill on the southern coast of Bi'r 'Alī bay and a fortress on top of the rock of Ḥuṣn al-Ghurāb, the find-spot of the famous South Arabian inscriptions now known as CIH 621 and CIH 728 (Wellsted 1838, 421–427).

Fig. 4.1 a. Ḥuṣn al-Ghurāb, view from the Halaniya island; b. Bi'r 'Ali Settlement (ancient Qana'), ruins of structures (view from the slope of Ḥuṣn al-Ghurāb).

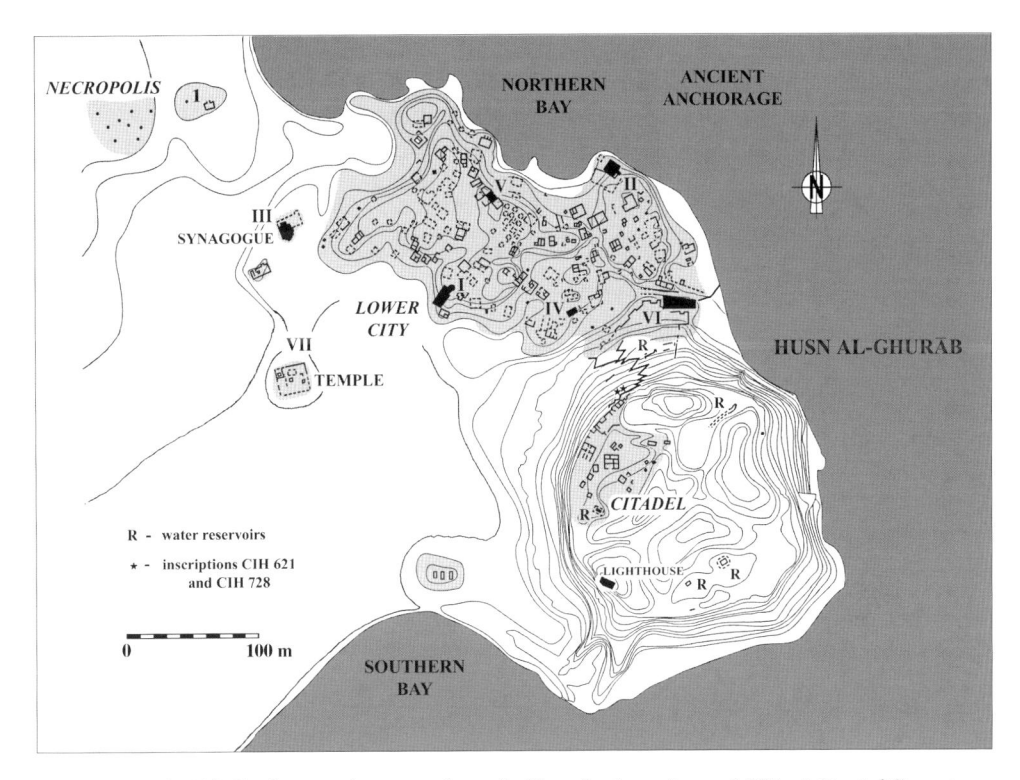

Fig. 4.2 Bi'r 'Alī Settlement (ancient Qana'). Sketch plan: Areas I-VII ; 1 Burial Structure.

Thus, the delightful ruins of the ancient Qana' or, according to our nomenclature, the Bi'r 'Alī settlement, were already known to scholars more than 150 years ago. In 1957 the site was visited and explored by B. Doe, who later, in 1961, published the first sketch-plan and rather detailed description of the ruins (Doe 1961, 191–198; 1964, 9–16). The archaeological excavations at the site started in 1972 with clearing the remains of a big building located at the highest point of Ḥuṣn al-Ghurāb (Shirinskij 1977, 202–205).[3] Since 1985, systematic excavations at Bi'r 'Alī settlement have been carried out by the Russian Archaeological Mission to the Republic of Yemen which, until the end of 1991, was called the *Soviet-Yemeni Joint Complex Expedition*. In several field seasons, (each campaign lasting from 2 to 4 weeks), it has been possible to identify the character of the city's buildings, the approximate chronological and territorial limits of the ancient town, and the stratigraphy of cultural deposits.

Description Of The Site

The ancient settlement is situated on the south-western side of the bay, about 3 km from the modern village of Bi'r 'Alī, at the foothill of the black volcanic rock, Ḥuṣn al-Ghurāb. In can conveniently be considered under three headings: the *Lower City* including separate structures outside the city limits; the *Citadel* on the summit of Ḥuṣn al-Ghurāb (fortress 'Urr Mawiyat according to the South Arabian inscriptions CIH 621 and CIH 728); and the *Necropolis* on the north-western edge of the city (Fig. 4.2).

Lower City. The tell, in the form of a rectangle consisting of two parts, constitutes the main part of the settlement. The size of the tell is about 300 × 500 m. The height of the north-western part is about 4.5–5.0 m (it measures about 300 × 320 m); the height of the south-eastern parts about 2.5–3.0 m. The long north-eastern side of the settlement opens to the Bi'r 'Alī bay. Even today this is the most suitable mooring for ships and boats, and for unloading them. There is a wide depression along the north-western side of the settlement, which separates the necropolis situated behind it. The south-eastern side of the settlement adjoins the foot of the rock Ḥuṣn al-Ghurāb.

The ruins of numerous ancient houses, in some cases with a very clearly visible layout, can be seen in this part of the settlement. There is no regular system of town planning, but sometimes streets and squares could be identified, particularly in the southern and south-eastern parts of the settlement. The number of ancient houses present is not clear, but probably was more than one hundred. The excavations suggest that the ordinary houses were combined into rather big dwelling complexes consisting of adjoining houses, separated by narrow streets and passages. The large buildings of the noblemen with wide courtyards were concentrated along the seashore in the northern and north-eastern parts of the settlement.

There are no traces of the city wall, and only some parts of the ancient town were fortified. We cannot exclude the possibility that the walls of the houses built along the perimeter served as defensive structures. One of the well-fortified areas was situated at the foot of Ḥuṣn al-Ghurāb and it was from this area that the road leading to the fortress 'Urr Mawiyat on the summit of Ḥuṣn al-Ghurāb started. The complex of structures at the foot of the hill had square towers and a narrow entrance from the sea.

A narrow and steep path to the summit led to the northern slope of Ḥuṣn al-Ghurāb. In some places the path became a kind of staircase supported by stone walls. The central part of the northern slope of Ḥuṣn al-Ghurāb, on both sides of the path, was consolidated with monumental stone walls made from basalt blocks which, most probably, were built to defend against landslides. There is a water-tank at the foot of one side of the walls. Ruins of tower-like buildings could also be traced on the slope.

Three structures lie outside the city limits. The western structure is about 44 × 64 m in size, and the excavations suggest it is a temple of a local deity (Fig. 4.3b). The structure to the north-west of the settlement in all probability is the ruins of a synagogue. A big dwelling or 'custom-house' lies on its own rather far from the border of the ancient town, on the coast of the so-called 'southern' bay.

Citadel. The north-western part of the summit of Ḥuṣn al-Ghurāb is occupied with the ruins of what was, in all probability, the fortress 'Urr Mawiyat. The entrance to the fortress was from the north-west where remains of fortifications (a wall with gates), could be traced. About 20 buildings constituted the fortress. On the top of Ḥuṣn al-Ghurāb was a huge structure, which was partly excavated in 1972, and could be identified as a lighthouse for incoming ships (Fig. 4.2–4.5; Fig. 4.3a). There are four huge water-tanks on the summit of Ḥuṣn al-Ghurāb in addition to the ruins of the fortress and lighthouse. They are rectangular or square in shape, and 6 × 12; 12 × 12; 4 × 14 m in size.

Necropolis. The ancient cemetery lies about 300 m to the north-west of the 'Lower City'. There are roughly 15 burial structures, most of them now completely ruined. The excavations suggest they were family tombs with rectangular surface structures and

Fig. 4.3 a. Ḥuṣn al-Ghurāb, ruins of a lighthouse on the summit; b. Bi'r 'Alī Settlement (ancient Qana'), temple of local deity (Area VII).

subterranean chambers. The funeral practice seems to have been collective inhumation in subterranean graves accompanied by grave goods such as pottery, personal ornaments, *etc*. The cemetery was in use during the 'middle' (BA-II) period of occupation, *i.e.* in the 2nd – 5th centuries AD (see below).

Stratigraphy of the Site

Systematic excavations at Bi'r 'Alī settlement (ancient Qana') have shed a great deal of light on various facets of the city's history: its topography, the character of the city's structures, the stratigraphy of the cultural deposits including its approximate chronological limits, and on different aspects of its material culture. The following is an attempt to summarize the preliminary results.

Excavations and soundings in various parts of the settlement made it possible to determine three main phases of Bi'r 'Alī occupation: the 'lower' (BA-I), 'middle' (BA-II) and 'upper' (BA-III) periods. Each period had its own chronological limits, and was characterised by specific pottery and numismatic assemblages, dwellings and building constructions. Imported pottery was dominant in all strata from the settlement and added up to 75% of all pottery finds.

The 'lower' (BA-I) period

Structures. The earliest structures unearthed during the excavations were located at the foot of Ḥuṣn al-Ghurāb (Area VI), at the beginning of the path leading to the fortress and the lighthouse on the summit. The excavated building ('Early Structure') revealed several adjoining large rooms, some of them covering an area of about 90 square metres (Fig. 4.6). In addition, we cannot exclude the possibility that some houses on the northern slope of Ḥuṣn al-Ghurāb, along the path to the summit, were also built during the BA-I period. Prior to the excavations such a supposition could not be justified with certainty, but the close similarity in the character of the stone masonry of these 'early' buildings should be noted.

Layers. Cultural deposits unearthed in the ruins of the 'Early Structure' in Area 6 above the 'initial' floors of its rooms are not very thick, suggesting a specific function of the building perhaps as a warehouse rather than a dwelling. Traces of a big fire exposed in the ruins show very clearly that the end of the 'Early Structure' was violent. In addition to Area 6, strata with similar pottery assemblages were unearthed in the soundings in Areas 2 and 4, but in both cases the deposits were a rather thin covering of the bedrock or virgin sand, with no structures exposed.

Pottery. The majority of the pottery fragments found in the strata of the 'lower' (BA-I) period can be identified as imports from the Mediterranean, Arabian Gulf and the Indian Subcontinent. Of special interest, is the rather small percentage of locally made pottery: it constitutes only about 25% of the total sherds. These are mostly large, hand-made storage vessels, the so-called *zirs* (Fig. 4.7, 4.1–8), but there are also a limited amount of kitchen and table ware (pedestal bowls). Parallels for locally made pottery could be found in the Wadi Ḥaḍramawt pottery assemblage of the last centuries BC – first centuries AD (phases LR-I – LR-III of the 'Late Raybun' Period) (Sedov 2003, 173–196).

A number of diagnostic forms can be identified in each category of pottery. In the storage pottery, the majority of the distinguishable pieces, about 58% of the RHB (rim, handle, base) fragments, belong to the so-called Koan type or Dressel 2–4 amphorae (Fig. 4.8, 1–6; 4.9, 1–6). At least three fabrics could be identified: (a) Koan and/or Eastern Aegean fabric, (b) Egyptian fabric, and (c) Campanian fabric.[4] The amphora types from

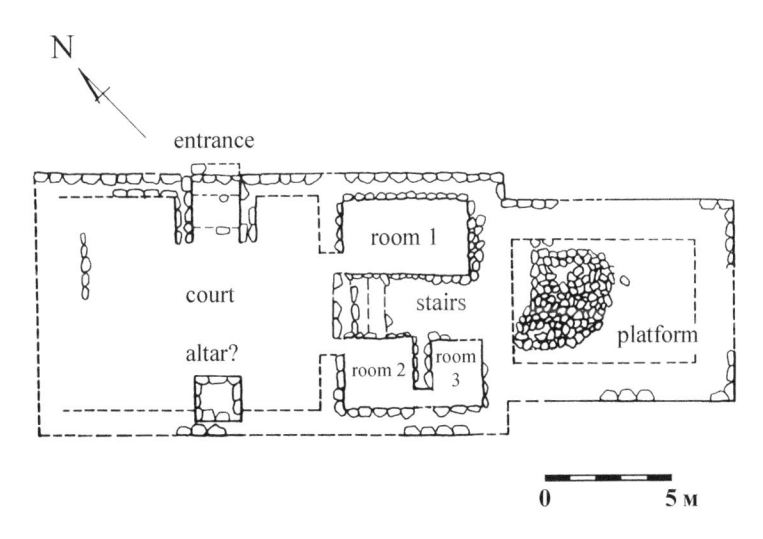

Fig. 4.4. Ḥuṣn al-Ghurāb. Structure on the summit (lighthouse), plan (after S.S. Shirinskiy).

Fig. 4.5. Ḥuṣn al-Ghurāb. Structure on the summit (lighthouse), variant of reconstruction.

the 'lower' (BA-I) period are not limited to the Dressel 2–4 forms. Fragments of probable Rhodian amphorae (6% of RHB fragments), Dressel 1B / Ostia XX / Class 4 and Dressel 7–11 / Ostia LII / Beltràn I / Class 17 (10% and 8% of RHB fragments accordingly) were found in the mixed contexts in the Area 2 and Area 6. All above mentioned types can be dated between the middle or late 1st century BC and the early or middle 2nd century AD (Panella 1970, 109; 1977, 504–515; Hayes 1976, 47–123; 1978, 83–84; Riley 1979, 134–135; Peacock and Williams 1986, 113–114, 120–121; Sciallano and Sibella 1994).

Fragments of a rather special type of a coarse, thick-walled storage vessel, the so-called 'black and grey ware' were found in the strata of the 'lower' (BA-I) period. It showed parallels with ed-Dur material and could be identified as Arabian Gulf production of the last centuries BC – first centuries AD (Salles 1984, 247; 1993, 513; De Paepe et al. 2003, 211–212).

The table pottery included pieces of the well known eastern sigillata wares. Some fragments can be classified as Eastern Sigillata A (ESA) wares (Fig. 4.10, 1–4, 14–17), but others are undoubtedly of western origin (Fig. 4.10, 5–13). The Eastern Sigillata A sherds range in date from the first half to the late 1st century AD, while those for Italian terra sigillata are between 15 BC and 15 AD (Goudineau 1968, 277–309, 341–347, 376–377; Hayes 1085, 15–17, 42, 55; Pucci 1985, 382–385, 389–391; Ettlinger et al. 1990; Ballet 1996, 822–825).

Fragments of elegant, thin-walled bowls and plates made of pink clay and painted inside with a red pattern were also found in the strata of the 'lower' (BA-I) period (Fig. 4.11, 1–2). They are undoubtedly of Nabatean origin and can be dated close to the 1st century BC – 1st century AD (Negev 1986, 36–62; Schmitt-Korte 1974, 70–93; 1984, 7–40).

A few pieces of fine slipped pottery, which show similarities with Indian Red Polished Ware (RPW), Rouleted Ware (RW) and Black-and-Red Ware (BRW), also occurred in the strata of the 'lower' (BA-I) period (Fig. 4.11, 3–9) (Orton 1991; Gurumurthy 1981, 230–275; Singh, 1982; Gupta 1995–96; Schenk 2001). The same strata revealed a small amount, *i.e.* about 8% of all pottery sherds, of the so-called green glazed pottery (Fig. 4.11, 10–15), which has similarities with the Parthian, or more generally, Mesopotamian pottery (Toll 1943).

The diagnostic forms of the kitchen pottery are globular or biconical jars and deep bowls, red slipped and burnished, made from red paste.

Coins. Altogether 61 coins attributed to different Ḥaḍrami series, as well as single pieces of Sabaean, Himyarite and Eastern Arabian series, were revealed in the strata of the 'lower' (BA-I) period. The coinage of Ḥaḍramawt is represented by the so-called 'early imitation' series (series head / owl, types 1.1, 1.2 and 3.0), the Shaqar / bull's head type (type 10.0) and head/eagle (type 4.0).[5] Foreign coinage is represented by Sabaean bronze series with "Bucranium" (*c.* very early 2nd – first half of the 3rd centuries AD), silver coin of 'Amdan Bayin Yuhaqbid, king of Saba' and dhu-Raydan (*c.* AD 80–100) (small fraction of his series with two heads), and a sole piece of the Eastern Arabian coinage, class XXXVIII (according to D.T. Potts' classification).

Dating. Judging from the preliminary analysis of the material, mostly Mediterranean

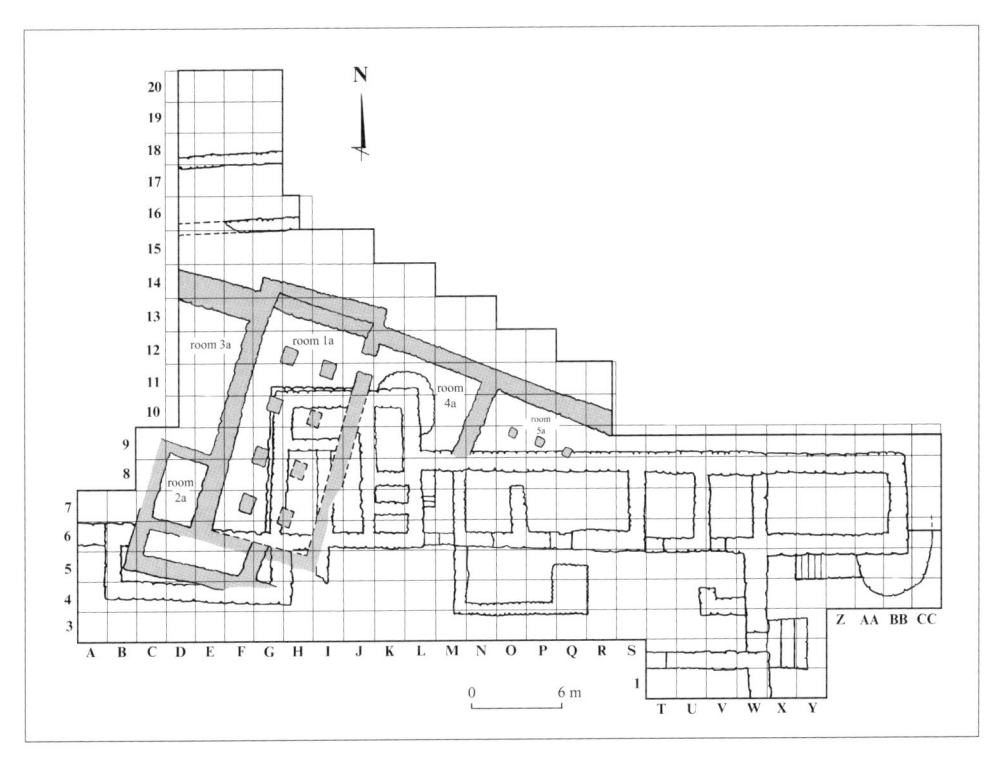

Fig. 4.6. Bi'r 'Alī Settlement (ancient Qana'). Area VI, 'lower' (BA-I) period, plan of excavated structures.

imports, the "lower" (BA-I) period of Bi'r 'Alī occupation can be placed between the second half of the 1st century BC and the middle or, more probably, the late 1st century AD.

The 'middle' (BA-II) period

Structures. Structures of the 'middle' (BA-II) period were revealed in various parts of the settlement (Areas II, III, IV, VI and VII) (Fig. 4.12–15). Particularly common were big multi-roomed dwellings sometimes with enormous enclosed courtyards (Areas II and VI), shops (Areas IV and VI) and religious buildings, a synagogue and a temple of local deity (Areas III and VII). Some of them were built on the ruins of previous structures (Area VI), while others were built on the basalt platform or virgin soil (Areas II, III, IV). It seems quite probable that buildings on the slope of Ḥuṣn al-Ghurāb as well as on its summit (fortress 'Urr Mawiyat and lighthouse) were still functioning.

Layers. Several phases of occupation connecting with different floors were distinguished in the buildings at the Areas II, III, V and VI. The thickness of cultural deposits testifies a rather long period of occupation. Unfortunately, the difference in the pottery assemblages between the 'early' and 'late' layers of the 'middle' (BA-II) period cannot be determined and is reflected only in the coin finds (see below).

Pottery. There are a lot of changes in the pottery of the 'middle' (BA-II) period of Bi'r 'Alī occupation, which can be explained, no doubt, as chronologically determined.

Dressel 2–4 and other early Mediterranean amphorae, terra sigillata and Nabatean pottery have completely disappeared at this time. The most typical forms of transportation pottery of the 'middle' (BA-II) period are vessels of apparently North African origin in which we can recognise a number of North African amphorae such as ?Tripolitanian types, made from red to dark-red paste with a large portion of white lime grits (Tripolitanian I and II), and Africana types, made from greyish to dark-red paste with white inclusions (Africana piccolo and Africana grande). The so-called "North Africa-Gallic" amphorae could be identified in the pottery assemblage of the period as well (Ostia V / Dressel 30 / Class 38 and Ostia LX / Pélichet 47 / Class 27). All these types were produced from the late 2nd to the 4th or early 5th centuries AD (Palma and Panella 1968, 105–106, tav. XXXIV, 523, XXXV, 525–528, XXXVI, 532, 533, XXXVII, 538, XXXVIII, 539; Panella 1973, 116, 143, 187, tav. XXIV, 131, XXIX, 190, 191, 193, XXXVI, 265, LX, 526–528, 530; 1977, 37, tav. XVII, 121, XXXVI, 262; Hayes 1976, 47–123; 1978, 83–84, fig. 27,39,43; Riley 1979, 195–197, fig. 84, 249–250, 85, 251–255; Peacock 1984, 130, fig. 39,56–62; Peacock and Williams 1986, 142–143, 153–157, 171–172; Sciallano and Sibella 1994).

Two forms are diagnostic of the vessels of the BA-II period: (1) handleless amphora-like vessels with triangular or oval pointed slightly vertical rim and, probably, long narrow body (Fig. 4.16, 1–11), and (2) handleless amphora-like vessels with collar stepped rim (Fig. 4.17, 1–6). They were manufactured from red or reddish-brown paste with a large portion of white lime grit and small portion of mica, and covered with yellowish to pink wash or, sometimes, reddish brown slip on the exterior. Most probably the origin of these storage jars was Palestine, where very similar forms have been produced at least from the Early Iron Age (Blakely 1988, 39, fig. 7, 7; Mazar and Mazar 1989, 61–121). Recently, the vessels with collar stepped rim were compared with Indian pottery from, for example, Amreli, and an Indian origin was postulated (Davidde, Petriaggi, and Williams 2004, 94–97).

Fragments of Egyptian 'bitronconique' amphorae also occurred in the layers of the 'middle'(BA-II) period (Ballet 1996, 825–826).

One more diagnostic form for the 'middle' (BA-II) period is a very specific type of oil lamp in the shape of a plate with a round bottom and small reservoir inside (Fig. 4.18, 12, 14, 15). The edge of reservoir is usually slightly burnt. Rather similar oil lamps were discovered in abundance during excavations of the Early Christian (4th to 7th centuries AD) sites along the Nile in Nubia (Bietak and Schwartz 1987, 171–172, fig. 24, 76449, 76460, 42, 76712, 76750, 76762, 44, 76687, 76688, 76713, 50, 76777–76779, 65, 76789–76795, Taf. 60, 76788–76795; see also Davidde, Petriaggi, and Williams 2004, 94), were revealed at the ancient settlements in India where they were usually interpreted as lids (Wheeler *et al.* 1946, fig. 23, 38a,c; Rao 1966, fig. 17, 52–53; Begley 1993, 105, fig. 15). A complete lamp and a rim sherd of this type were found in Shabwa in the layers XI–XIV, dated close to the 2nd–4th centuries AD (Badre 1992, 280, fig. 16, 331, 334).

Table pottery is characterised by the presence of sherds of fine orange painted ware representing beaker fragments (Fig. 4.18, 5–8). The direct analogies for such pottery can be found at Tepe Yahya in the strata of Periods I–IA dated to the Partho-Sassanian

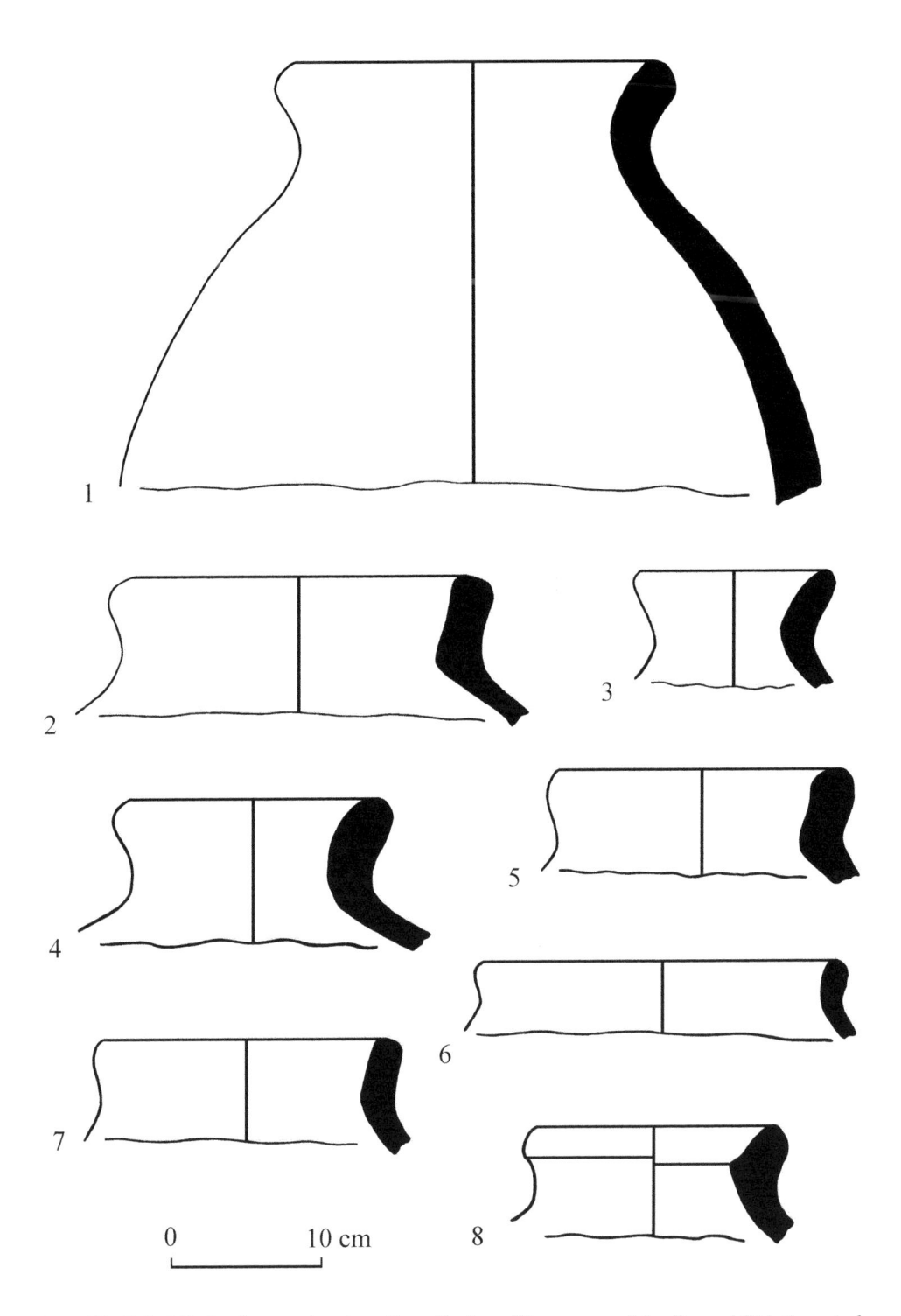

Fig. 4.7. Bi'r 'Alī Settlement (ancient Qana'). Area VI, pottery of the 'lower' (BA-I) period.

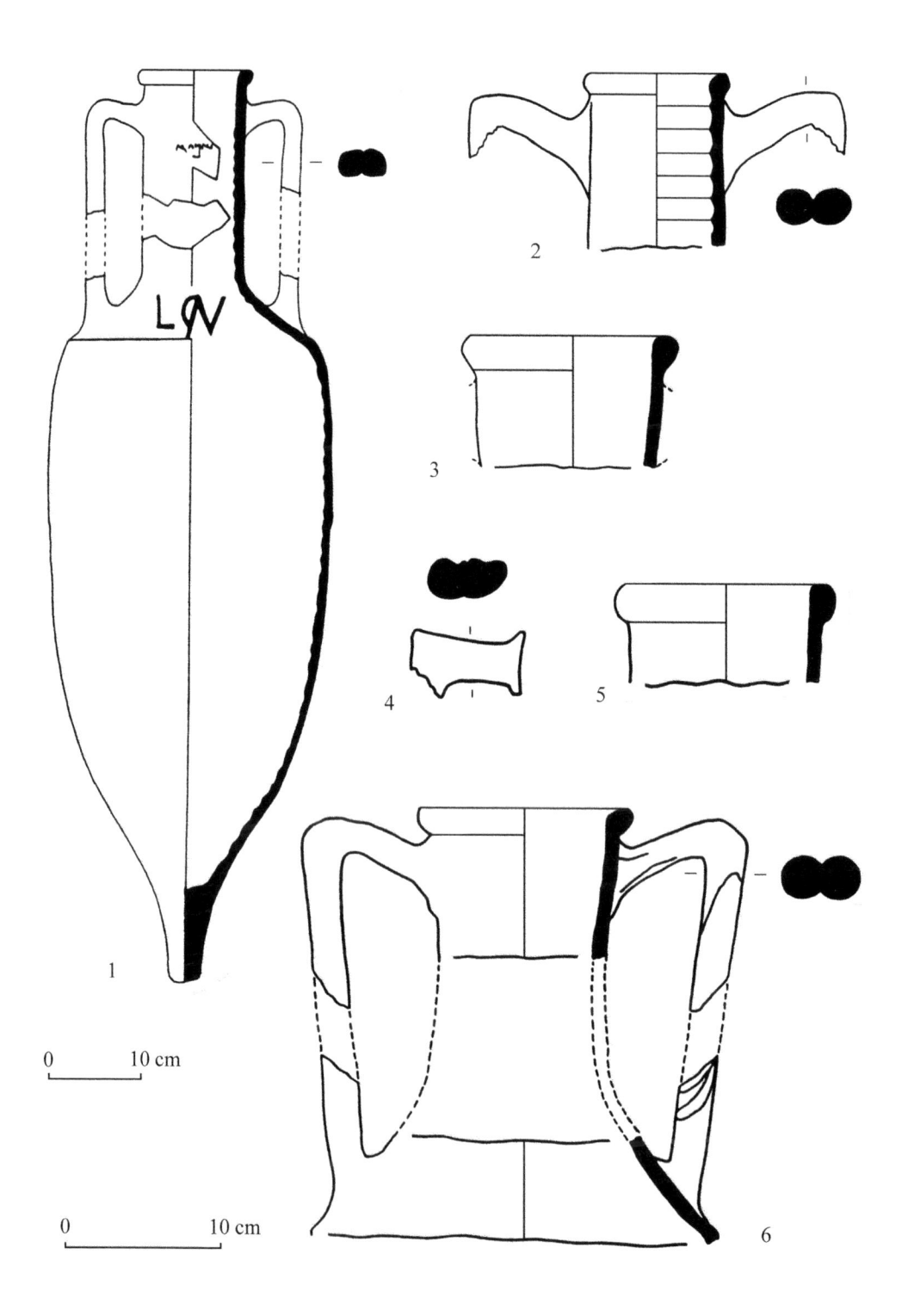

Fig. 4.8. Bi'r 'Alī Settlement (ancient Qana'). Area VI, pottery of the 'lower' (BA-I) period.

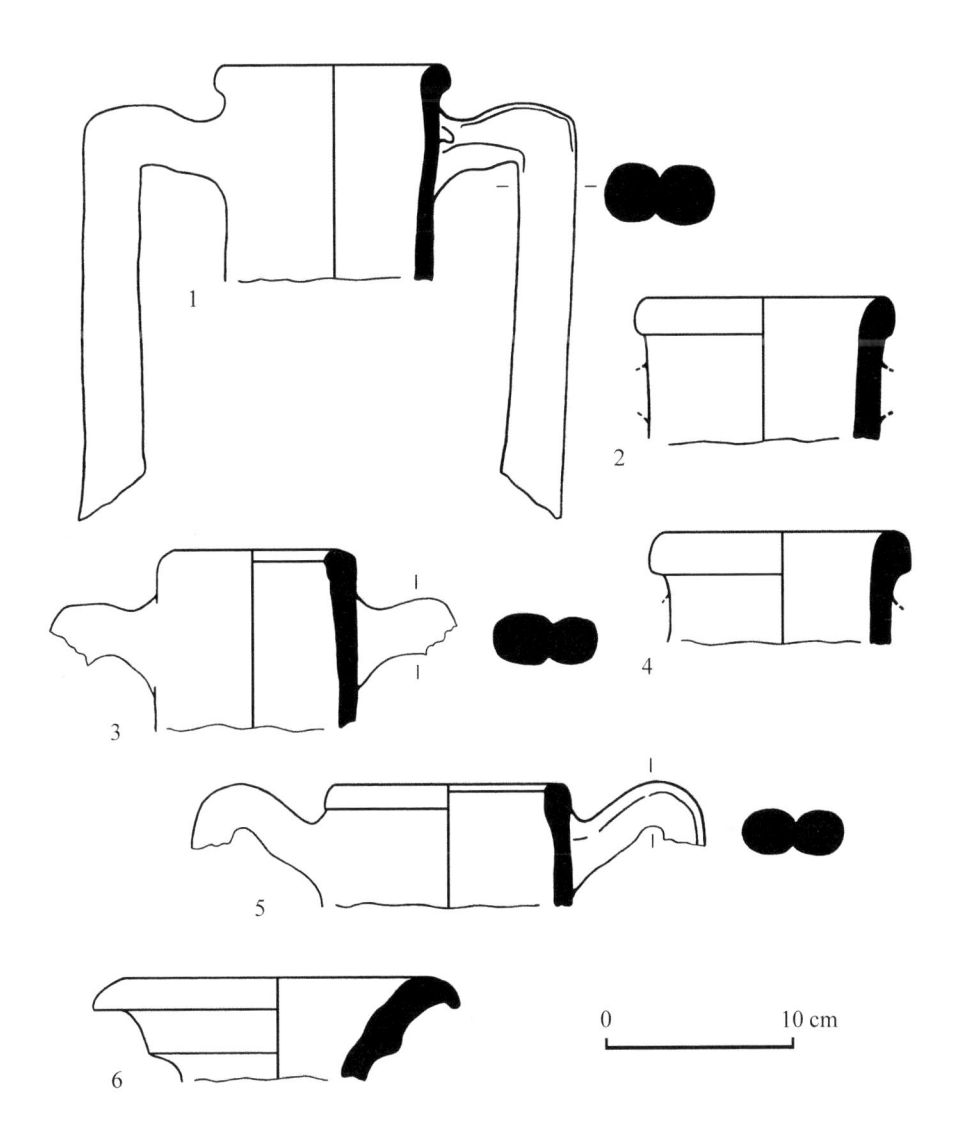

Fig. 4.9. Bi'r 'Alī Settlement (ancient Qana'). Area VI, pottery of the 'lower' (BA-I) period.

period (*c.* 0–500 AD), as well as at some other southern Iranian sites, and in monuments located on the Arabian coast of the Gulf (in the Sasanian layers of Qala' at al-Bahrain dated close to the 3rd–4th centuries AD) (Lamberg-Karlovsky 1972, 89–91; Whitehouse and Williamson 1973, 38, fig. 5–6; de Cardi 1975, 57–58, fig. 9, 40–65; Mouton 1992; Lecompte 1993, 195–217, fig. 12, 1–4; Hojlund 1997, 213–215, fig. 886–895; Potts 1998, 207–220). The percentage of glazed wares of Mesopotamian origin (Fig. 18, 9–11) (Toll 1943) and the so-called Indian RPW (Fig. 18, 1, 3, 4) (Orton 1991, 51, fig. 4.1, no. 2–4, 65, fig. 4.15, no. 2, 52–53, fig. 4.2, no. 3, 67, fig. 4.18, no. 2, 3; Whitehouse and Williamson 1973, 38–39, fig. 5, 7; Zarins 1997, 615–689), known from the previous strata in very few

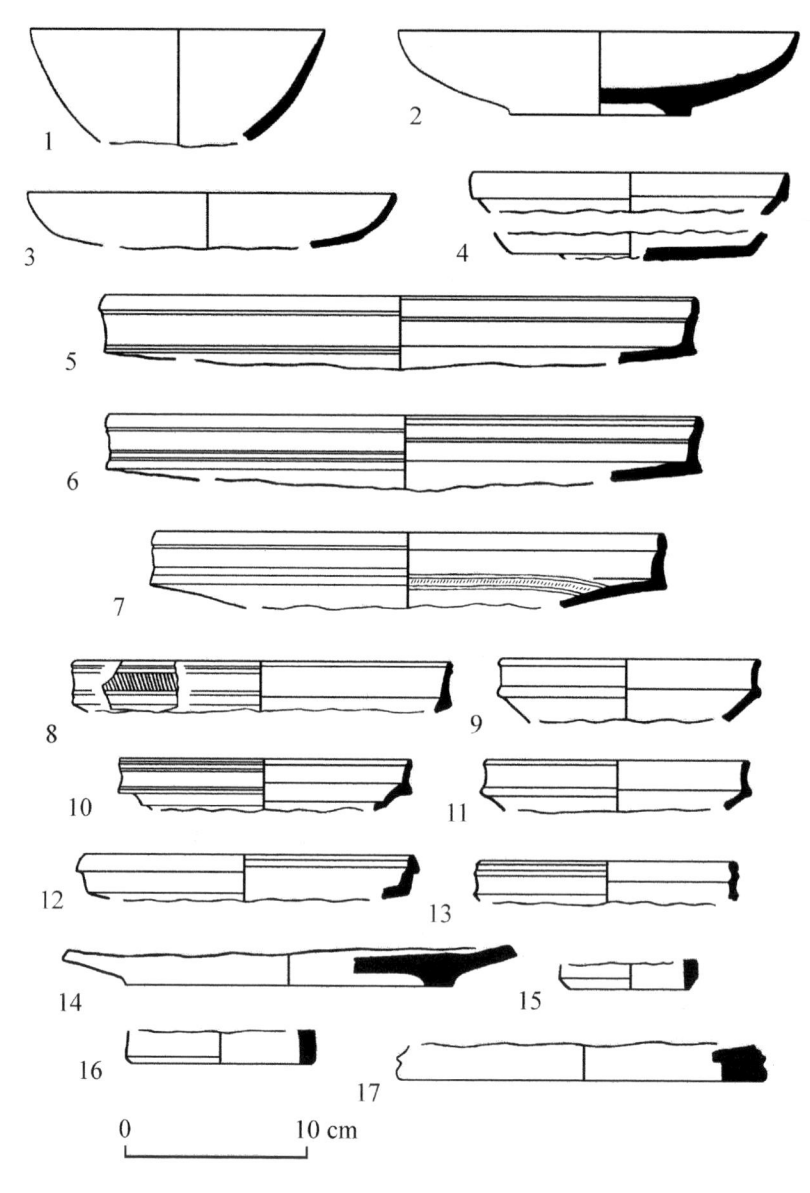

Fig. 4.10. Bi'r 'Alī Settlement (ancient Qana'). Area VI, pottery of the 'lower' (BA-I) period.

numbers, increases in the layers of the 'middle' (BA-II) period. At the end of the 'middle' (BA-II) period, Aksumite pottery suggesting perhaps East African connections, appears for the first time in the Bi'r 'Alī pottery (Munro-Hay 1989, 290–311). Fragments of local, Ḥaḍrami pottery remain scarce, represented exclusively by large storage vessels made from coarse and porous yellowish or greenish-yellow paste.

Coins. The Ḥaḍrami series (59 pieces) were found exclusively in the 'early' layers of the

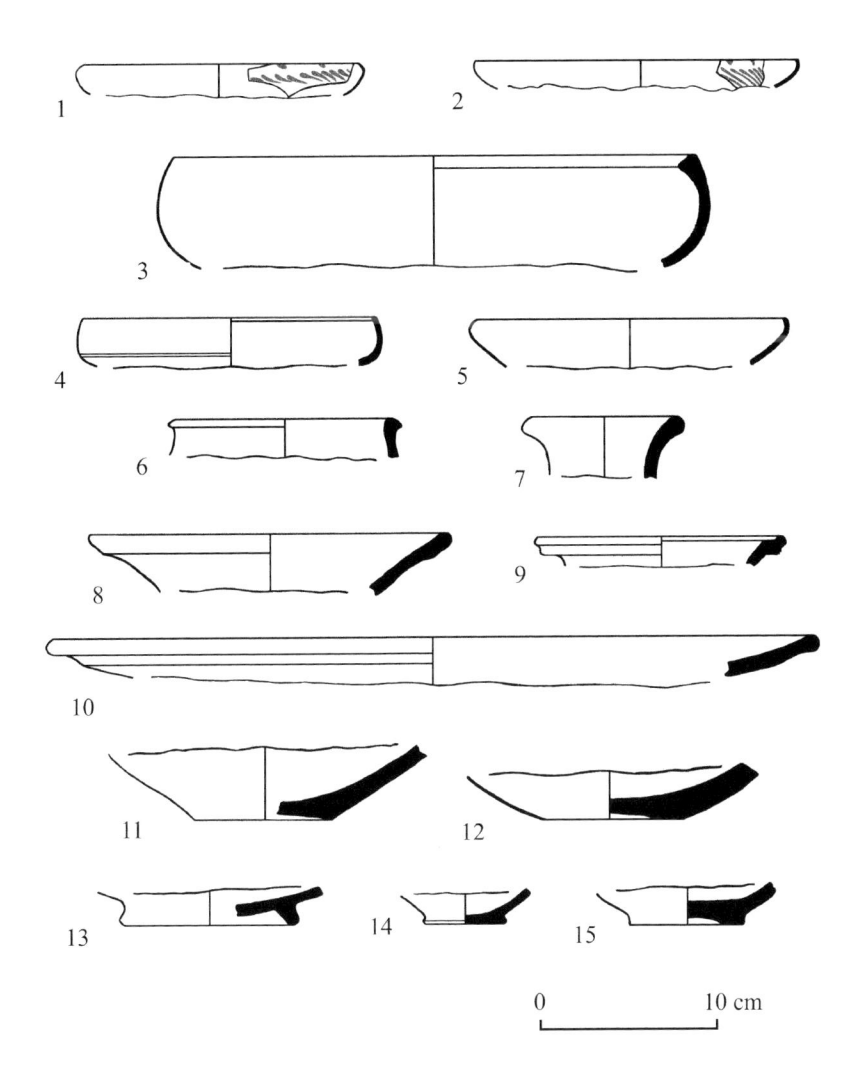

Fig. 4.11 Bi'r 'Alī Settlement (ancient Qana'). Area VI, pottery of the 'lower' (BA-I) period.

'middle' (BA-II) period of Bi'r 'Alī occupation. This series comprises radiates of head / winged caduceus (type 3.0), issues attributed to Yashhur'il Yuhar'ish, son of Abiyaśa', mukarrib of Ḥadramawt (series head/eagle, type 4.0), a radiate series with head / bull (type 5.3), head / bull (types 6.1, 6.2 and 7.1), Shaqar / bull (type 8.1) and Shaqar / bull's head (type 10.0). 'Late' layers of the 'middle' (BA-II) period of Bi'r 'Alī occupation revealed 716 coins: 424 attributed to Ḥadrami series, Sabaean and Himyarite series and 253 identified as late Himyarite series with "Bucranium", together with a single bronze coin of the Aksumite king Ouazebas (*c*. 4th century AD).

Thus, the main difference between 'early' and 'late' layers of the 'middle' (BA-II) period of Bi'r 'Alī occupation is the presence or absence of the late Himyarite bronze series with 'Bucranium'. They are among the smallest, lightest and the most numerous

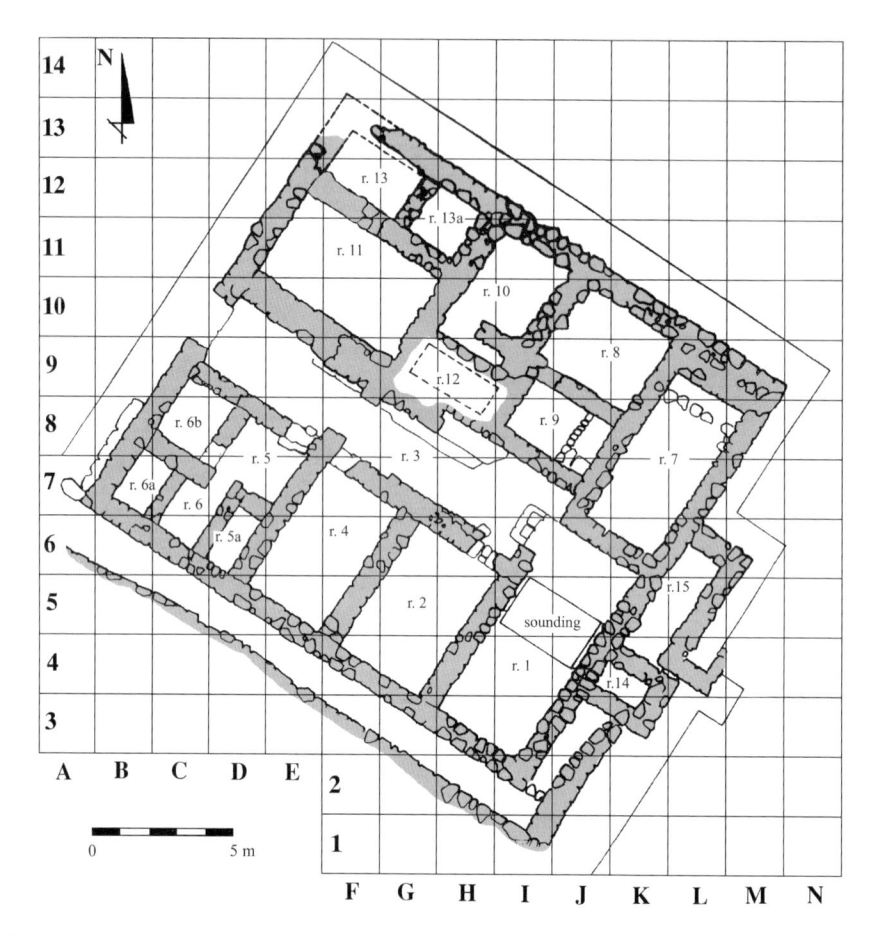

Fig. 4.12. Bi'r 'Alī Settlement (ancient Qana'). Area II, plan of excavated structure.

issues ever minted in South Arabia. The finds from Bi'r 'Alī showed very clearly that the custom of withdrawing old pieces from circulation when the new ones appeared on the market, was not practised in Ḥaḍramawt.

Dating. Judging from the preliminary analysis of the pottery assemblage, the 'middle' (BA-II) period of Bi'r 'Alī (ancient Qana') occupation can be placed between the 2nd and 5th centuries AD. It might be concluded also that 'early' layers were formed before ancient Qana' was integrated into the political and economic system of the Himyarite Empire, *i.e.* before the late 3rd century AD.

The 'upper' (BA-III) period

Structures. Structures of the 'upper' (BA-III) period were revealed in the south-western (Area I) and central (Area V) of the settlement (Fig. 4.19 & 20), usually characterised by big multi-roomed houses separated from each other by small narrow streets.

Layers. Several phases of occupation connecting with different floors were traced in the excavated buildings.

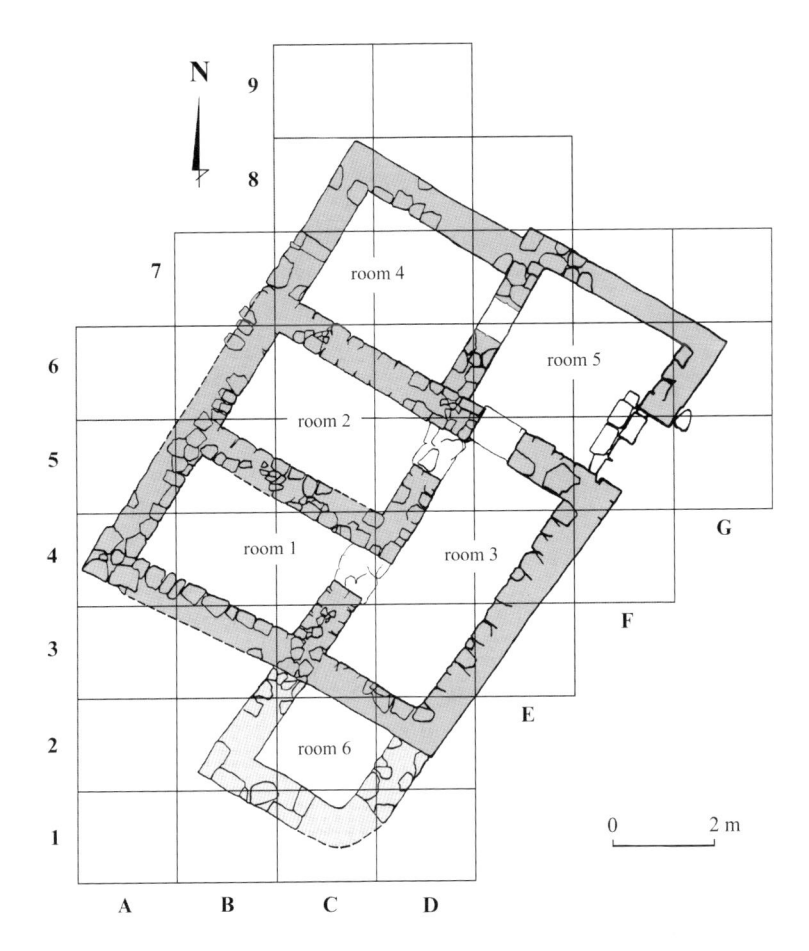

Fig. 4.13. Bi'r 'Alī Settlement (ancient Qana'). Area IV, plan of excavated structure.

Pottery. New types of storage pottery are characteristic of the strata of the 'upper' (BA-III) period of Bi'r 'Alī.

Amphorae with a ribbed body constitute the majority of sherds (Fig. 4.21, 1–8; 4.22, 1–4). The vessels were made of reddish gritty clay, containing mica, white lime inclusions and large granulated quartz. They have cream, nearly pink, or greyish wash on the exterior and a vertical rim with a step inside, a high neck and a rather narrow body widely spaced by ridges. Their handles were massive, oval or semi-oval in section. Rather often the vessels had graffiti, dipinti or painted design with black or red on the exterior.

The amphorae with ribbed body are comparable to the Ayla-Aksum type distributed in the Red Sea region during the 5th, 6th and early 7th centuries (Tomber 2004). The majority of the Qana' vessels were produced, probably, at the region of Aqaba (ancient Ayla), where kilns of the early 7th century AD have been discovered (Whitcomb 1989, fig. 5).

Another diagnostic type is the vessels made of brown to drab brown clay sometimes with a greyish wash on the exterior.[6] They had a small everted or slightly vertical rim and

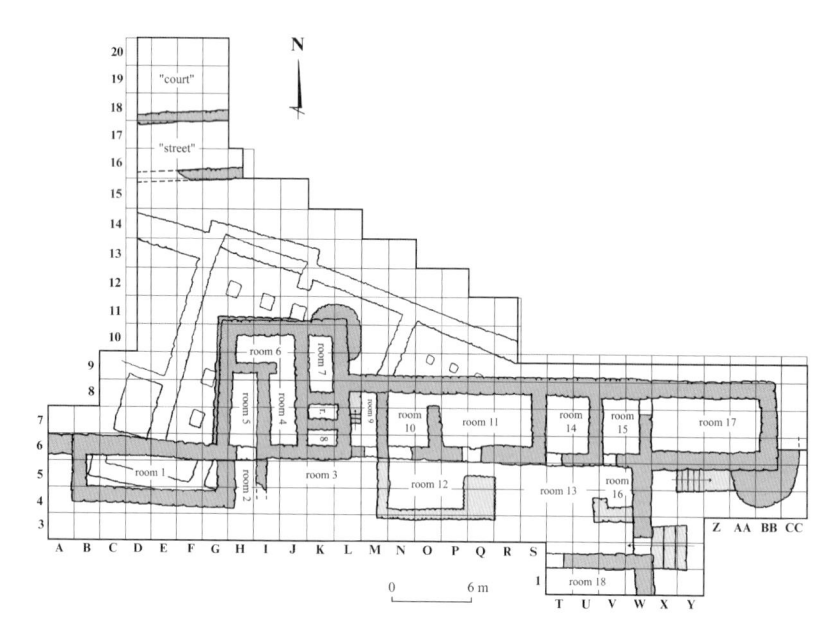

Fig. 4.14. Bi'r 'Alī Settlement (ancient Qana'). Area VI, plan of excavated structures of the 'middle' (BA-II) period.

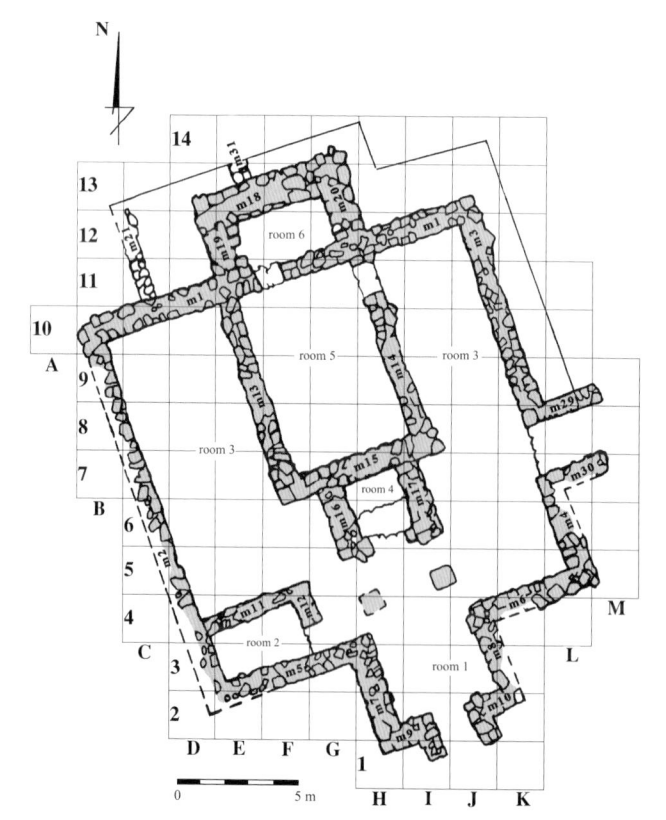

Fig. 4.15. Bi'r 'Alī Settlement (ancient Qana'). Area III, 'late synagogue', plan of excavated structure.

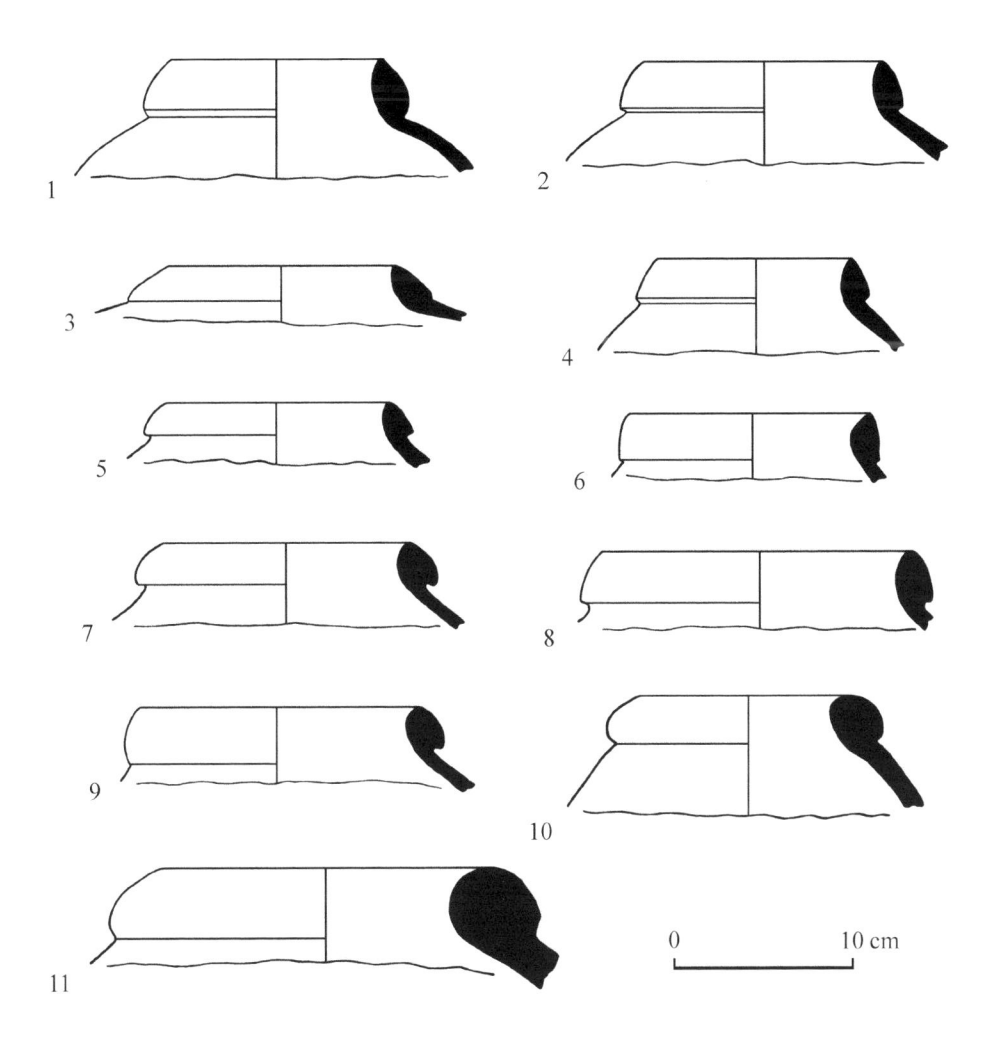

Fig. 4.16. Bi'r 'Alī Settlement (ancient Qana'). Area VI, pottery of the 'middle' (BA-II) period.

rough, loop handles on the shoulders (Fig. 4.22, 5–9). This is the well-known Gaza type or Late Roman Amphora 4, produced in Palestine in the late 4th to the late 7th centuries AD (Egloff 1977, 117; Riley 1979, 219–222; Peacock and Williams 1986, 198–199; Sciallano and Sibella 1994; Ballet 1996, 827; Majcherek 1995, 163–178).

The strata of the 'upper' (BA-III) period revealed a great amount of handmade pottery (Fig. 4.22, 10; 23, 1–11) with close parallels in Aksum monuments (Munro-Hay 1989, 290–311; Ballet 1996, 828).

Coins. Only two coins were found in the strata of the 'upper' (BA-III) period occupation. The first could be attributed to the Ḥaḍrami series, radiate head/bull (type 5.3), while identification of the second one is uncertain.

Dating. Judging by the analysis of the pottery, the 'upper' (BA-III) periods of the Bi'r 'Alī (ancient Qana') occupation should be placed between the 6th and early 7th centuries AD.

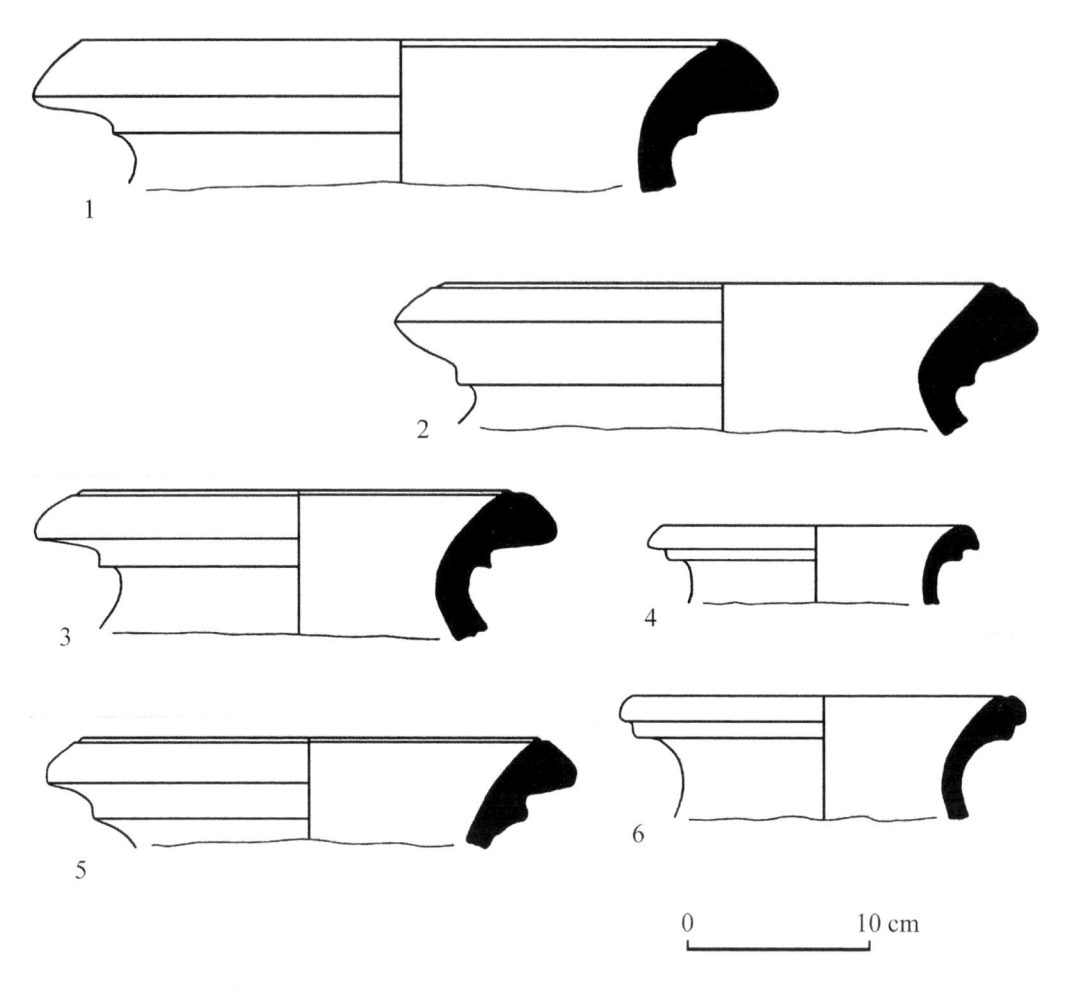

Fig. 4.17. Bi'r 'Alī Settlement (ancient Qana'). Area VI, pottery of the 'middle' (BA-II) period.

Development of the Site

As stated above, some scholars consider that the earliest attestation of Qana' occurs in the first quarter of the 6th century BC. However, others believe that the reference of Ezekiel should be attributed to Cana situated in Galilee. It is hard to imagine, in my opinion, that such a small place on the then practically uninhabited southern coast of the Arabian Peninsula, so far from Palestine, would be mentioned in the Bible.

The earliest structures of the Bi'r 'Alī settlement unearthed during the excavations were located at the foot of Ḥuṣn al-Ghurāb (Area VI), at the beginning of the path leading to the fortress and to the lighthouse on the summit. The excavated building ('Early Structure') revealed several adjoining big rooms, some of them covering an area of about 90 square metres, with columns once supporting the roof.[7] The rooms had been cut into the base of the rock. Judging from the exposed remains, the building was used as a warehouse for

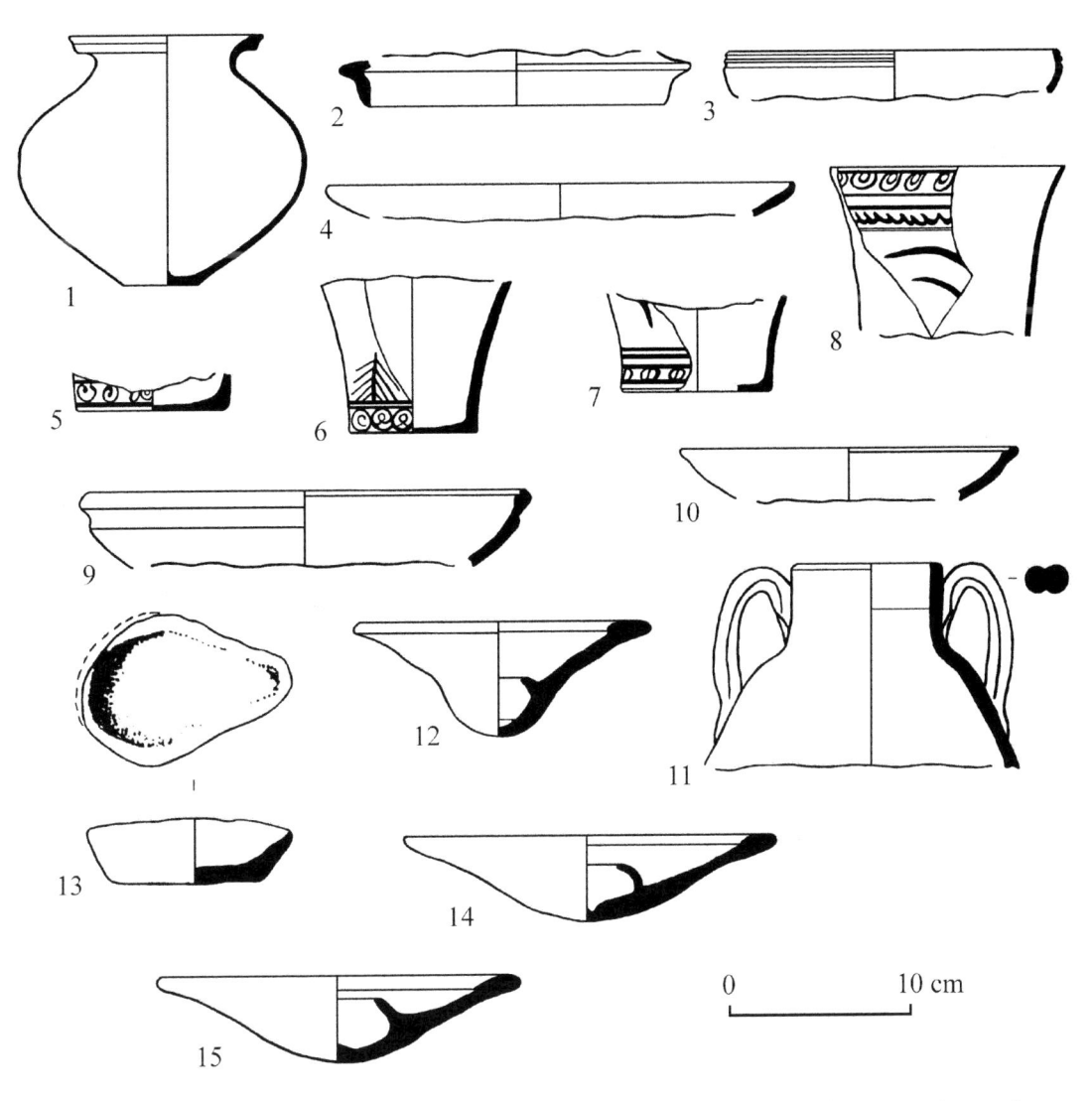

Fig. 4.18. Bi'r 'Alī Settlement (ancient Qana'). Area II, pottery of the 'middle' (BA-II) period.

holding incense, the main export item of the Ḥaḍramawt Kingdom. Its rooms were badly damaged by fire and a large amount of burnt incense was found all over its floors. The remnants of burnt incense were also discovered in baskets or big bags made of palm, which once stood in the corners of the rooms. These containers were used in ancient Ḥaḍramawt to carry and hold incense, which finds correspondence with the modern practice.

We cannot exclude the possibility that some houses situated on the northern slope of Ḥuṣn al-Ghurāb along the path to the summit also belonged to the period of 'Early Qana''. Prior to the excavations such a supposition could not be justified with certainty, but close similarity in the character of the stone masonry of these 'early' buildings must be noted. The fragment of Dressel 2–4 amphora found during the excavation of the lighthouse on the very top of Ḥuṣn al-Ghurāb confirms the existence of the building from the very beginning of the city's history. It seems quite probable that some structures constituted the ruins of the fortress 'Urr Mawiyat on the top of the rock, as well as at least three big water cisterns, which were also constructed during the earlier days of the city.

Of special importance is the absence of remains of any structures in the BA-I strata exposed at the Areas 2 and 4. Judging by this, it seems quite probable that the 'Early Qana'', Qana' of the time of the *Periplus Maris Erythraei*, was limited to the areas at the foot of Ḥuṣn al-Ghurāb, where the warehouse for holding incense was situated, as well as structures on the summit.

The period between the early 2nd and 5th centuries AD was, probably, the heyday of the Bi'r 'Alī settlement. Its territory grew up very intensively and at that time covered an area of more than 5 ha. Big multi-roomed houses with the central corridor system, sometimes with enormous courtyards, were built along the seashore of the bay (Area II), while shops were apparently concentrated in the southern part of the city (Areas IV and VI). A huge temple probably dedicated to Sayin, the supreme god of Ḥaḍramawt, was built to the south-west of the settlement (Area VII).[8] On the north-western outskirts of the city a building used as a synagogue was erected (Area III). A cemetery consisting of rectangular crypts with subterranean chambers was founded to the north-west of the city. The warehouse at the foot of Ḥuṣn al-Ghurāb was abandoned. A long defensive wall with rectangular bastions surrounding the foot of the hill and protecting the path to the 'Urr Mawiyat fortress was erected on its ruins. The bastions were divided into small adjoining rooms. There were also oblong adjoining rooms along the wall. The rooms unearthed along the wall and in bastions seem to have been used as dwellings, shops and storage. A building discovered close to the north-west of this defensive area might also have been a shop as many small bronze and silver Ḥaḍrami, Sabaean and Himyarite coins of various types were found on the floors of the rooms.

On the north-western outskirts of the settlement, a building was excavated which appears to have had a religious function. This is suggested both by the ground plan (Fig. 4.15) and the nature of the finds recovered within it. The building comprised several sections: a big courtyard, a vestibule, a main prayer hall with a very small rectangular chamber on a high platform added to its northern side (an apse oriented towards Jerusalem and intended for holding an Ark of the Law or Torah shrine?), and some structures adjoining the north-eastern corner of the courtyard. From its layout, the building was identified as a synagogue. A stone basin for ablutions once stood in the vestibule, a large piece of frankincense, a part of a marble chancel screen (?), fragments of limestone and bronze candlesticks and a large number of Ḥaḍrami and Himyarite bronze coins of various types (an unusually large number for dwelling- or store-house) were found there.

The structure was erected above what we identified as the ruins of an 'early synagogue' with different layout. The Greek graffito incised on a fragment of gypsum plaster was found on the floor of one of the rooms of the building (Fig. 4.24). The text is a part of a prayer of a certain Kosmas (?) to the Almighty and to His Temple to keep his (Kosmas') caravan and ship safe and sound during the journey and to grant him (*i.e.* Kosmas) success during his voyage. According to its palaeography, the inscription can be dated close to the second half of the 4th century AD, which, most probably, is also the date of construction of the entire building (Vinogradov 1989, 162–167; Bowersock 1993, 3–8; Sedov 2005a, 165–171).

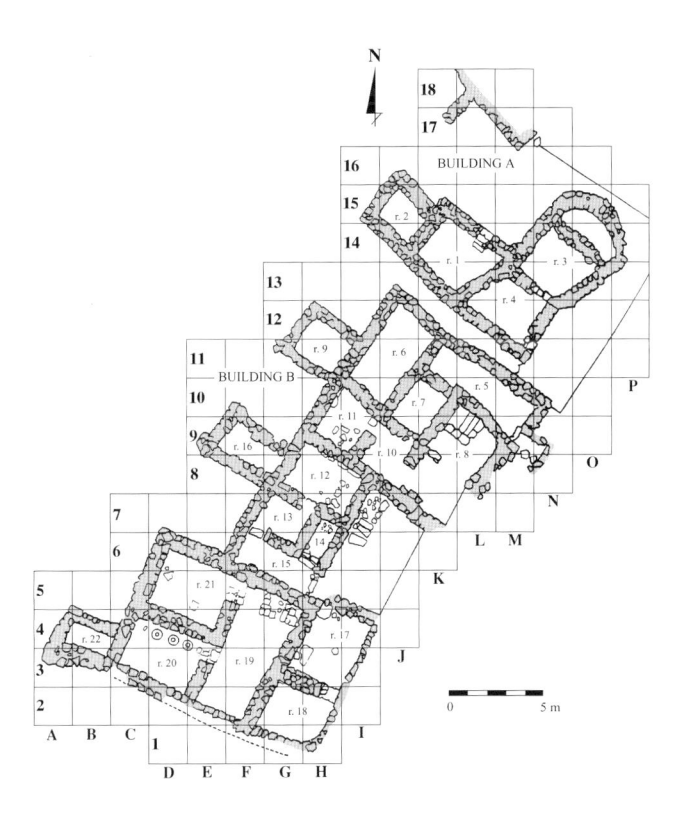

Fig. 4.19. Bi'r 'Alī Settlement (ancient Qana'). Area I, plan of excavated structures.

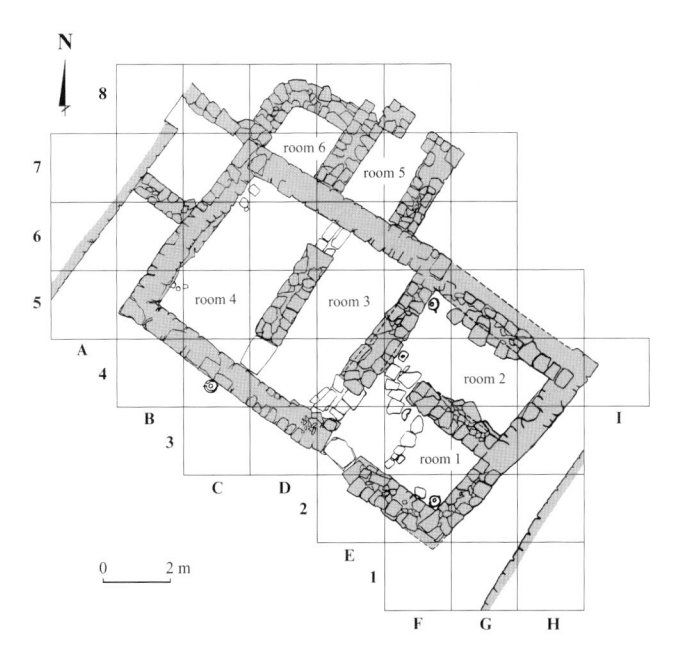

Fig. 4.20. Bi'r 'Alī Settlement (ancient Qana'). Area V, plan of excavated structure.

In the 6th – early 7th centuries AD the ancient town of Qana' occupied the north-western part of the settlement only, which is about 130 × 155 m in size. Houses consisting of several dwellings (Areas I and V) covered its reduced territory. Each dwelling had two or three (rarely more), small rooms and a separate entrance. Small narrow streets separated the structures from each other. According to the South Arabian inscription CIH 621 cut on the rock of Ḥuṣn al-Ghurāb, the fortress 'Urr Mawiyat was rebuilt on the top of the rock around AD 525.

In all probability, the Bi'r 'Alī settlement was abandoned around the early 7th century AD, perhaps as a result of political and religious changes on the Arabian Peninsula. It seems, however, that the desolation of the individual districts of the city did not happen simultaneously. While life continued in the central parts of the town, the south-western and south-eastern districts fell into a state of neglect. Burials were found in the ruins of abandoned houses (Areas I and VI), and probably the last inhabitants of the city were buried there. Later, only pilgrims on their way to Mecca used the ruins of the settlement as temporary shelters.

Place of Qana' in the Rome – Indian Sea Trade

Frankincense and myrrh, two of the best aromatic resins, well-known in antiquity (Müller 1979, 79–92), grew only in the south-western parts of the Arabian Peninsula, and in some parts of East Africa, in the present Somaliland on the so-called African Horn, Eritrea and Ethiopia. It is usually considered that frankincense and myrrh were luxury goods, and there was not a temple or private house, administrative building or palace in Greece and Italy, Egypt and Palestine, Persia and Babylonia, Central Asia and India where aromatics were not burnt on some occasion. It is widely accepted also that the prosperity of the ancient South Arabian kingdoms was based on the incense trade (Doe 1983, 93–105). However, aromatic resins were not only the luxury goods: they were used for medicine, religious and funerary practice as well, thus comprising part of daily-life (Groom 1981, 1–21; Faure 1987). The economy of the South Arabian civilisation was, no doubt, based on agriculture and not on trade (Groom 1981, 214–228; Robin 1992, 45–54; 1997, 37–56). This is clear because surveys indicate that well-developed irrigation systems were established around practically all ancient oases as well as every ancient town and village. It is well known, for instance, that the famous Mārib dam blocked the Wadi Dhana and helped to cultivate about fifteen thousand hectares in the ancient oasis.

But of course, the commercial ties between South Arabia and the Mediterranean and Mesopotamian regions existed, and the Incense Road was, perhaps, one of the most ancient routes of international trade. One route led from South Arabia, *i.e.* from Qtataban, Saba' and the Ḥaḍramawt kingdoms, through Najrān to Gaza in Palestine and further to Egypt; it covered a total distance of almost 3400 kilometres. Another led to Gerrha in the eastern part of the Arabian Peninsula and on to Mesopotamia. It is usually thought that not only production but also trade of aromatic goods were in the hands of ancient South Arabians (Groom 1981, 165–213; de Maigret 1997, 315–332; Macdonald 1977, 333–350). Very often one can also find a statement that maritime trade routes along the South Arabian shore were established as early as caravan routes via the Peninsula.[9] For this supposition to be upheld, we must have at least the following categories of evidence: (1) existence of

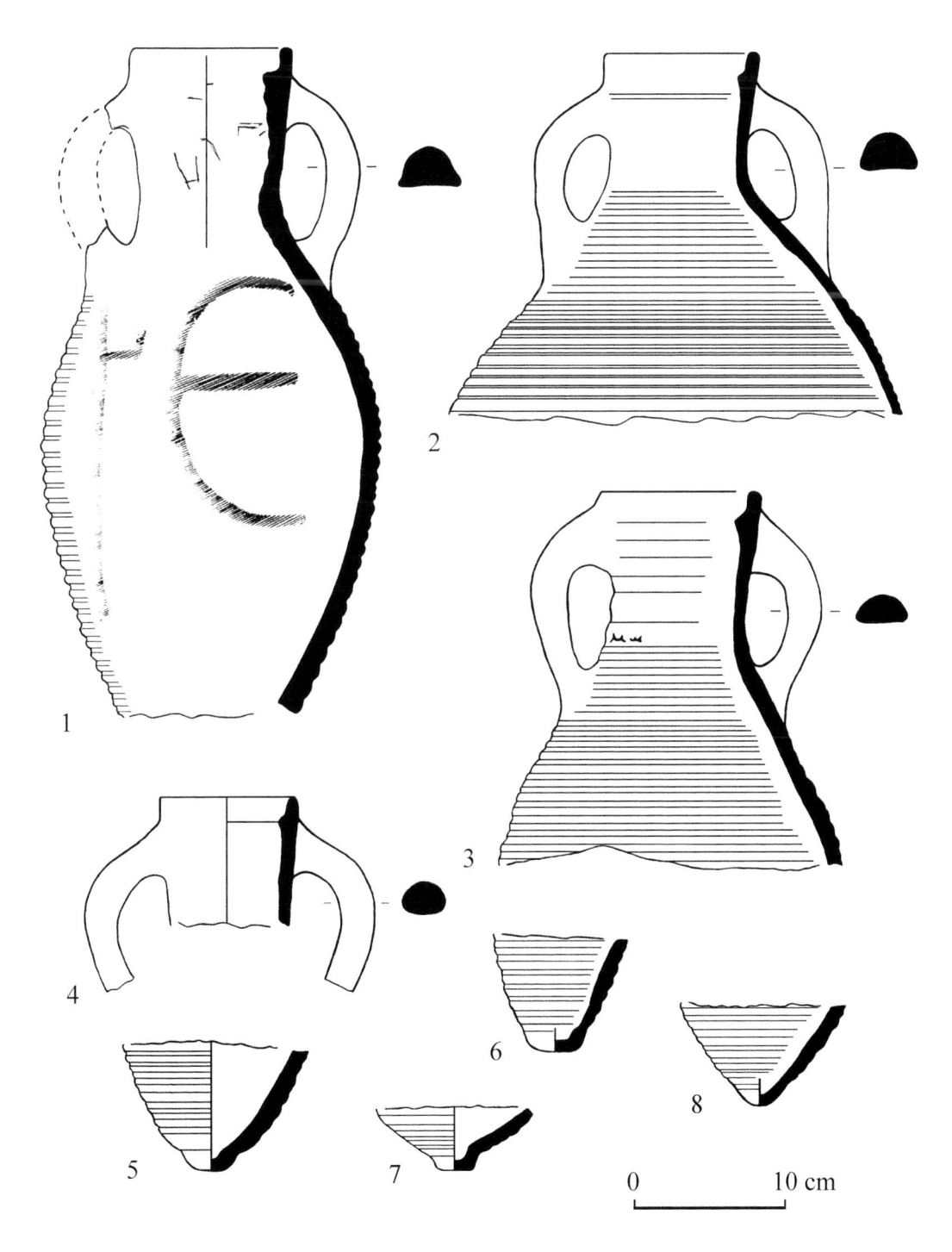

Fig. 4.21. Bi'r 'Alī Settlement (ancient Qana'). Area I, pottery of the 'upper' (BA-III) period.

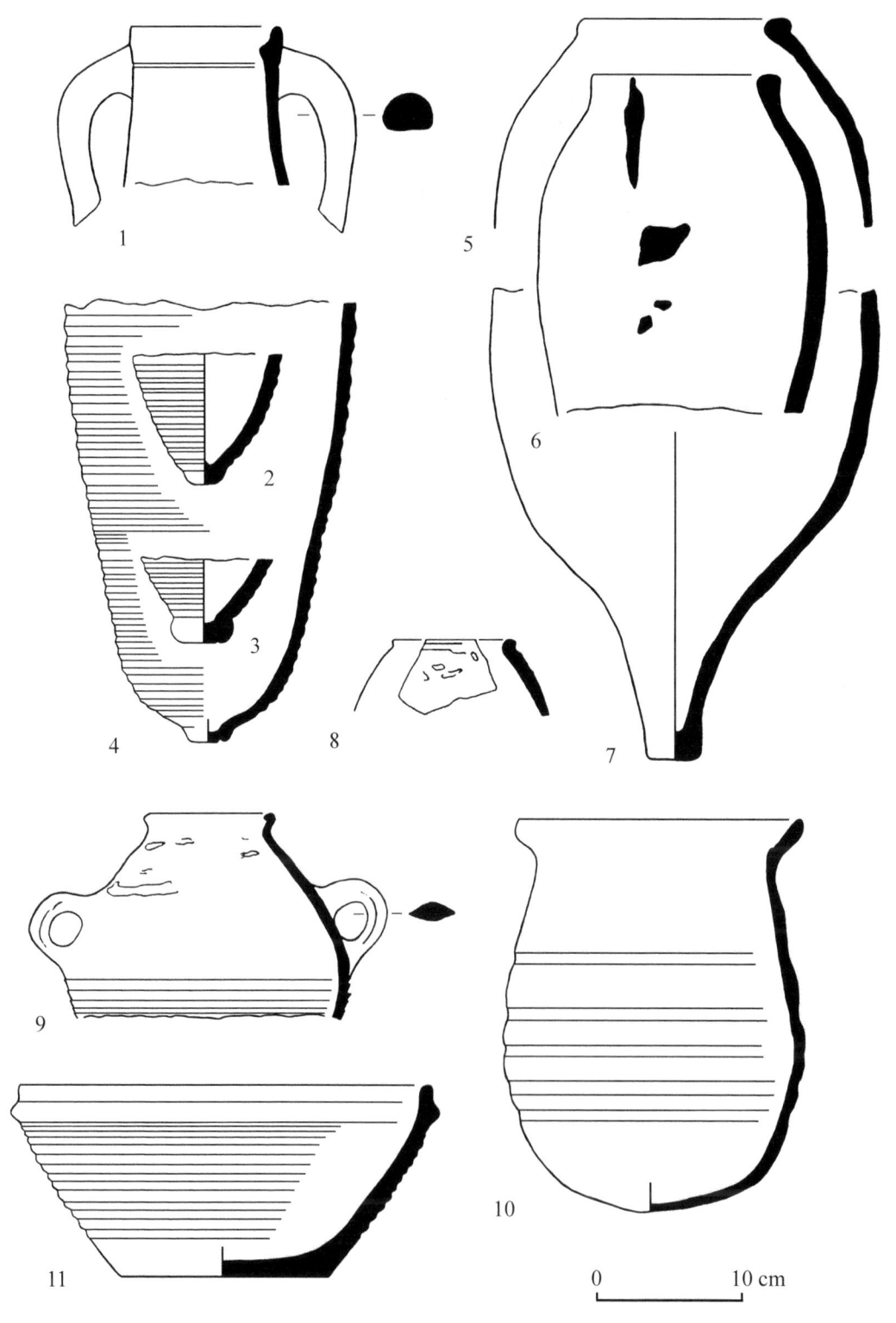

Fig. 4.22. Bi'r 'Alī Settlement (ancient Qana'). Areas I and IV, pottery of the 'upper' (BA-III) period.

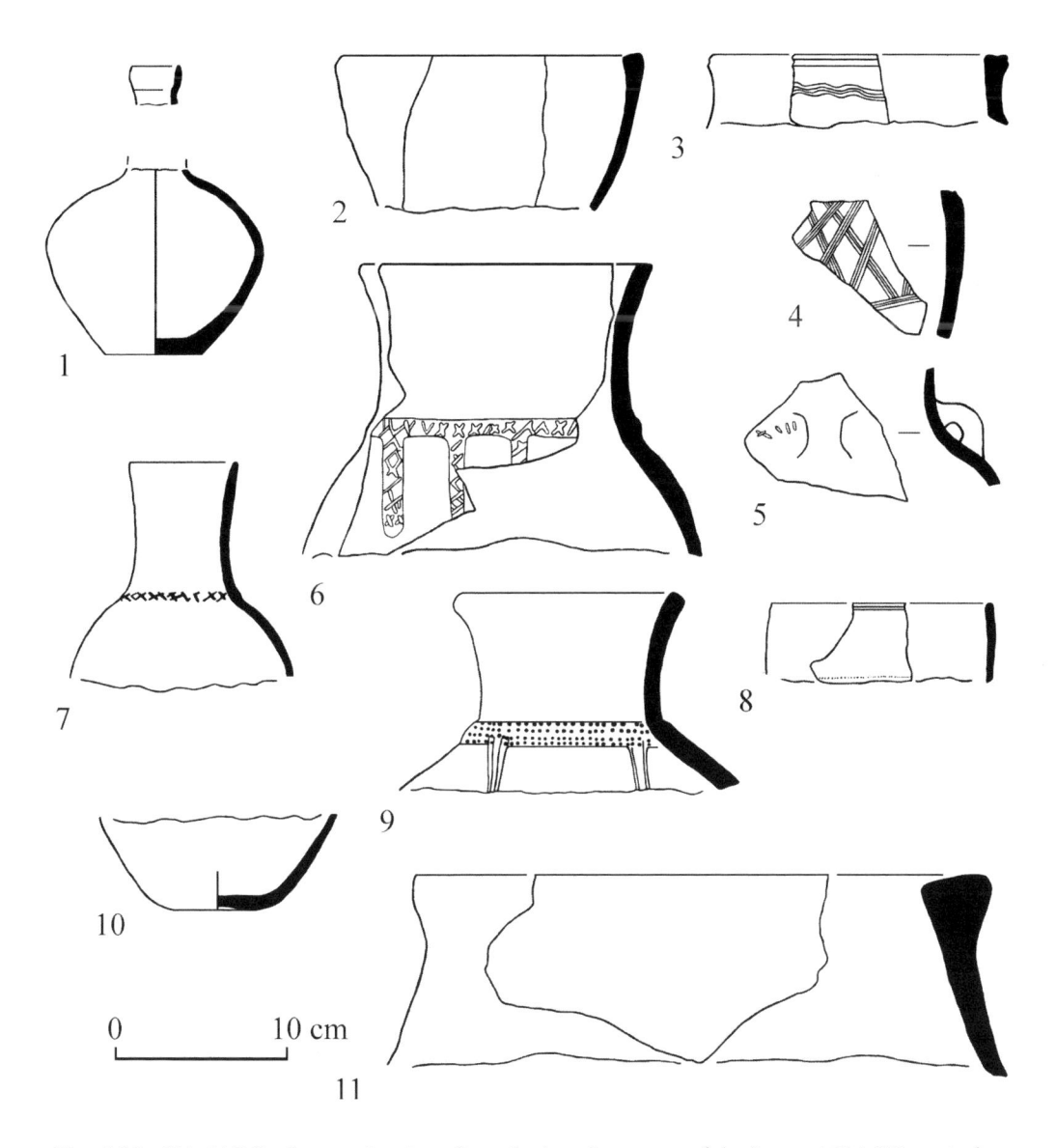

Fig. 4.23. Bi'r 'Alī Settlement (ancient Qana'). Area I, pottery of the 'upper' (BA-III) period.

ancient sea-ports on the southern coast of the Peninsula belonging to South Arabians, (2) material and / or literary evidence of using sea-boats in the coastal and / or far-distance trade and (3) material traces of some products, which were exclusively or mostly transported by the sea (traces which can be found during archaeological excavations). Unfortunately, in the present state of our knowledge, these criteria can seldom be met in full.

It is a commonplace in scientific literature, that from the time of the first Ptolemaic kings of Egypt, in the early 3rd century B.C., and perhaps from the time of Alexander the Great, the maritime trade between the Mediterranean basin and the Red Sea-Indian Ocean countries existed and flourished (Sidebotham 1986, 1–12; 1989, 195–223). At that time, no doubt, cabotage along the coast would have been the rule. The coastline extending along the northern part of the Indian Ocean forms a natural link between Africa and the Indian Subcontinent. There are a lot of small but good harbours, which make coastal sailing rather easy and safe. Small local craft probably took commodities from Indian ports and brought them somewhere to the south-western point of the Arabian Peninsula, where, as we know from the classical sources, a big international market was situated. Greek merchants from Egypt also brought their goods by ships through the Red Sea to this market. Here cargoes were exchanged: goods from India were shipped to Egypt and further to Greece, Palestine, Asia Minor and other parts of the Mediterranean world, as well as Mediterranean goods to India. At the same time some commodities could be off-loaded in the South Arabian kingdoms. The most suitable place for this international market was, supposedy, the present Aden (Casson 1989, 190).

The first archaeological evidence of the existence of a large and important pre-Islamic site, port-city or village, revealed during the last few years, is at the port of Aden. The presence of Sabir-related pottery in Little Aden (adjacent to the modern town[10]) suggests that the coastal site was permanently inhabited since at least the late 3rd – early 2nd millennia BC onwards. In the last centuries BC a village of fishermen was, probably, transformed into a large settlement with a good harbour. On the northern outskirts of the modern town, in the district of Bir Fadl, a big pre-Islamic cemetery was found, where unsystematic excavations revealed inhumations in subterranean graves accompanied by personal jewellery (stone and coral beads, silver bracelets and finger-rings), bronze, glass and ceramic vessels. Silver Qatabanian coins dated approximately close to the late 2nd – early 1st centuries BC were found in the graves.[11]

Thus, the first archaeological evidence from the region supports the idea of the existence of a big and well-developed ancient port-city in the Aden area. As we know from the *Periplus* (26:8.31–32), 'Caesar' sacked the town and market place not long before the middle of the 1st century AD, the proposed date of the Periplus.

Changes took place in the south Arabian maritime commerce after the discovery of monsoons by Hippalus, a seaman from Egypt. This discovery led to the establishment of direct sailing between Egypt and India (Tchernia 1993, 525–534; 1997, 250–276). It is usually thought that as a result of this discovery, the South Arabians lost their monopoly in the trade with India. In my opinion, to the contrary, direct sailing from the Egyptian Red Sea ports to the ports on the Indian coast was rare, and usually in reality it involved the southern Arabian states, which made possible an increased flow of Mediterranean goods and materials to South Arabia.

The most important source for maritime commerce in the beginning of our era is the *Periplus Maris Erythraei*, a handbook written by an anonymous author, probably around the middle of the 1st century AD, for merchants and skippers who sailed in the Red Sea and northern part of the Indian Ocean.[12] It lists the ports and the objects of trade that could be bought and sold in each. In other words, it gives detailed information on the commerce of the area.

The author mentions only two main ports on the Southern Arabian coast apart from places like Okêlis, 'an Arab village ...a harbour, watering station' located near the Bab al-Mandab strait (25:8.19), 'a fortress to guard the region, a harbour, and a storehouse for the collection of frankincense' near Syagros, the modern Ra's Fartak (30:9.32–33), and 'a designated harbour for loading the Sachalite frankincense, called Moscha Limên' on the present day Dhofari coast (32:10.30).

The first one was Muza (21:7.19), which was situated more or less where Mocha (al-Makha) is today. Muza was 'a legally limited port of trade' in what the author described as the Kingdom of two nations, 'the Homerite [=Himyarites] and the one, lying next to it, called the Sabaean'. In spite of several campaigns by different scholars, no archaeological remains of this port of trade have been found so far.

According to the Periplus, Egypt exported to Muza goods of different kinds (24:8.3–11): textiles and clothes, metal (silver?) in money, foodstuff (wine and grain), drugs and cosmetics, a number of luxury items for the royal court (gold, silver and copperware, expensive clothing, and even horses and pack mules). In return, Egyptian merchants took from Muza local products, principally 'myrrh, the select grade and stactê', white marble as well as re-exported commodities 'from Adulis across the water'. From the same source we know that South Arabian trade connections extended eastward as well: ships from Muza made a short run to the island of Dioscuridês, *i.e.* Socotra (31:10.20–21), and even a long run to Barygaza (21:7.22–23), the chief port on the north-western coast of India.

The second port was Qana' (Kanê in the Periplus), the chief port of the 'frankincense-bearing land', *i.e.* the Ḥaḍramawt Kingdom. Qana' was the port to where 'all the frankincense grown in the land is brought'. It carried on trade 'with the ports across the water – Barygaza, Skythia, Omana – and with its neighbour, Persis' (27:9.8–12). It is interesting to note that, according to the Periplus, ships from India, Lamyriké or Barigaza, which traded with Ḥaḍramawt, occasionally wintered at Moscha Limên, the harbour ancillary to Qana'. As we know from the excavations at the site in the Khor Rori lagoon, which without doubt must be identified with Moscha Limên (Sumhuram of the Ḥaḍrami texts), objects of pure Indian origin, so rare in South Arabia, were found (Albright 1982; Pirenne 1975, 81–96; Beeston 1976, 39–42; Wissmann 1977; Goetz 1963, 187–189; Sedov 1992, 126).

According to the *Periplus*, Qana', in a similar way to Muza, carried on an active

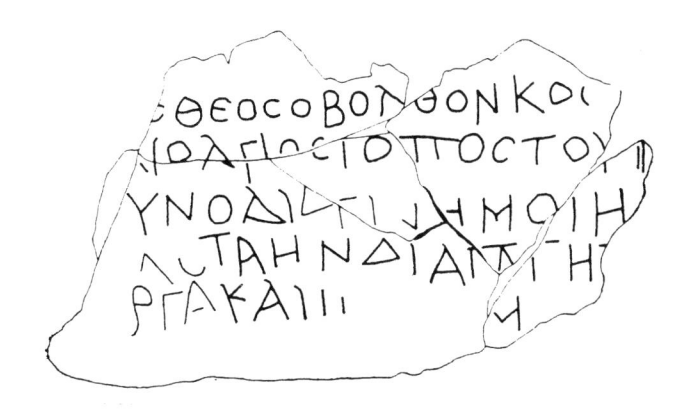

Fig. 4.24. Bi'r 'Alī Settlement (ancient Qana'). Area III, 'early synagogue', Greek graffito (tracing).

trade with Roman Egypt, exchanging its frankincense for the same products for which Muza exchanged myrrh (28:9.13–20). As we know, Ḥaḍramawt also exported aloe, which may have come from Socotra. At the time of the Periplus, the island was a part of the 'frankincense-bearing land' and a number of Arabian, Indian and Greek merchants were settled on the island (31:10.19–20).

Not far from the modern village of Suk on the northern coast of the island a settlement named Hajrya was found. It is the biggest ancient settlement on the island covering the area of more than 1 ha. A defensive stone wall surrounded it. Both from the surface of the settlement, and in soundings, numerous fragments of local handmade pottery were discovered. Alongside this pottery were sherds of an entirely different character. There are sherds of dark green glazed pottery, which probably originated from the Persian Gulf area and can be dated between the 10th and 13th centuries AD, as well as fragments of Roman amphorae and fine red paste cups and bowls of Mediterranean origin dated close to the first centuries AD. Furthermore, fragments of black and grey ware of apparently Arabian Gulf origin, and dated to the 1st – 4th centuries AD were found. Thus, the preliminary analysis of the material permits us to conclude that the settlement of Hajrya was, in all probability, founded in the early 1st century AD. Life on the settlement must have ended close to the 12th or 13th centuries AD (Naumkin and Sedov 1993, 569–623).

It is interesting to note, that the huge areas of the island's northern plateau as well as its western part, around the modern town of Qallansiya, are divided into plots by stone boundary walls. Brian Doe, one of the first explorers of the island's antiquities, states that they 'formed alignments enclosing areas of private ownership' (Doe 1970, 152). In one of his latest books, he wrote that the walls were dividing the plots of land and farms for growing incense, aloe and Dragon tree (cinnabar) (Doe 1983, 19).

An alternative explanation that these walls were boundaries, which in antiquity divided plantations of fragrant trees and aloe, seems closer to the truth. In this case they should be dated close to the period when Socotra was a major supplier of aloe, frankincense and cinnabar, *i.e.* to the early centuries of our era.

It seems, on archaeological evidence, that Qana' was founded sometime in the 1st century BC, (most probably close to the beginning of its second half), and that its foundation was directly connected with the establishment and expansion of the regular sea-trade between Egypt and India, with the rise of the Ḥaḍramawt Kingdom.

The late 1st century BC and the beginning of the Christian era was very important in the history of one of the South Arabian states, the 'frankincense-bearing land', *i.e.* the ancient Ḥaḍramawt Kingdom (Müller 1984, 125–131). Ḥaḍrami troops led successful wars against the neighbouring countries and occupied their territories. The settlement at Khor Rori lagoon, ancient Sumhuram according to the Ḥaḍrami texts, or Moscha Limên according to the Periplus, was founded, or better to say rebuilt, in the late 1st century BC or in the beginning of the 1st century AD. It was founded on the Dhofari coast by colonists from Shabwa, 'the servants of the king of Ḥaḍramawt', to guard the easternmost extension of the Kingdom, which includes now the main frankincense producing areas of South Arabia (Robin 1984, 211–213). The island of Socotra became the possession of the Kingdom probably also around that time. Thus, from the early 1st century AD, Ḥaḍramawt became the largest and probably one of the most powerful kingdoms among the South Arabian states. Frankincense and aloe, the main local products traditionally exported from Ḥaḍramawt via caravan routes, started to be sent now in large quantities by sea through Qana' and Sumhuram. On the other hand the direct sailing between Egypt and India, the so-called monsoon sailing, which became regular and very intensive from the late 1st century BC – early 1st century AD, probably necessitated the foundation of transit points on the southern coast of the Arabian Peninsula supplying water and food products. It is unlikely that those stations were founded by Greek and Roman sailors or merchants, but no doubt by their local partners. We have, at least, evidence of the presence of such partners in late Hellenistic times: altars with Minean and Ḥaḍrami dedications from the sanctuary of Artemis on Delos island in the Aegean Sea (*c.* mid-2nd century BC); a famous sarcophagus from Giza with funerary inscription telling about a certain Minean who was a priest in the Egyptian temple and was involved in the incense trade (died around the late 2nd – early 1st century BC) (Robin 1992a, 62). They were in existence, no doubt, in the late 1st century BC – early 1st century AD.

The location of Qana' is rather surprising. The coastal area around the site is wild and unpleasant with sand, black volcanic stones, salt water even in the wells, and very little vegetation. It is interesting to note that further east there are a lot more plausible and suitable harbours for ships and places for settlement. We can suggest at least two explanations: (1) the bay of Qana' with its offshore islands and huge black volcanic rock, known now as Ḥuṣn al-Ghurāb, was impossible to miss and so it was a favourite place for mooring ships, or (2) there were good and suitable caravan roads connecting Qana' and Shabwa, the capital of the Kingdom (probably, along the Wadi Hajar full with sweet water), Qana' and Mayfa'at (modern Naqb al-Hajar), the chief-town of the region of al-Mashriq, the so-called Western Ḥaḍramawt, one of the largest and most important parts of the ancient Kingdom.

Archaeological investigations show that the main structures at Qana' at the time of the *Periplus* were storage-houses at the foot of the hill to hold incense, water-tanks, a lighthouse and probably some buildings (the fortress) on the summit of Ḥuṣn al-Ghurāb and on its northern slope. The ceramic material from the excavations gives an excellent opportunity, in addition to the written sources, to trace the general links of trade connections of this port, and to identify the main products exported by sea to the Ḥaḍramawt Kingdom.
According to the *Periplus*, amongst the 'imports from Egypt (to Qana' – A.S.) are: wheat, a limited quantity, and wine...' (28:9.13–14). Some wine and dates were imported to Arabia, i.e. to Qana' as well, from the Arab-Persian Gulf ports, Apologos and Omana, most probably by the local middlemen (36:12.10–11).

The main type of amphora found in the strata of the 'lower' (BA-I) period is Dressel 2–4. This is the most popular type of amphora used during the period of the Early Roman Empire in the Mediterranean region. It is thought that the principal content of Dressel 2–4 amphorae was wine (Riley 1979, 150; Peacock and Williams 1986, 105–106). Rhodian amphorae, found in the strata of the 'lower' (BA-I) period in small numbers, were used for the transportation of Rhodian wine (Riley 1979, 134–135).

We know that Italian wine was transported all over the Empire from Britain and the northern Provinces to the Red Sea, Arabian Peninsula, Arab-Persian Gulf and Indian Subcontinent. According to the Periplus, Adulis, the African Red Sea port, and Barygaza, the port on the western Indian coast, were markets for 'wine of Laodicea and Italy' (6:2.32–33; 49:16.20–21) and this statement is true for Qana' as well.

However, many of the Dressel 2–4 amphorae found at the Bi'r 'Alī settlement were produced in Egyptian kilns. What kind of products were carried in these containers after they had served as wine jars? Could it be the wheat mentioned in the Periplus? It is interesting to note that according to Riley 'a secondary use of the later Gaza amphora (known in large numbers in the strata of the 'upper' (BA-III) period of Bi'r 'Alī settlement, was for wheat and amphorae were used as a measure of volume in Egypt' (Riley 1979, 222).

It is known from the *Periplus* that Arabian wine was imported to India (49:16.20–21). Most probably, this product was picked up in some South Arabian ports like Qana' or Muza by transit vessels sailing to India. The local traders could also deliver it there. The only storage jars known in the local pottery are big hand-made vessels of coarse porous paste, the so-called *zirs*. No doubt it was impossible to carry wine in such vessels. Did South Arabians re-use the Dressel 2–4 amphorae for such purposes and fill them with local wine somewhere on the coast?

Wine and dates from the Arab-Persian Gulf ports, Apologos and Omana, could be carried in black and grey ware representing, very likely, the type of local containers produced in the Gulf area.

It is known that Dressel 7–11 / Ostia LII / Beltran I amphorae, fragments of which were also found in the strata of the 'lower' (BA-I) period, have been manufactured along the southern Spanish coast and carried fish-based products and fish sauces (Peacock and Williams 1986, 113–114, 120–124). Most probably, these contained small quantities of delicious food destined for foreign residents, as well as for local officials or other important persons living in Qana' or in Shabwa, the capital of the Ḥaḍramawt Kingdom. Thus, the trade links of 'Early Qana'', Qana' of the time of the Periplus, covered an extensive region from the western Mediterranean countries like southern Spain and the Italy (fish sauces, wine and some luxuries like terra sigillata and glass vessels) to Egypt, Palestine and Asia Minor (wine, wheat and the fine pottery such as Eastern Sigillata wares and Nabatean bowls). The presence of the black and grey ware (containers for dates?) and green glazed pottery (luxury vessels?) indicates the trade connections with another part of the ancient world – with the Mesopotamian and Arab-Persian Gulf countries.

Of particular note are an extremely small number of artefacts, which could be connected with the Indian imports to southern Arabia. This is rather strange, especially if we compare this with the larger number of western artefacts. Of course, we can suppose that goods from India did not leave any material evidence, which might be found in excavations. On the other hand, lack of artefacts could be satisfactorily explained as an indication of much less intensive trade contacts between Southern Arabia and India than between southern Arabia and Roman Egypt. The demand for frankincense, traditional export from Ḥaḍramawt, was, probably, greater in the Mediterranean world than in India, although we know about the presence of this good on the Indian markets as well (Periplus: 39:13.8).

Although the Periplus points out the local sea-trade carried on between Qana' and 'the ports across the water – Barygaza, Skythia, Omana' (27:9.10–12) we have practically no indication in the guide about Indian imports to the south Arabian ports. There are only two exceptions: Indian imports to the island of Socotra (31:10.20–24) and the exceptional case of Moscha Limên. As stated in the Periplus, when some vessels 'from Limirikê or Barygaza that passed the winter [*sc.* at Moscha] because of the season being late, by arrangement with the royal agents take on', *i.e.* got a cargo of frankincense 'in exchange for cotton cloth and grain and oil' (32:11.1–5).

According to the *Periplus*, Qana' was one of the departure points for transit vessels on their run to India (57:19.7). But did they use the same point on their run back when some Indian products could be off-loaded?

Very probably the majority of the above mentioned products and other commodities known from the Periplus were carried to the southern coast of the Arabian Peninsula by private merchants from Egypt. On the other hand, undoubtedly Ḥaḍrami middlemen were also involved in the sea-commerce as well.

The heyday of Qana', as well as for South Arabian maritime commerce in general, was probably between the late 2nd and 4th centuries AD. The territory of the settlement grew very intensively and covered an area of more than 5 ha. Strong fortifications were erected above the earliest structures at the foot of Ḥuṣn al-Ghurāb. Big houses with enormous courtyards were built along the seashore of the bay, while shops were apparently concentrated in the southern part of the city. A huge temple probably dedicated to Sayin, the supreme god of Ḥaḍramawt, was built to the south-west of the settlement. On the north-western outskirts of the city, a building used as a synagogue was erected. A cemetery consisting of rectangular crypts with subterranean chambers was founded to the north-west of the city. No doubt these changes resulted from the successful political and economic development of the chief port of the ancient state during the reign of 'Ili'adh Yalut, son of 'Amidhakhar, king of Ḥaḍramawt (*c*. AD 200?–225?), when ambassadors from India, probably arriving via Qana', and Palmyre took part in an official ceremony led by the king (Jamme 1963, 44). According to some Sabaean inscriptions (Ry 533, Ir. 13), around the beginning of the 3rd century AD Qana' was destroyed during the military raid of Sabaean troops, when ships were burnt in its bay. However, the archaeological evidence shows that the ancient port-city was rebuilt very quickly. From the late 3rd century AD Qana' was no doubt a possession of Himyarite kings (more than 36% of all coin finds of this period could be identified as Himyarite coinage).

It is important to note that Ptolemy listed more villages and towns on the Arabian coast (*Geography*, VI, 7). According to him, Okêlis, for instance, was an emporium, and not a watering station as stated in the Periplus (25:8.19–20). No doubt, these changes were a reflection of successful development of the South Arabian maritime commerce. At this time Judaism (from the late 4th century AD) widely penetrated into south Arabia. A majority of Himyarite kings of the late 4th – early 6th centuries AD owed allegiance to Judaism. As Beeston states, 'evidently by this time there was a well-established Jewish community (or communities) of some wealth and standing, fully integrated into the social structure and enjoying the patronage of the king'. On the other hand, 'it must be concluded that [in the 5th century] – Judaism did not prevail at any time among more than a minority of the population' (Beeston 1984, 277). Anyway, we can assume that the synagogue erected on the north-western outskirts of the ancient city was used, in all probability, not only by foreign residents but also by local people converted to Judaism.

Unfortunately, there is no guide like the Periplus for the 2nd to the 5th centuries AD, *i.e.* for the 'middle' (BA-II) period of Bi'r 'Alī occupation. The analysis of the trade connections must therefore be based exclusively on the materials from the archaeological excavations.

The ceramic finds of the 'middle' (BA-II) period of Bi'r 'Alī occupation demonstrate that the trade connections between the Ḥaḍramawt and later Himyarite port of trade and the Mediterranean region were preserved and even extended. Wine was still imported. The 'North Africa-Gallic' amphorae found in the strata of the 'middle' (BA-II) period probably originate in the south of France, and it is thought to have normally carried wine (Peacock and Williams 1986, 142–143, 171–172). North African types of amphorae are thought to have carried olive oil and, less frequently, fish products (Peacock and Williams 1986, 153–169). Very probably this kind of food continued to be imported for foreign residents in Qana' or, more generally, in the Ḥaḍramawt and Himyarite Kingdoms.[13] The amphora-like vessels or storage jars with the inner coating show the establishment of permanent trade connections with the Palestine region, which became more regular and intensive in the next, 'upper' (BA-III) period of Bi'r 'Alī occupation. The content of these vessels is unknown. It is thought that the vessels usually carried wine, and the resinous substance served as a kind of protector of direct contact between wine and fabric of the vessel (Adan-Bayewitz 1986, 97–99; Peacock and Williams 1986, 18).

The increased numbers of the green glazed pottery fragments, and the presence of black and grey ware and fine orange painted ware indicate, no doubt, more intensive contacts with the Mesopotamian, Arab-Persian Gulf and even southern Iranian regions. Most probably some products from those countries like wine, dates and luxury vessels continued to arrive at Qana'. A large number of pottery sherds of undoubtedly Indian origin (RPW) came from the strata of the 'middle' (BA-II) period. It seems Ḥaḍramawt still preserved and even increased its commerce with the countries to the east of Arabia.
It is very important to note that the objects of Indian origin revealed at Khor Rori, ancient Sumhuram or Moscha Limên, by the American Expedition have chronological ranges which are close to the 'middle' (BA-II) period at Qana'. The Indian bronze figurine representing a female deity or spirit, probably a yakshi in the so-called *salabhanjika* pose, may be attributed to the beginning of the 3rd century AD (Goetz 1963, 187–189). The bronze coin of the Kushana king Kanishka I was also found in the «level of late habitation» dated approximately to the early 4th century AD (Albright 1982, 50; Sedov 1992, 126). Of no less interest is the statement of the late V. Begley based on the new investigations at Arikamedu, that 'some – commerce took place in the 4th century. and later' (Begley 1993, 105).

In general, the impression can be summarised as follows. The trade connections with the Mediterranean region, which were reduced, probably, in the late 1st century AD, were no doubt re-activated in the 2nd – 5th centuries AD although, perhaps, not at the same level as before. At the beginning of the BA-II period, *i.e.* in the 2nd – early 3rd centuries AD, Qana' was transformed from a small coastal settlement used mostly as a transit station for vessels on their run from Egypt to India, and as 'a warehouse' for frankincense, into an extensive port-city of the Ḥaḍramawt and, later, Himyarite Kingdoms. The increased material evidence of the imports from Arabian Gulf countries, Mesopotamia and India as well as the reduction of Mediterranean objects show, very likely, that, in contrast with the previous period, there were some changes in the character of the sea-trade. The commerce now was concentrated in the hands of middlemen from Ḥaḍramawt and/or foreign merchants who had their permanent residence in the ancient kingdom. It seems quite probable that Ḥaḍrami middlemen tried to find a kind of balance between 'western' and 'eastern' imports.

In the 6th – early 7th centuries AD the ancient town of Qana' occupied the north-western part of the settlement only, which is about 130 × 155 m in size. Small houses separated by narrow streets covered the reduced territory. This period was dominated by conflict between the Himyarite Empire and the Aksumite Kingdom, and, according to the inscription CIH 621, the 'Urr Mawiyat fortress on the top of Ḥuṣn al-Ghurāb was rebuilt around AD 525 as a stronghold of some local Himyarite tribes (Yaza'nites) against the Ethiopians.

Amphora material from the 'upper' (BA-III) period shows very strong trade links between 'Late Qana'' and the regions of southern Palestine or south-west Jordan. The principal content of the amphorae produced in the Aqaba kilns is unknown, but most likely it was wine or oil as it was assumed for the similar type of amphorae from Berenice and Carthage (Riley 1979, 215). It is thought that amphorae from Gaza carried the famous white wine from that region. However, there is evidence that olive and sesame oil was occasionally carried in such vessels (Riley 1981, 120; Peacock and Williams 1986, 185–187, 198–199; Blakely 1988, 35–38). The storage jars with inner coating which probably carried wine as well continued to arrive in Qana' from somewhere in Palestine.

The connections with the Indian subcontinent were reduced drastically. On the other hand, from the strata of the 'upper' (BA-III) period we have a rather important but curious find indicating the very early contacts between the Arabian Peninsula and Far Eastern countries. A fragment of Chinese celadon, slightly greyish, nearly white in colour, with part of the Chinese letter of van, which means "king", was found.[14]

A great amount of Aksumite hand-made pottery including kitchen wares as well as other finds attest the permanent and very close contacts between Qana' and the north-eastern coast of the African continent during the last decades of the town's existence. It is hard to say with certainty that the population of Qana' at that time directly came from Aksum, but no doubt the sailing across the Bab al-Mandab Strait and connections with the Aksumite Kingdom were very close and intensive.

The evidence of intensive trade contacts with Palestine, *i.e.* with the regions of Byzantine Empire, fits very well with the political situation in South Arabia at that time, when Christian Aksumite Kingdom dominated the area. We can suppose that middlemen from Aksum now controlled the sea-trade of the ancient city (Munro-Hay 1996, 403–416).

In all probability, Qana' was abandoned around the early 7th century AD, perhaps, as a result of general political and religious changes on the Arabian Peninsula, including a change of the directions of trading links. The prophet Mohammed begun a new chapter in the history of Arabian Peninsula, and the majority of pre-Islamic centres went into a state of neglect. New ones appeared and begun to flourish, like al-Mukalla, one of the most beautiful Yemeni cities, and as-Shihr, which were founded 100 kilometres to the east of Qana'. Al-Mukallā and ash-Shiḥr became new port-cities of Ḥaḍramawt, and new centres of Arabian seafaring.

Notes

1. On the date of the *PME* see Robin 1991; Fussman 1991.
2. See Yacut's geographisches Wörterbuch, aus den Handschriften zu Berlin, St. Petersburg, Paris, London und Oxford ... Bd. VI. Hrsg. von F. Wüstenfeld. Leipzig, 1866–1870, S. 273; see also Ibn al-Mujāwir 1954, 270; Doe 1964, 12, note 3; Griaznevich 1995, 280.
3. See also Adwā 'al-l-athār al-Yamaniya. Taqrīr l-'alam as-sufyatiy Sirji Shirinski 'an al-athār fi al-Yaman ad-dumuqrati. Aden, 1975.

4. Bibliography on Dressel 2–4 amphorae is very numerous, see, for example, Grace 1961; Ettlinger and Simonett 1952, 90; Callender 1965, 9–11; Beltran Lloris 1970, 358–367; 1978, 172; Ricerche a Pompei 1984, 278–279; Robinson 1959, 10, 83–85; Tchernia and Zevi 1972, 35–67; Farinas del Cerro, Fernadez de la Vega and, Hesnard 1977, 179–206; Panella and Fano 1977, 133–177; Peacock and Williams 1986, 105–106; Sciallano and Sibella 1994; about Dressel 2–4 amphorae in India (Arikamedu) see Wheeler *et al.* 1946, 17–124; Wheeler 1954, 146; Slane 1991, 204–215; 1996, 351–368; Will 1991, 151–156; 1996, 317–350; Tchernia 1993, 525–534 and bibliography in the last five works; about the production of Dressel 2–4 amphorae in Egypt see Empereur 1986, 599–608; Empereur and Picon 1992, 145–152.
5. On the typology of Ḥaḍramawt series see Sedov 2005, 359–419.
6. The Gaza type amphorae first occurred in the 'late' layers of the 'middle' (BA-II) period of Bi'r 'Alī (ancient Qana') occupation.
7. Cf. similar storage rooms, "the bins" (especially room K3), excavated at the site in Khor Rori lagoon (ancient Sumhuram): Albright 1982, 33; pl. 4; 12, fig. 19.
8. Temple was partly excavated in 1995–96 by the French team under the leadership of Dr. Michel Mouton; see Sedov 2005a, 161–165.
9. But *cf.* Crone 1987, 12–50.
10. The site of an-Nabwa was the subject of exploration by the joint German-Russian team under the direction of B.Vogt and H.Amirkhanov in 1999–2000.
11. The material is being kept now in the Aden National Museum.
12. See the last edition of the manuscript: *The Periplus Maris Erythraei. Text with Introduction, Translation, and Commentary* by Lionel Casson. Princeton, 1989.
13. We now have considerable evidence testifying the presence of foreign temporary residents in Ḥaḍramawt in 2nd–4th centuries AD: the evidence about Palmyrene and Indian ambassadors in Shabwa; the prayer of certain Kosmas, who was, most probably, a temporary resident in Qana'; the Christian ostracon from Qana' bearing the Greek name with Christian affiliation; Syriac graffiti found along with the Kosmas inscription; a structure at Qana', which could be identified as a synagogue, and was erected initially, most probably, for foreign residents rather than for local people. In 1988 M. Piotrovskij and P. Griaznevich found a Greek inscription adorned with a cross above it, unfortunately in bad condition, in the vicinity of Wadi Hajar. The inscription was incised on the rock at the side of an ancient caravan road leading from Qana' to Shabwa and was tentatively dated to the 'early Byzantine period' (M.B. Piotrovskij, pers. com.).
14. Could a Chinese vessel have been dropped by a late visitor to the site probably in the 10th or 11th centuries AD, and later one of the fragments was accidentally placed into the upper strata of the settlement?

Bibliography

Adan-Bayewitz, D., 1986. The Pottery From Late Byzantine Building (Stratum 4) and Its Implications. In Levine, L.I., and Netzer, E. *Excavations at Caesarea Maritima. 1975, 1976, 1979 – Final Report.* Jerusalem, 97–99.

Albright, F.P., 1982. *The American Archaeological Expedition in Dhofar, Oman, 1952–1953.* Washington, DC.

Badre, L., 1992. Le sondage stratigraphique de Shabwa 1976–1981. In Breton, J.-F, (Ed) *Fouilles de Shabwa. II. Rapports préliminaires.* Paris, 229–314.

Ballet, P., 1996. De la Méditerranée a l'océan Indien. L'Égypte et le commerce de longue distance a l'époque romaine: les données céramiques. *Topoi,* 6/2, 809–840.

Beeston, A.F.L., 1976. The Settlement at Khor Rori. *Journal of Oman Studies,* 2, 39–42.

Beeston, A.F.L., 1984. Judaism and Christianity in Pre-Islamic Yemen. Arabie du Sud. Histoire et civilisation. Tome I. In Chelhod, J. (Ed), *Le peuple yéménite et ses racines*. Paris, 271–278.
Begley, V., 1993. New investigations at the port of Arikamedu. *Journal of Roman Archaeology*, 6, 93–108.
Beltran Lloris, M., 1970. *Las ánforas romanas en España*. Zaragosa.
Beltran Lloris M., 1978. *Cerámica Romana. Typologia y Classificacion*. Zaragosa.
Bietak, M. and Schwartz, M., 1987. *Nag 'El-Scheima: eine befestigte christliche Siedlung und andere christliche Denkmäler in Sayala-Nubien. T. I. Die österreichischen Grabungen 1963–1965*. Vienna.
Blakely, J.A., 1988. Ceramics and Commerce: Amphorae from Caesarea Maritima. *Bulletin American Society Oriental Studies*, 271.
Bowersock, G.W., 1993. The New Greek Inscription from South Yemen. In Langdon, J.S., *et al.*, (eds.) *TO ELLHNIKON. Studies in Honour of Speros Vrynos, Jr. Volume I. Hellenic Antiquity and Byzantium*. New Rochelle, 3–8.
Callender, M.H., 1965. *Roman Amphorae with Index of Stamps*. London.
de Cardi, B., 1975. Archaeological Survey in Northern Oman, 1972. *EW*, n.s., 25, no. 1–2, 9–75.
Casson, L., 1989. South Arabia's Maritime Trade in the First Century A.D. L'Arabie préislamique et son environnement historique et culturel. In Fahd, T. (ed), *Actes du Colloque de Strasbourg 24–27 juin 1987*. Leiden, 187–194.
Crone, P., 1987. *Meccan Trade and the Rise of Islam*. Oxford.
Davidde, B., Petriaggi, R., and Williams D.F., 2004. New data on the commercial trade of the harbour of Kanê through the typological and petrographic study of pottery. *Proceedings South Arabian Seminar*, 34, 85–100.
De Paepe, P., Rutten, K., Vrydaghs, L., and Haerink, E., 2003. A Petrographic, Chemical and Phytolith Analysis of Late Pre-Islamic Ceramics from ed-Dur (Umm al-Qaiwain, U.A.E.). Archaeology of the United Arab Emirates. In Potts, D., al-Nabbodah, H., Hellyer, P. (eds.), *Proceedings of the First International Conference on the Archaeology of the U.A.E.* Trident Press, 207–228.
Doe, B., 1961. Ḥuṣn al-Gurâb and the site of Qana'. *Le Muséon*, 54, 191–198.
Doe, B., 1964. Ḥuṣn al-Gurâb and the site of Qana'. *Department of Antiquities Publication. Bulletin* 3. Aden, July 1964.
Doe, B., 1970. *Socotra. An Archaeological Reconnaissance in 1967*. Miami, 152.
Doe, B., 1971. *Southern Arabia*. London.
Doe, B., 1983. *Monuments of South Arabia*. Cambridge.
Egloff, M., 1977. *Kellia. La poterie copte. Quatre siècles d'artisant et d'échanges en Basse-Égypte*. Genève.
Empereur, J.-Y., 1986. Un atelier de Dressel 2–4 en Egypte au IIIe siècle de notre ère. In Empereur, J.-Y., et Garlan, Y. (eds.), *Recherches sue les amphores grecques*. Paris, 599–608.
Emperior, J.-Y., and Picon, M., 1992. La reconnaissance de productions des atelier céramiques: l'exemple de la Maréotide. In Ballet, P. (Ed), *Cahiers de la céramique égyptienne. Ateliers de potiers et productions céramiques en Égypte*. Cairo, 145–152.
Ettlinger, E., and Simonett, C., 1952. *Römische Keramik aus dem Schutthügel von Vindonissa*. Basel.
Ettlinger, E., *et al.* 1990. *Conspectus formarum terrae sigillatae italico modo confectae*. Bonn.
Farinas del Cerro, L., Fernadez de la Vega, W., and Hesnard, A., 1977. Contribution à l'établissement d'une typologie des amphores dites «Dressel 2–4». *Méthodes classiques et méthodes formelles dans l'étude de amphores*. Rome, 179–206.
Faure, P., 1987. *Parfums et aromates de l'Antiquité*. Paris.
Fussman, G., 1991. Le Périple et l'histoire politique de l'Inde. *Journal asiatique*, 279, no. 1–2, 31–38.

Goetz, H., 1963. An Indian Bronze from South Arabia. *Archaeology*, 16, no. 3, 187–189.
Goudineau, Chr., 1968. *La céramique arretine lisse*. Paris.
Grace, V.R., 1961. *Amphoras and the Ancient Wine Trade*. Princeton.
Griaznevich, P.A., 1995. Morskaja torgovlja na Aravijskom more: Aden i Kana (Sea-trade in the Arabian Sea: Aden and Qana'). Ḥaḍramaut. *Arheologicheskie, etnograficheskie i istoriko-kul'turnie issledovanija. Trudi Sovetsko-Yemenskoj kompleksnoj ekspedicii. Tom I (Ḥaḍramawt. Archaeological, Ethnological and Historical Studies. Preliminary Reports of the Soviet-Yemeni Joint Complex Expedition. Volume I)*. Moscow, 1995, 273–301.
Groom, N., 1981. *Frankincense and Myrrh. A Study of the Arabian Incense Trade*. London.
Gupta, S., 1995–96. Beyond Arikamedu: macro stratigraphy of the Iron Age – early historic transition and Roman contact in South India. Puratattva. *Bulletin of the Indian Archaeological Society*, 26, 50–61.
Gurumurthy, S., 1981. *Ceramic traditions in South India (down to 300 A.D.)*. Madras.
Hayes, J.W., 1976. Pottery: Stratified groups and typology. In Humphrey, J.H. (ed.), *Excavations at Carthage 1975 conducted by the University of Michigan*. Vol. I. Tunis, 47–123.
Hayes, J.W., 1978. Pottery Report – 1976. In Humphrey, J.H. (Ed), *Excavations at Carthage 1976 conducted by the University of Michigan*. Vol. IV. Ann Arbor, 23–98.
Hayes, J.W., 1985. Sigillate orientali. *Enciclopedia dell'arte antica. Classica e orientale. Atlante delle forme ceramiche. II. Ceramica fine romana nel bacino Mediterraneo (tardo ellenismo e primo impero)*. Rome, 1–70.
Højlund, F., 1997. Sasanian painted pottery. In Højlund, F., Andersen, H.H., *Qala'at al-Bahrain. Vol 2. The Central Monumental Buildings*. Aarhus.
Ibn al-Mujāwir, 1954. *Descriptio arabiae meridionalis... qui liber inscribitur Ta'rīh al-Mustabṣir.* Pt. 1–2. Ed. by O. Löfgren. Leiden.
Jamme, A., 1963. *The al-'Uqlah Texts*. Washington D.C. (Documentation Sud-Arabe, III).
Khulusi, S., 1976. A Thirteenth Century Poet from Bahrain. *Proceedings of the Society for Arabian Studies Seminar*, 6, 91–102.
Lamberg-Karlovsky, C.C., 1972. Tepe Yahya 1971 – Mesopotamia and the Indo-Iranian Borderlands. *Iran*, vol. 10.
Lecompte, O., 1993. Ed-Dur, les occupations des 3e et 4e s. ap. J.-C.: contexte des trouvailles et matériel diagnostique. *Materialen zur Archäologie der Seleukiden- und Partherzeit im südlichen Babylonien und im Golfgebiet. Ergebnisse der Symposien 1987 und 1989 im Blaubeugen*. Tübingen, 196–217.
Macdonald M.C.A. 1997. Trade Routes and Trade Goods at the Northern End of the «Incense Road» in the first Millennium B.C. In Avanzini, A. (ed.), *Profumi d'Arabia. Atti del convegno*. Rome, 333–350.
Madjid, Ahmad, 1984. *Kniga pol'z ob osnovah i pravilah morskoj nauki. Kriticheskij tekst, perevod, kommentarij, issledovanie i ukazateli T.A. Shumovskogo*. II. Moscow.
de Maigret, A., 1997. The Frankincense Road from Najrān to Ma'ān: a Hypothetical Itinerary. In Avanzini, A. (ed.), *Profumi d'Arabia. Atti del convegno*. Rome, 315–332.
Majcherek, G., 1995. Gazan Amphorae: Typology Reconsidered. 'Hellenistic and Roman Pottery in the Eastern Mediterranean – Advances in Scientific Studies. In Meyza, H., and Mlynarczyk, J. (eds.), *Acts of the II Nieborów Pottery Workshop. Nieborów, 18–20 December 1993*. Warsaw, 163–178.
Mazar, E. and Mazar, B., 1989. *Excavations in the South of the Temple Mount. The Ophel of Biblical Jerusalem*. Jerusalem.
Mouton, M., 1992. *La péninsule d'Oman de la fin de l'âge du Fer au début de la période sassanide (250 av. – 350 ap. J.-C.)*. Thèse de doctorat. Université de Paris I (Panthéon-Sorbonne).
Müller, W.W., 1979. Arabian Frankincense in Antiquity According to Classical Sources. *Studies in the History of Arabia*. Vol. I. Sources for the History of Arabia. Riyadh, 79–92.

Müller, W.W., 1984. Survey of the History of the Arabian Peninsula from the First Century A.D. to the Rise of Islam. *Studies in the History of Arabia. Volume II. Pre-Islamic Arabia.* Riyadh, 125–131.

Munro-Hay, S.C.H., 1989. *Excavations at Aksum. An Account of Research at the Ancient Ethiopian Capital Directed in 1972–4 by the Late Dr. Neville Chittick.* London.

Munro-Hay, S.C.H., 1996. Aksumite overseas interests. In Reade, J. (ed.), *The Indian Ocean in Antiquity.* London, 403–416.

Naumkin, V.V., and Sedov, A.V., 1993. Monuments of Socotra. *Topoi,* 3/2, 569–623.

Negev, A., 1986. *The Late Hellenistic and Early Roman Pottery of Nabatean Oboda. Final Report.* Jerusalem.

Orton, N.P., 1991. Red Polished Ware in Gujarat: A Catalogue of Twelve Sites. In Begley, V. and de Puma, R.P. (eds), *Rome and India. The Ancient Sea Trade.* Madison, 46–81.

Palma, B., and Panella, C., 1968. Anfore. *Ostia I. Le terme del Nuotatore. Scavo dell'ambiente IV.* Roma.

Panella, C., 1970. Anfore. *Ostia II. Le terme del Nuotatore. Scavo dell'ambiente I. Roma,* 102–156.

Panella, C., 1973. Anfore. *Ostia III. Le terme del Nuotatore. Scavo dell'ambiente V et di un saggio nell'area.* Roma.

Panella, C., 1977. Anfore. *Ostia IV. Le terme del Nuotatore. Scavo dell'ambiente Xve dell'area XXV.* Roma, 116–265.

Panella, C., and Fano, M., 1977. Le anfore con anse bifide conservate a Pompei: contributo ad una loro classificazione. *Méthodes classiques et méthodes formelles dans l'étude des amphores.* Rome, 133–177.

Peacock, D.P.S., 1984. The Amphorae: Typology and Chronology. In Fulford, M.G., and Peacock, D.P.S., Excavations at Carthage: the British Mission. Vol. I, 2. *The avenue du président Habib Bourguiba, Salambo: the pottery and other ceramic objects from the site.* London, 116–140.

Peacock, D.P.S., and Williams, D.F., 1986. *Amphorae and the Roman Economy: an Introductory Guide.* London-New York.

Pirenne, J., 1975. The Incense Port of Moscha (Khor Rori) in Dhofar. *Journal of Oman Studies,* 1, 81–96.

Potts, D.T., 1998. Namord Ware in Southern Arabia. *Arabia and its Neighbours.* In Phillips, C.S., Potts, D.N. and Searight, S. (eds), *Essays on prehistorical and historical developments presented in honour of Beatrice de Cardi.* Brepols (Abiel II. New Research on the Arabian Peninsula), 207–220.

Pucci, G., 1985. Terra sigillata italica. Enciclopedia dell'arte antica. Classica e orientale. *Atlante delle forme ceramiche. II. Ceramica fine romana nel bacino Mediterraneo (tardo ellenismo e primo impero).* Roma, 361–406.

Ar-Rafik, 1966. *An-Nafi''ala durub manzumatay al-mallah Ba Ta'i'. Ta'lif Muhammad 'Abd al-Qadir Ba Matraf.* Al-Mukalla, 82–83.

Rao, S.R., 1966. *Excavations at Amreli. A Kshatrapa-Gupta town.* Baroda.

Ricerche a Pompei, 1984. *Ricerche a Pompei: L'insula 5 della Regio VI dalle origini al 79 d.c. I (campagne di scavo 1976–1979).* Rome.

Riley, J.A., 1979. *The Coarse Pottery from Berenice.* In Lloyd, J.A. (ed.), *Excavations at Sidi Khrebish Benghazi (Berenice). Vol. II,* Tripoli, 91–497.

Riley, J.A., 1981. The pottery from the cisterns 1977.1, 1977.2 and 1977.3. In Humphrey, J.H., (ed.), *Excavations at Carthage 1977 conducted by the University of Michigan. Volume VI.* Ann Arbor, 85–124.

Robin, Chr., 1984. La civilisation de l'Arabie méridionale avant l'Islam. In Chelhod, J. (ed.), *L'Arabie du Sud. Histoire et civilisation. 1. Le peuple yéménite et ses racines.* Paris, 195–224.

Robin, Chr., 1991. L'Arabie du Sud et la date du Périple de la Mer Érythrée (nouvelles données). *Journal asiatique*, 279, no. 1–2, 1–30.
Robin, Chr., 1992. Cités, royaumes et empires de l'Arabie avant l'Islam. L'Arbie antique de Karib'îl à Mahomet. *Nouvelles données sur l'histoire des Arabes grâce aux inscriptions*. Aix-en-Provence, 45–54.
Robin, Chr., 1992a. Quelques épisodes marquants de l'histoire sudarabique. L'Arbie antique de Karib'îl à Mahomet. *Nouvelles données sur l'histoire des Arabes grâce aux inscriptions*. Aix-en-Provence, 55–70.
Robin, Chr., 1997. Arabie Méridionale: l'état et les aromates. In Avanzini, A. (ed.), *Profumi d'Arabia. Atti del convegno*. Rome, 37–56.
Robinson, H., 1959. *Pottery of the Roman Period*. Princeton (The Athenian Agora. V).
Salles, J.-F., 1984. Céramiques de surface à ed-Dur, Émirats Arabes Unis. *Arabie Orientale, Mésopotamie et Iran Méridionale de l'âge du fer au début de la période islamique* (Réunion de travail, Lyon, 1982, Maison de l'Orient). Sous la direction de R.Boucharlat et J.-F.Salles. Paris, 241–270.
Salles J.-F. 1993. The Periplus of the Erythraean Sea and the Arab-Persian Gulf. *Topoi*, 3/2, 493–524.
Schenk, H., 2001. The development of pottery at Tissamaharama. In Weisshaar, H.J, Roth, H. and Wijeyapala, W. (eds), *Ancient Ruhuna: Sri Lankan-German archaeological project in the Southern Province. Vol. I*. Mainz am Rhein, 59–196.
Schmitt-Korte, K., 1974. *Die Bemalte nabatäische Keramik, Vebreitung, Typologie und Chronologie. Petra und das Königreich der Nabatäer*. München, 70–93.
Schmitt-Korte, K., 1984. *Nabatean Pottery. A Typological and Chronological Framework. Studies in the History of Arabia. Pre-Islamic Arabia*. Riyadh, 7–40.
Sciallano, M., and Sibella, P., 1994. *Amphores. Comment les identifier?* Aix-en-Provence.
Sedov, A., 1992. New Archaeological and Epigraphical Material from Qana' (South Arabia). *Arabian archaeology and Epigraphy*, 3/2, 110–137.
Sedov, A.V., 2003. Notes on stratigraphy and pottery sequence at Rayban I settlement (Western wādī Ḥaḍramawt). Arabia. *Revue de sabéologie*.1.173–196.
Sedov, A.V., 2005. Drevnij Ḥaḍramaut. Ocherki arheologii i numizmatiki (*Ancient Ḥaḍramawt. Essays on Archaeology and Numismatics*). Moscow.
Sedov, A.V., 2005a. Temples of Ancient Ḥaḍramawt. *Arabia Antica* 3.
Shihab, Hasan Salih., 1984. '*Ulum al-'arab al-bahriya (Dirasat mukarana)*. Al-Kuwait.
Shirinskij, S.S., 1977. Novij pamjatnik juznoarabskoj arhitekturi I v. do n.e. (A new monument of the South Arabian architecture of the 1st century B.C*.). Istorija i kultura antichnogo mira (History and Culture of the Classical World)*. Moscow, 202–205.
Sidebotham, S.E., 1986. *Roman Economic Policy in the Erythra Thalassa 30 BC – AD 217*. Leiden.
Sidebotham, S.E., 1989. Ports of the Red Sea and the Arabia-India Trade. *L'Arabie préislamique et son environnement historique et culturel*. Actes du Colloque de Strasbourg 24–27 juin 1987. Éd. par T. Fahd. Leiden, 195–223.
Singh, H.N., 1982. *History and archaeology of Black-and-Red Ware (Chalcolithic period)*. Delhi.
Slane, K.W., 1991. Observation on Mediterranean Amphoras and Tablewares Found in India. In Begley, V., and de Puma, R.P. (eds), *Rome and India. The Ancient Sea Trade*. Madison, 204–215.
Slane, R.W., 1996. Other Ancient Ceramics imported from the Mediterranean. In Begley, V., *The Ancient Port of Arikamedu. New Excavations and Researches 1989–1992. Vol. 1*. Pondichéry / Paris, 351–368.
Sprenger, A., 1864. *Die Post- und Reiserouten des Orients. Abhandlungen für die Kunde des Morgenlandes,* Band III, no. 3. Leipzig.

Tchernia, A., 1993. Rome et l'Inde: l'archeologie toute seule? (Begley, V., and de Puma, R.D, 1991. *Rome and India. The Ancient Sea Trade*). *Topoi*, 3/2, 525–534.

Tchernia, A., 1997.Winds and Coins: From the Supposed Discovery of the Monsoon to the Denarii of Tiberius. In De Romanis, F., and Tchernia, A. (eds), *Crossings. Early Mediterranean Contacts with India*. New Delhi, 250–276.

Tchernia, A. and Zevi, F., 1972. Amphoras vinaires de campanie et de tarraconaise à Ostie. *Recherches sur les amphores romaines*. Rome, 35–67.

Toll, N., 1943. The Green Glazed Pottery. In Rostovtzeff, M.I., Bellinger, A.R., Brown, F.E. and Welles, C.B. (Eds), *The Excavations at Dura-Europos Conducted by Yale University and the French Academy of Inscriptions and Letters. Final Report IV*. Pt. I, fasc. 1. New Haven.

Tomber, R., 2004. Amphorae from the Red Sea and their contribution to the interpretation of late Roman trade beyond the Empire. In Eiring, J., and Lund, J., *Transport amphorae and trade in the Eastern Mediterranean*. Mon. Danish Inst. Athens, 5, 393–402.

Vinogradov, Ju.G., 1989. Grecheskaja nadpis'iz Juzhnoj Aravii (Greek Inscription from South Arabia). *Vestnik drevnej istorii*, 2, 162–167.

Wellsted, J.R., 1838. *Travels in Arabia. Volume II*, London.

Wheeler, R.E.M., 1954. *Rome beyond the Imperial Frontiers*. London.

Wheeler, R.E.M., *et al.* 1946. Arikamedu: an Indo-Roman Trading-station on the East Coast of India. Ancient India. *Bulletin of the Archaeological Survey of India*, 2, 17–124.

Whitcomb, D., 1989. Evidence of the Umayyad Period from the Aqaba Excavations. In Bakhit, M.A., and Schick, R. (eds), *The Fourth International Conference on the History of Bilad al-Sham during the Umayyad Period. Vol. 2*. Amman.

Whitehouse, D., and Williamson, A., 1973. Sasanian Maritime Trade. *Iran,* vol. XI, 29–49.

Will, E.L., 1991. The Mediterranean Shipping Amphoras from Arikamedu. In Begley, V., and de Puma, R.P. (eds), *Rome and India. The Ancient Sea Trade*. Madison, 151–156.

Will, E.L., 1996. Mediterranean Shipping Amphorae at Arikamedu, 1941–50 Excavations. In Begley V., *The Ancient Port of Arikamedu. New Excavations and Researches 1989–1992*. Vol. 1. Pondichéry/Paris, 317–350.

Wissmann, H. von, 1964. Ḥimyar, Ancient History. *Le Muséon*, 77, 3–4, 429–497.

Wissmann, H. von, 1977. Das weihrauchland Sa'kalān, Samārum und Moscha. *Mit. Beiträgen von W.W. Müller.* Wien.

Zarins, J., 1997. Persia and Dhofar: Aspects of Iron Age, International Politics and Trade. In Young, G.D, Chavalas, M.W., and Averbeck, R.E. (eds), *Crossing Boundaries and Linking Horizons*. Bethesda, Md., 615–689.

Chapter 5: Frankincense in the 'Triangular' Indo-Arabian-Roman Aromatics Trade

Sunil Gupta

This paper endeavours to show that a rapid increase in the south Arabian frankincense exports to the Roman world created the problem of reciprocal supplies for the Romans. There was a need to provide more than the traditional elite goods (wine, fine cloth, statuary) to the Ḥaḍramawt. This forced the Romans to augment their exports to Arabia with Indian foodstuff and cloth that had a steady demand in the arid peninsula. In particular, the Romans exchanged Indian essentials for frankincense at the harbour of Kanê, taking advantage of the old trade in Indian basic goods (cereals, sesame oil, cloth and iron) operational along the arc from western India to the southern Red Sea.

The rapid growth of the south Arabian incense trade with the Mediterranean during the BC – AD transition was a consequence of direct Roman maritime contact with Yemen and the southern Oman (Dhofar) regions. The sailing guide of the 1st century AD, *Periplus Maris Erythraei*, informs us that myrrh and frankincense, two aromatic resins from trees native to south Arabia, were exported from harbours about the Gulf of Aden to Roman Egypt. South Arabian incense trade with the northern Red Sea region was extant since the 2nd millennium BC when Pharaonic trading missions first ventured to the legendary land of Punt, most probably the present day Yemen (Meeks 2003, 53–80; Gupta 2004, 133–160). There are repeated references to the myrrh and frankincense of Punt in Egyptian hieroglyphic records of the 2nd – 1st millennium BC (Schoff 1912, 120–126; Kitchen 1993, 587–608). In the early 1st millennium BC, caravan routes emanating from south Arabia cut across the Arabian peninsular to the northern Red Sea region and the Persian Gulf. Myrrh and frankincense consignments moved along these routes. The rock cut city of Petra in Jordan, capital of the Nabataean kingdom, grew rich with the flow of the overland incense trade from south Arabia in the BC–AD transition. The conquest of Ptolemaic Egypt by the Romans in 30 BC extended the frontiers of the empire to the Red Sea coast and opened access to the resources of the Indian Ocean lands, including the myrrh and frankincense of south Arabia.

Our concern here is with the south Arabian frankincense trade and its implications for the flourishing sea commerce between the Roman world and the Indian subcontinent in the early centuries AD. While frankincense exports to the Mediterranean region and the Persian Gulf littoral are fairly well recorded in Greco-Roman historical sources of this period, the textual records are mostly silent on the issue of frankincense supplies to the Indian subcontinent. The *Periplus Maris Erythraei*, compiled by an anonymous mariner in the mid 1st century AD, has a solitary reference to the import of frankincense to the harbour of Barbarikon on the estuary of the river Indus (*PME* 39; Casson 1989, 75, 191). While Indian textual records

Frankincense in the 'Triangular' Indo-Arabian-Roman Aromatics Trade 113

of the early historic period mention a number of aromatics, there is no reference to myrrh or frankincense. Only one source comes close. The ancient Indian economic treatise, the Arthasastra (broadly dated between 3rd century BC to 3rd century AD), mentions (Indian) aloe (*Arth.* 2.11.57–58) and 'aloe from across the seas' (*Arth.* 2.11.59) in its treasury list. The latter must surely be the Arabian aloe mentioned in the Periplus (section 28) as a major export, together with frankincense, from the port of Kanê. 'It (Kanê) exports local wares, namely frankincense and aloe' (Casson 1989, 67). Kartunnen (1998, 151–2) distinguishes between the Indian and Arabian types of aloe, 'The names *agallochum* and *aloe* refer to two different products, the Indian wood of *Excoecaria agallocha* (so-called eagle-wood, also known as *Aloexylon aagallochum* and *Aquilaria agallocha*, OIA *agaru, aguru*, MIA *agulu*) and the Arabian leaf of *Aloe vera* (*A. barbadensis*) and *Aloe perryi*, also called medicinal Aloe'. These aromatics, one a resin and other a leaf, grew together in the Ḥaḍrami territories and there is every reason to believe that frankincense came with aloe to India as the Periplus (section 27) mentions frankincense and aloe as major exports of the Ḥaḍramawt. Recently, Russian archaeologists exploring the island of Socotra off the Yemen coast found frankincense and aloe trees growing in abundance (Naumkin and Sedov 1993, Photo 2–1). As I shall discuss, frankincense became a major fixture in a 'triangular' trade involving Romans, Indians and Arabians in the Arabian Sea.

Frankincense was grown in eastern Yemen (Ḥaḍramawt), south Oman (Dhofar), on the island of Socotra off Yemen and the Somalian coast (discussions in Schoff 1912, 120–143; Casson 1989, 162–167). Most of the frankincense exports were routed through two major ports of trade of the kingdom of Ḥaḍramawt, Kanê Emporium and Moscha (see *PME* sections 28 and 32) (Fig. 5.1). The two ports serviced different frankincense producing

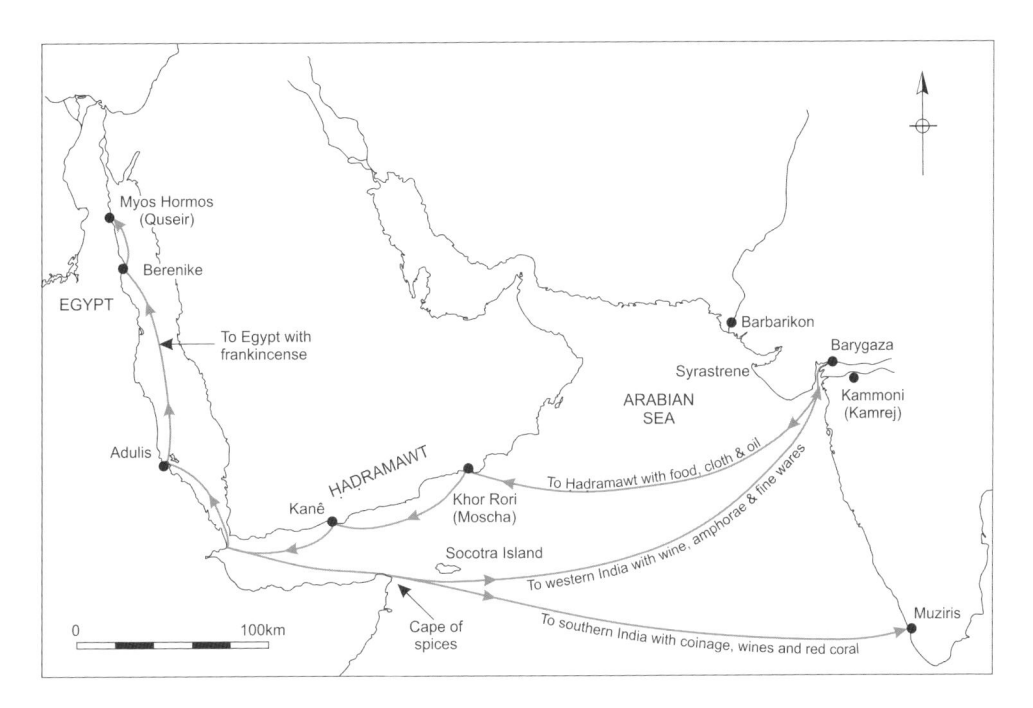

Fig. 5.1. Map of the Arabian Sea showing the 'triangular' trade.

regions. Kanê Emporium received the frankincense produced in the Ḥaḍramawt Valley and from Moscha, the frankincense from the coastal tracts of the Dhofar, isolated from the Ḥaḍramawt by high mountains of the Qara range (Fig. 5.1). According to the author of the Periplus the frankincense in the Dhofar region was called Sachalitic frankincense (PME 29, 32; see commentaries by Schoff 1912, 129–130; see descriptions of the Dhofar coast in Fiennes 1992). In fact, the royalty of Ḥaḍramawt specifically developed Moscha for the trade in Sachalitic frankincense, sending military officers and settlers to open the mosquito ridden coast in the late 1st century BC (Pirenne 1975, 81–96; Beeston 1976, 39–42). The initiation of trade in Sachalitic frankincense, over and above the Ḥaḍrami variety, must have made large amounts of the aromatic available for foreign markets.

The ports of Kanê and Moscha have been identified with the sites of Bir 'Alī (Ḥuṣn al Ghurāb) and Khor Rori (Fig. 5.1) (Schoff 1912, 116; Casson 1989, 161; van Beek, 1958, 142; Avanzini, 1994, 55; Avanzini *et al.*, 2002). Archaeological excavations at the sites of Kanê (modern Bi'r 'Alī) and Moscha (modern Khor Rori) have brought to light structures (warehouse at Kanê and sea fort at Moscha) and Roman, Indian and Parthian wares. Work at Bi'r 'Alī is summarized, for example, by Sedov (1992, 110–37; 1996, 11–35 and chapter 4 above) and Salles and Sedov (2002) while for Moscha / Khor Rori (see Avanzini (2002)), all with references to earlier work. It appears that Khor Rori was fortified in the late 1st century BC and continued until 5th century AD. The presence of Roman amphorae in good numbers at Bi'r 'Alī and Khor Rori, together with conspicuous amounts of pottery from the Indian subcontinent and the Persian Gulf region corroborate the Periplus'conception of Kanê and Moscha as 'international' ports of trade (Fig. 5.2). The component of Roman ceramics dominated the pottery corpus from the Kanê excavations, constituting almost 75 % of the total wares registered by the Russian-Yemen excavation team (Sedov 1992, 116). The situation at Khor Rori was similar, except that Roman pottery was in hundreds and not thousands as at Kanê /Bi'r 'Alī (Sedov and Benvenuti 2002, 11–12). The Indian pottery at Khor Rori comprised mainly cooking vessels (Sedov and Benvenuti, 11–12). Some specific types, characterized by coarsely fired red fabric, were circulating in a wide arc from western India through the Gulf of Aden region right up to the Egyptian coast. Also present on the Ḥaḍhramī coast are fine wares inspired by the Indian Red Polished Ware (RPW) tradition (Sedov 1996, 11–35). The origin of the RPW has been associated with the Roman *terra sigillata* tradition. Archaeologists have been at pains to distinguish between an Arabian imitation of *sigillata* and Indian Red Polished Ware excavated from Kanê and Khor Rori (Yule and Kervran 1993, 69–106). The inference that can be drawn is that a syncretic red ware tradition, inspired by fine Roman red wares, had grown on both sides of the Arabian Sea during the BC – AD transition. The exotic ceramics point to the coming together of Arabian, Roman and Indian mercantile interests at the Ḥaḍramawt ports.

Crucial information in the Periplus points to this happening. The relevant information, concerned with trade activity at Moscha, is contained in section 32 of the Periplus,

'...those sailing by from Limyrike or Barygaza that passed the winter (sc. At Moscha) because of the season being late, by arrangement with the royal agents take on, in exchange for cotton cloth and grain and oil, a return cargo of frankincense...'

(Casson 1989, 71)

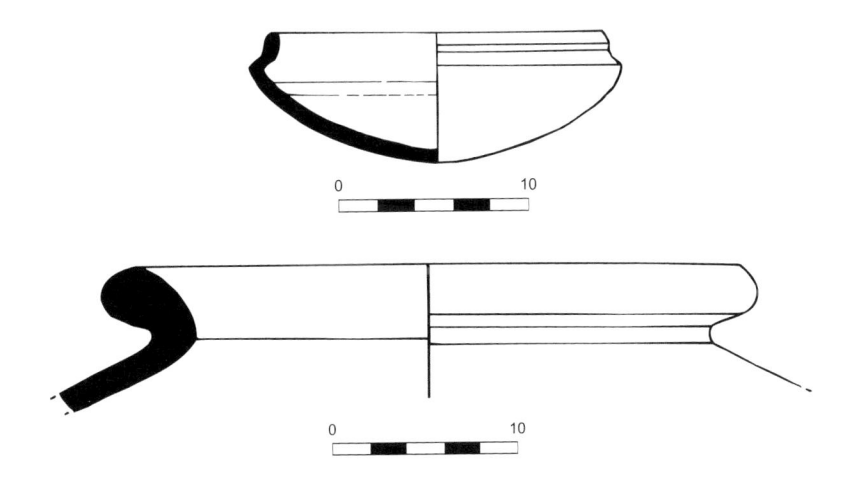

Fig. 5.2. Indian cooking wares from Kamrej, Khor Rori.

Who were the shippers coming from India and 'sailing by' Moscha? Schoff (1912, 140–141) has nothing to say on the identity of ships exchanging wheat for frankincense. His use of the term 'returning' instead of 'sailing by' is suggestive of Roman ships on their way back to Egypt after delivering consignments in India. Presumably, some of these returning ships wintered at Moscha (Schoff 1912, 34–5) and Casson (1989, 71), whose translation is excerpted above. The statement that latecomers wintered at Moscha suggests that normally the port they were sailing to would have been further, namely Kanê. Furthermore, Casson (1989, 172–3) assumes the sailors to be Indian. Salles (1993, 516) is of the opinion that the shippers who took food consignments from Barygaza to the Arabian Peninsula were Arabs and Persians. In my opinion, the vessels making landfall at Moscha belonged to Arabo-Persians, Indians, Romans; all important players in the maritime trade of the Arabian Sea. This is indicated by the substantial deposition of Roman amphorae and Indian cooking wares at Moscha / Khor Rori, besides the Arabian and Parthian ceramics. The Periplus (section 30) mentions that Persian, Indian and Greek expatriate merchants residing in the nearby island of Socotra. The same situation must have obtained at Moscha and Kanê.

The Periplus informs us that some of the cloth and grain and sesame oil traded at Moscha was sourced in western India. This is established by the reference to Barygaza as one of the sources of the consignments reaching Moscha. The basic goods traded at Moscha/Khor Rori are the same set of essentials the Periplus mentions as the traditional products of Syrastrene (Saurashtra) in western India. Of the goods of Syrastrene, section 41 of the Periplus informs, 'The region, very fertile, produces grain, rice, sesame oil, ghee, cotton and the Indian cloths made from it, those of ordinary quality' (Casson 1989, 77). A similar set of goods were shipped from the great harbour of Barygaza (modern Bharuch, western India) to the inhabitants of Socotra island, the Somali 'far side' ports and the Aksumite port of Adulis near the southern Red Sea (PME 6, 14, 31, 32). The

Fig. 5.3. The site of Kamrej.

internal evidence of the Periplus suggests that Moscha was integral to a maritime network supplying Indian essential goods from Oman through the Gulf of Aden and up to the southern Red Sea during the BC – AD transition.

The evidence from my recent excavations at Kamrej, an early historic port on the west coast of India, corroborates the information provided by the Periplus (Gupta *et al.* 2004, 9–33). Early historic Kamrej, located on the banks of the river Tapi some 40 km upstream of the Gulf of Khambhat, has been identified as the settlement of Kammoni mentioned in the Periplus (Gupta 1993, 119–127) (Fig. 5.3). We discovered large quantities of rice grains close to a kiln producing the type of Indian transport vessels found at Moscha and Quseir. Rice is mentioned in the Periplus as one of the basic exports from western India (Fig. 5.4). White fibrous material embedded in the sections close to the riverside is suspected to be remnants of cotton (Fig. 5.5), another major item of export to the Arabian peninsula. Also a large number of iron furnaces came to light. I have made the assertion that Kamrej was a major iron making center exporting iron and steel to Ethiopia (Gupta 1993, 119–127). This projection has been given credibility by the identification by Tomber (2005) of an amphora-like handle found at Kamrej as part of an Aksumite vessel dating to the 4th century AD (Fig. 5.6). This is the first Aksumite vessel of the Early Historic period to be found in India. The material indicators for long distance trade at Kamrej strongly corroborate the critical references in the Periplus to the Indian trade in essentials in the western Indian Ocean sphere. This trade extended from western India to the southern Red Sea, forming a powerful maritime network. The trade was old, rooted in the antiquity of the Bronze Age. The Harappan and Late Harappan ceramic deposition in Oman has been associated with the export of food from agriculturally rich western India to the semi-arid Lower Gulf region (Cleuziou 1992, 93–103). The Harappan – Early Historic parallelism suggests that the 'food' networks were still enduring after the collapse of the Harappan

Fig. 5.4. Rice from Kamrej excavations.   *Fig. 5.5. Cloth remains from Kamrej.*

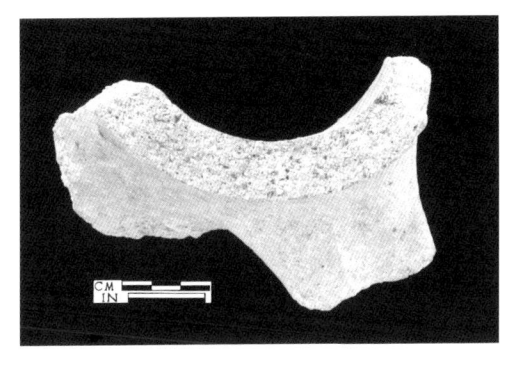

Fig. 5.6. Aksumite sherd from Kamrej.

Civilization. In fact, the trade in essentials still carries on, with dhows laden with flour and onions regularly setting sail from western India to the Gulf (Sahani 1997, 9–18). Clearly, two distinct networks are visible in the western Indian Ocean during the time of the Periplus, the old trade conduits dealing in essentials and the robust and new Indo-Roman commodity exchange focused on high value commodities.

It must have made sense for Roman shippers returning to Egypt from India to take advantage of the Indian food supply lines to the Gulf of Aden region. Liquid stock like sesame oil and perishables like grain/wheat/rice brought from western India to Moscha and Kanê must have generated a high demand for container wares. In this context, the amphorae, as reusable containers essentially constructed for sea transport, must have come in good use. As pointed out, the majority of foreign wares in the Lower Period at Kanê are typically containers for wine. The bulk of the amphorae fragments have been identified as the Dressel 2–4, a popular container for wine in the 1st century BC to 2nd century AD (Peacock and Williams 1986). Similarly, the Dressel 2–4 form was the dominant type at Moscha/Khor Rori. In western India, a Dressel 2–4 amphora 'continuum' has been delineated at the Early Historic site of Nevasa (Gupta *et al.* 2001, 7–18) (Fig. 5.7). It is not far fetched to imagine a scenario where Roman shippers carrying wine amphorae to India held back part or whole of their amphorae after selling off the wine at Indian

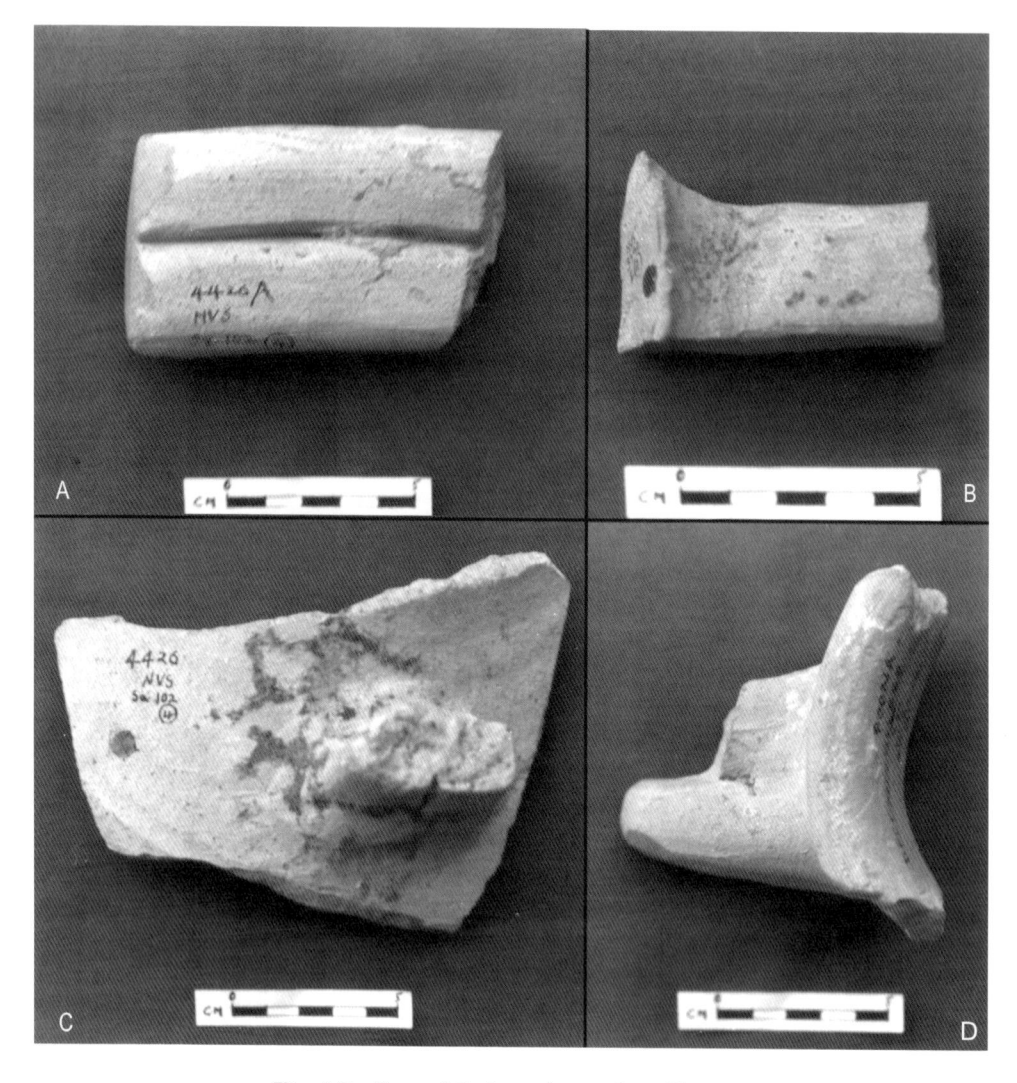

Fig. 5.7. Dressel 2–4 amphorae from Nevasa.

ports and filled the excess containers with sesame oil and wheat for Arabian markets. The circulating amphorae would have been constantly replenished as the broken ones were discarded. Numerous broken amphorae reused as a buoyancy aid were found in the harbour front at Quseir in Egypt, but these could derive from a wreck at the mouth of the harbour (Peacock *et al.* 2000; 2001; 2006). The large amphora deposition at Kanê and Khor Rori was probably formed by accumulation of discards created by constant exchange, breakage and replenishment of stock. The large numbers of Indian storage jars at Khor Rori suggest the same process.

An important theme emerging from the archaeo-historical evidence is the strong Ḥaḍrami, as compared to the Himyarite, engagement with Indo-Roman sea trade dynamics. The conspicuous Roman presence on the Ḥaḍrami coast, together with deep linkages with

India visible in the archaeological record, are expressive of the broader 'Indo-Roman' scheme into which Ḥaḍramawt had been drawn. The historical and material indicators suggest that the dramatic rise in demand for supplies of frankincense from the south Arabian coast forced the Romans to think of other supply strategies for the trade. This developed as the 'triangular' trade involving south Arabians, Romans and Indians in a unique relationship. We have instances of such trade in other times, the most dramatic being the substitution of opium for the gold the British were paying the Chinese for tea and other goods in the 19th century (Vinacke 1960, 34–5; Fairbank *et al*. 1989, 448–57; Perkins 1999, 368–9).

'While the first trade was entirely one sided, Chinese products being paid for in specie or bullion, an exchange of commodities was gradually built up….it was only after opium began to figure largely in the imports that specie was no longer needed to settle a balance adverse to the foreigners'

(Vinacke 1960, 34–5)

The port of Calcutta (modern Kolkata) in eastern India was developed by the British as the supply route for Indian opium to China, saving the British treasury of a 'drain of wealth'. These events sparked the infamous Opium Wars in the 19th century. Nearly two millennia ago, Pliny shared the sentiments of the colonial British, complaining in the Roman senate of the adverse balance of Roman trade with India and of the Indian practice of draining the Romans of their gold in return for spices and diaphanous cloth. Given the situation, the Romans could not afford to supply large quantities of gold and silver coins to south Arabians in return for incense. The Romans were already pumping their specie into India. It is interesting to note that although large quantities of coin were imported into Kanê (Casson 1989, 67) overall imports into India were on a far greater scale than those to Arabia (*cf*. Turner 1989; Sidebotham 1989). Neither could they conquer south Arabia militarily, as Gallus' aborted mission of 25–16 BC proved. The strategy of making cheap Indian essentials pay for frankincense supplies to lucrative markets in the Mediterranean must have seemed a ready and worthwhile solution. The 'aromatics for food' trade, as it regularised, must have contributed in part to the heavy deposition of Mediterranean amphorae and Indian trade potteries in the Ḥaḍrami ports.

Bibliography

Albright, F.P., 1982. *The American Archaeological Expedition to Dhofar, Oman 1952–53.* Washington D.C., Publication of the American Foundation for Study of Man.
Avanzini, A., 1994. *The Red Sea and Arabia, in Ancient Rome and India*. In R.M. Cimino (ed.). Ancient Rome and India. 53–59. Delhi-Rome
Avanzini, A., 2002. *Khor Rori Report 1.* Pisa.
Avanzini, A., Buffa, V., Lombardini, A., Orazi, R. and Sedov, A. 1999–2000. Excavations and Restoration of the Complex of Khor Rori MID's Interim Report (1999–2000), *EVO* 22–23 (1999–2000*), 189–228.
Beeston, A.F.L., 1976. The Settlement at Khor Rori, *Journal of Oman Studies,* 2, 39–42.
Casson, L., 1989. *Periplus Maris Erythraei*. Princeton.

Cleuziou, S., 1992. The Oman Peninsula and the Indus Civilization, A Reassessment, *Man and Environment,* 17 (2), 93–103.

Cleveland, R.L., 1960. The 1960 American Expedition to Dhofar, *Bulletin of the American School of Oriental Research,* 159, 14–26.

Fairbank, J.F., Reischaner, E.O., and Craig, A.M., 1989. *East Asia, Tradition and Transformation.* Delhi.

Fiennes, R., 1992. *Atlantis of the Sands.* London.

Gupta, S., 1993. The Location of Kammoni (Periplus 43), *Man and Environment,* (Journal of the Indian Society for Prehistoric and Quaternary Studies), 18, 119–127.

Gupta, S., 2004. Monsoon Environments and the Indian Ocean Interaction Sphere in Antiquity, 3000 BC – AD 300. In Y. Yasuda and V. Shinde (eds.) *Monsoon and Civilization,* 133–160. Delhi.

Gupta, S., Williams, D., and Peacock, D., 2001. Dressel 2–4 Amphorae and Roman Trade with India, the evidence from Nevasa. *Journal of South Asian Studies,* 17, 7–18.

Gupta, S.P., Sunil Gupta, Tejas Garge, Rohini Pandey, Anuja Geetali and Sonali Gupta, 2004. On the fast Track of the Periplus, Excavations at Kamrej – 2003. *Journal of Indian Ocean Archaeology,* 1, 67–79.

Kitchen, K.A., 1993. The Land of Punt. In T. Shaw, Sinclair, P. and Okpoko, A. (eds) *The Archaeology of Africa.* London and New York. 587–608.

Meeks, D., 2003. Locating Punt. In D. O'Connor and S. Quirke (eds) *Mysterious Lands.* London, Institute of Archaeology, UCL. 53–80.

Naumkin, V.V., and Sedov, A.V., 1993. Monuments of Socotra, *Topoi,* 3, 569–622.

Peacock, D., and Blue, L., 2006. *Myos Hormos – Quseir al-Qadim, Roman and Islamic ports on the Red Sea. Volume 1, Survey and excavations 1999–2003.* Oxford.

Peacock, D., Blue, L., Bradford, N. and Moser, S., 2000. *Myos Hormos / Quseir al Qadim, A Roman and Islamic Port on the Red Sea Coast of Egypt.* Interim Reports of Excavations. Southampton, University of Southampton.

Peacock, D., Blue, L., Bradford, N., and Moser, S., 2001. *Myos Hormos / Quseir al Qadim, A Roman and Islamic Port on the Red Sea Coast of Egypt.* Interim Reports of Excavations. Southampton, University of Southampton.

Peacock, D., and Williams, D., 1986. *Amphorae and the Roman Economy. An Introductory Guide.* London and New York.

Perkins, D., 1999. *Encyclopaedia of China.* London.

Pirenne, J., 1975. The Incense Port of Moscha (Khor Rori) in Dhofar. *Journal of Oman Studies,* 1, 81–96.

Sahani, L., 1997. Ethnoarchaeology of Harappan Sea Trade. *Man and Environment,* 22(1), 9–18.

Salles, J-F., 1993. The Periplus of the Erythraean Sea and the Arab-Persian Gulf. *Topoi,* 3(2), 493–523.

Salles, J-F, and Sedov, A., 2002. *Qani, le port antique du Hadhramawt entre la Méditerranée, l'Afrique et l'Inde, Fouilles ruses, 1985–94.* Leiden.

Schoff, W.H., 1912. *The Periplus of the Erythraean Sea.* (reprint 1995). New Delhi.

Sedov, A.V., 1992. New Archaeological and Epigraphical material from Qana' (South Arabia). *Arabian Archaeology and Epigraphy,* 3, 110–137.

Sedov, A.V., 1996. Qana' (Yemen) and the Indian Ocean, the Archaeological Evidence. In H.P. Ray and J-F. Salles (eds) *Tradition and Archaeology, Early Maritime Contacts in the Indian Ocean,* 11–35. Delhi.

Sidebotham, S.E., 1986a. *Roman Economic Policy in the Erythra Thalassa (31 BC – 217 AD).* Leiden.

Tomber, R., 2005. Aksumite and other Red Sea Ceramics from Kamrej. *Journal of Indian Ocean Archaeology,* 2, 99–102.

Sedov, A.V., and Benvenuti, C., 2002. The Pottery of Sumhuram, general typology. In A. Avanzini (Ed) *Khor Rori Report 1*. Pisa. 177–148.
Turner, P.,1989. *Roman Coins from India*. Institute of Archaeology. London. Occasional Paper No.12 and Royal Numismatic Society Special Publication No.22.
Yule, P., and Kervran, M., 1993. More than Samad in Oman, Iron Age pottery from Suhar and Khor Rori. *Arabian Archaeology and Epigraphy,* 4, 69–106.
Vinacke, H.M., 1960. *A History of the Far East in Modern Times*. London.

Chapter 6: Incense in Mithraic Ritual: The Evidence of the Finds

Joanna Bird

This paper was originally published in *Roman Mithraism: the evidence of the small finds*, edited by Marleen Martens and Guy De Boe, Brussels 2004. We are grateful to the editors and publishers for permission to include it here.[1]

Summary

The paper discusses the evidence for the use of incense in Mithraic ritual. This comes mainly from finds made in *mithraea,* and includes both smaller objects, such as pottery vessels and iron altar-shovels, and more substantial monuments, such as sculptures, mosaics and wall-paintings. The evidence indicates that incense was an important element in the rites, and that the fourth grade of initiation, the Lion, was instrumental in its use. The commonest finds are pottery censers or thuribles, of which three types have been identified; the decoration on some of these vessels is of particular relevance. One specific type of incense, the cones of *Pinus pinea,* may have been used in rituals associated with the god's birth.

By the later 1st century AD, the period when Mithraism began to spread into the western Roman provinces, the custom of burning incense was already more than 3000 years old. In the Roman world it was an intrinsic feature of public and domestic religious ritual, of religious and ceremonial processions and of purificatory and funerary rites, and it was also used in celebrations such as weddings, triumphs and feasts (Atchley 1909, 46–60). As well as the aromatic gums which form the usual base for incense, spices, scented woods and perfumed oils could be added, and for some rites very precise and elaborate formulae were prescribed (Miller 1998, 26). Myth and legend surrounded the source and collection of incense and spices, which were all believed to come from Arabia, a land open to the full fiery power of the sun. This hot dry origin was seen as endowing them with their fragrance and incorruptibility, qualities which fitted them for their role as a food and sacrifice for the gods, and as a medium of communication between gods and men (Detienne 1997, especially 6–19). In fact, while frankincense, myrrh and balsam are native to south Arabia, many other perfumes and spices were brought from much further east, part of a complex and costly trade in luxury goods for which Arabia and the Red Sea were major points of entry (Miller 1998, especially 98–109, map 5).

That incense played an important role in Mithraic ritual is demonstrated by one of the painted inscriptions on the walls of the Santa Prisca *mithraeum* in Rome. Two superimposed layers of painting show processions of members of the fourth grade of initiation, the Lion, bringing offerings to the Father of the community. The figures are identified as Lions by the inscriptions above their heads, and their gifts include animals, a cockerel, loaves, candles and, carried by the Lions Niceforus, Heliodorus and Phoebus, three large craters (Vermaseren 1956/1960, nos 481, 1–6, and 482, 1–8). An inscription on the lower layer of painting, above the meal of Sol and Mithras, reads: *accipe thuricremos pater accipe sancte leones/ per quos thura damos per quos consumimur ipsi* (Vermaseren 1956/1960, no. 485). While the precise Mithraic sense of the last phrase, 'by whom we are ourselves consumed', may be open to interpretation, the earlier part – 'receive the incense-burners, Father, receive the Lions, holy one, through whom we offer incense' – clearly implies that the Lions offered incense on behalf of all. For the Lions to be responsible for the burning of incense would be appropriate, since the grade was under the tutelage of Jupiter and was associated with fire; Tertullian describes the Lions as 'of a dry and fiery nature' (*aridae et ardentis naturae*: *Adversus Marcionem*, 1.13.4), and in the Santa Prisca paintings they are dressed in red. In addition to its more customary use as an offering in its own right, incense would have been a component in Mithraic fire rituals: these are indicated by a number of finds, including an inscribed stone basin from Königshoffen with traces of pitch inside (Vermaseren 1956/1960, no. 1370; Clauss 2000, fig. 84) and an altar from Heddernheim *mithraeum* I with a bowl cut into the top in which a fire could be ignited from below (Vermaseren 1956/1960, no. 1095; Huld-Zetsche 1986, no. 3). The *mithraeum* near San Martino ai Monti in Rome contained seven torches of fir-wood coated with 'tar' (Vermaseren 1956/1960, no. 356).

The attributes of the Lion grade shown on the mosaic floor of the *mithraeum* of Felicissimus at Ostia consist of Jupiter's thunderbolt, a *sistrum* or rattle, and a *vatillum*, a fire- or altar-shovel (Vermaseren 1956/1960, no. 299, 8; Becatti 1954, pl. 25, 4; Clauss 2000, fig. 101). The Santa Prisca wall-paintings also include superimposed processions of the seven grades, and on both layers the Lion is carrying what is probably a *vatillum*, with the inscription above *Nama Leonibus tutela Iovis* : 'Hail to the Lions, under the protection of Jupiter' (Vermaseren 1956/1960, nos 480, and 484). Two reliefs showing members of the grade wearing their lion masks and carrying altar-shovels have been recovered from *mithraeum* III at Heddernheim (Vermaseren 1956/1960, nos 1123 and 1126/1134; Huld-Zetsche 1986, nos. 33 and 39/61; for the restoration of Vermaseren 1956/1960, nos 1126/1134 as one sculpture, Wamser 2000, 406, Katalog 179c). A second mosaic from Ostia, from the *mithraeum* 'degli Animali', shows a shaggy-haired figure, perhaps wearing a lion mask, holding a *vatillum* and a sickle, which on the Felicissimus mosaic is an attribute of the fifth and seventh grades, the Persian and Father (Vermaseren 1956/1960, no. 279; Becatti 1954, pl. 18, 1; Clauss 2000, figs 102, 104). In the *mithraeum* at Carrawburgh on Hadrian's Wall remains of an iron altar-shovel were found which held traces of a charcoal composed of pine-cones – a source of incense, discussed further below – and hazel-wood (Richmond and Gillam 1951, 20, 87, pl. 15B, fig. 4).

A number of *mithraea* in the north-western provinces have now produced evidence for the burning of incense. This usually consists of the pottery vessel type known in Britain as a tazza and in Germany as a *Räucherkelch* or *Räucherschale;* it has long been

Fig. 6.1. 1: handled tazza from Friedberg (after Horn 1994). 2: pierced-rim vessel from Zeughausstrasse, Köln (after Binsfeld 1960–61). 3: pierced-rim vessel from Köln mithraeum I (after Behrens 1952). 4: pierced-rim vessel from Mainz (after von Pfeffer 1960 and Huld-Zetsche 1984). 5: pierced-rim vessel from Stockstadt mithraeum II (after Schleiermacher 1928 and a photograph courtesy of M. Marquart, Museen der Stadt Aschaffenburg).

identified as an incense burner from its occurrence in religious and funerary contexts and from the traces of soot or burning that are frequently found on the interior.[2] Both the form, a carinated dish or bowl on a pedestal foot, and the decoration, 'pie-crust' frilling or heavy bands of notched or rouletted ornament, are distinctive and characteristic. The pots were usually made in a light-coloured, relatively coarse fabric which was probably deliberately selected to prevent cracking when hot charcoal was placed inside. Some *mithraea* have now produced significant numbers of these vessels (Schatzmann 1997, 35; 2004, 13), and over one hundred came from the ritual pit found at the *mithraeum* at Tienen in Belgium (Martens 2004a, 32–34, fig. 5, 4). A lid from Tienen has applied and incised decoration showing a man's head with a lion's mane, a crater and a snake (the lion, snake and crater triad is discussed further below), and is heavily soot-stained underneath; it is of the right dimensions to have been used with an incense-burner of this type (Martens 2004a, 34, fig. 9, 2). It is perhaps relevant to note here a relief from the *mithraeum* at Königshoffen which shows the Mithraic winged god (unusually human-headed rather than lion-headed) accompanied by a lion; the animal's head is bent over a snake-entwined crater and there is an upturned pot, presumably the lid of the vessel, on the ground (Vermaseren 1956/1960, no. 1326). The winged god was associated with fire, and a relief from Rome shows him, lion-headed, holding a pair of torches and igniting an altar fire with his breath (Vermaseren 1956/1960, no. 383; Clauss 2000, fig. 121); the Königshoffen image may thus reflect the role of the Lion grade in the rituals of fire and incense.

A larger deeper version of the form, requiring the addition of two handles, was recovered from the *mithraeum* at Friedberg (Fig. 6.1:1). It is decorated with applied motifs, a scorpion and a three-runged ladder on one face and a snake twining up each handle; the number of rungs indicates that it was a votive offering from an initiate who had attained the third grade, the Soldier (Vermaseren 1956/1960, no. 1061; Schwertheim 1974, no. 47, l, Taf. 10; Bird 2001, 304, 306, fig. 29.3).[3] A fragment of what is probably a vessel of similar form comes from *mithraeum* III at Heddernheim; it is in a fine pale fabric with narrow rouletted lines and red-painted lattice decoration, and has an applied snake climbing up towards the rim; the snake is decorated with incised rings (Huld-Zetsche 1986, no. 53, Abb. 28). A second fragment, also from Heddernheim but its precise findspot unknown, consists of the rim and part of one handle with a crested snake's head on the top; it is in a white-slipped fabric with frilled rim and rows of rouletting, and the snake is decorated with incised lines and the remains of red paint. The interior is soot-stained (Huld-Zetsche 1986, no. 64, Abb. 29).

A second, much smaller, group of pottery vessels probably also functioned as censers. These are two-handled jars or craters with a broad inner rim that is pierced with between five and eight holes; their occurrence in *mithraea* strongly suggests a ritual purpose, and use as censers or thuribles would fit both the unusual shape and the associated decoration (Bird 2001, 304; Zabehlicky-Scheffenegger 1985, 364–365). The incense and glowing charcoal would have been placed inside the pot, with a lid covering the central opening so that the scented smoke would seep from the holes. Although no lids have been found in association with the pots, the inner lip is shaped to carry one, and a lid found in Breitestrasse, Köln, decorated with an applied snake and of approximately the right size, shows the sort of lid that might be expected (Ristow 1974, no. 36, Taf. 20, Abb. 24). An alternative possibility is that the scented smoke drifted out of the central opening while the holes in the rim held slender tapers. This would produce a wreath of light, recalling the pierced radiate crowns on certain images of Mithras-Sol which could be illuminated during the rituals (Clauss 2000, 125–126), but the occurrence of this and other similar types of pierced-rim pot from non-Mithraic contexts shows that this was not part of the primary design (cf. Zabehlicky-Scheffenegger 1985).

At least five pierced-rim censers have either been recovered from *mithraea* or bear distinctively Mithraic decoration; they are described in detail in Bird (2001). The most

Fig. 6.2. Detail of the vessel shown on Fig. 6.1: 2, with Sol-Mithras offering incense; the altar is largely missing (after Ristow 1974).

significant comes from the probable *mithraeum* on Zeughausstrasse, Köln (Fig. 6.1:2). It has a lion on one handle and a snake winding from the base of this handle, along the back of the pot and up the other handle, originally to the rim. The front carries barbotine and painted decoration showing Sol-Mithras standing between Cautes and Cautopates and casting incense on a flaming altar; his left hand holds a round object which may be a small jar for the incense, but it is decorated with crossed bands and so may represent the celestial globe (Fig. 6.2). Both faces are ornamented with painted stars, reinforcing the cosmic imagery; on the back the stars are placed between the coils of the snake (Binsfeld 1960–61, Abb. 4; Ristow 1974, no. 14, Taf. 16, Abbn 18, 19; Schwertheim 1974, no. 15, a, Taf. 5; Bird 2001, 303, fig. 29.1, 1). The figure of Sol-Mithras clearly associates the pot with the offering of incense, and also shows that incense was cast on altar fires in *mithraea,* as was customary in the Roman world (Atchley 1909, 46–56, 90–91, and illustration opposite 319). A motif of seven flaming altars occurs on a number of cult reliefs, such as that from the *mithraeum* near Santa Lucia in Selge in Rome (Vermaseren 1956/1960, no. 368; Clauss 2000, fig. 50). In this context, the lion on the rim of the pot would seem to refer to the role of the Lion grade in the ritual.

A second of these pots, from the Richmod *mithraeum (mithraeum* I) in Köln, also carries a snake and lion on the handles with a raven on the rim between them, probably indicating a votive gift from an initiate of the first grade, the Raven (Fig. 6.1:3) (Vermaseren 1956/1960, no. 1020; Behrens 1952, Abb. 3; Ristow 1974, no. 9, Taf. 13, Abb. 14; Schwertheim 1974, no. 10, b; Bird 2001, 303, 306, fig. 29.1, 2). A third example, from Mainz, is in fine red-painted Wetterau ware; one face carries a scene of Mithras surrounded by stars and pursuing the bull, the other has a hilly landscape of pine or cypress trees painted among the windings of an applied snake (Fig. 6.1:4). A scorpion sits on the rim, suggesting that this was an offering from a member of the same grade as the Friedberg pot (von Pfeffer 1960; Schwertheim 1974, no. 94, a, Taf. 23; Huld-Zetsche 1984, no. 12, Taf. 8; Bird 2001, 303, 306, fig. 29.1, 3). The motifs on the handles have broken away, but the differential firing of surface and core has left the shape of a lion's front paws discernible above the handle on one side. Although the handle seems rather small for a lion mount, the terra sigillata crater handle from Tienen also has a relatively large lion applied to it, with a snake on the companion handle (Martens 2004a, 34, fig. 9, 1; Thomas 2004, 204, fig. 7). The less complete scar on the second handle of the Mainz censer would have been left by the head of the snake on the wall.[4]

A fourth pierced-rim censer was recovered from *mithraeum* II at Stockstadt am Main.

Unfortunately this pot did not reach museum care, and only a drawing, published in 1928, and a rather dark photograph now survive. Fig. 6.1:5 is based on the photograph, which shows four animals at the rim. The two on the handles are larger, and it is tempting to suggest that they are couched lions but the details are by no means clear; at least one of the creatures between them is a long snake, its body marked by incised lines (Vermaseren 1956/1960, no. 1220; Schleiermacher 1928, Abb. 8; Ulbert 1963, Abb. 7; Schwertheim 1974, no. 117, h; Bird 2001, 303–4, fig. 29.1, 4; photograph courtesy of M. Marquart). A further example comes from the *mithraeum* at Dieburg; it is similar in shape to the painted one from Mainz but slightly larger, with less elaborately moulded rim and handle. It has no applied animals at the rim, but the upper wall apparently bears very faint traces of reddish paint (Vermaseren 1956/1960, no. 1269; Behrens 1952, Abb. 2; Schwertheim 1974, no. 123, r; Bird 2001, 304). Finally, a vessel of what seems to be a similar form in terra sigillata, decorated with an elaborately scaly snake and carrying part of an incised dedication above barbotine figures of Mithras, Cautes and Luna, was found at the *mithraeum* at Biesheim in Alsace (Pétry and Kern 1978, fig. 6, A; Bird 2001, 304, 306, fig. 29.1, 5; Thomas 2004, 204, fig. 8).

A further type of pottery incense burner is attested from *mithraea* at Rome. This is a small altar-shaped vessel some 15 cm high, its square top hollowed for the burning of incense; there is usually a lamp attached at each side, though occasionally only one lamp has been added. The type is manufactured in a beige fabric, often with a reddish slip, and dates from the later 1st century to the 3rd; its distribution suggests local production. Finds from *mithraea* include three from the *Castra Peregrinorum mithraeum*, where they were still *in situ* in niches in the podium walls, and others from the Crypta Balbi and Santa Prisca *mithraea* and probably the *mithraeum* near Porta Maggiore. Examples found among the dumped material at the Terme di Nuotatore at Ostia may have come from the nearby *mithraeum* of Felicissimus (Saguì 2004, 173, fig. 15).

Another group of ceramic objects may have been used with tazze to disperse incense in a particularly dramatic way. These are 'lamp chimneys', hollow, open-based square or circular towers of pottery or tile; they normally stand around 50 cm high and are built up in tiers with openings on each level. They vary considerably, from simple versions with arched or triangular openings and frilled or rouletted bands between the layers to much more elaborate architectural structures (for a range of types, see Loeschcke 1909, Abb. 19; Lowther 1976, Group A). Placed over a lamp or glowing censer, they would be illuminated from inside, recalling structures such as signal-towers and light-houses where guidance was provided by smoke or fire beacons. Although only one has been recorded from a *mithraeum*, a soot-stained fragment of a square tower from Heddernheim *mithraeum* III (Huld-Zetsche 1986, 14–15, no. 54), they have been found elsewhere in temples of both oriental and Celtic deities (Henig 1984, 159, fig. 80). A tall barrel-shaped vessel with two rows of ovoid holes in the side, found in the *mithraeum* at Rudchester, may have served a similar function, with its open end at the base (Gillam and MacIvor 1954, fig. 12).

In use, both types of pottery censers would have been placed on altars or side-tables, as shown in the reconstructions of *mithraea* II and III at Heddernheim (Huld-Zetsche 1986, Abbn 12, 14). Neither could have been safely suspended or swung when full of hot charcoal and incense, and comparable vessels that could be so used, such as church censers and mosque lamps, have at least three suspension rings to provide stability (for example,

British Museum 1921, fig. 68; Campbell 1987, no. 12; Bloom and Blair 1997, figs 149 and 213). An eccentric and rather crudely worked Mithraic relief, now at Mannheim but likely to have come originally from Ladenburg, shows what is probably a member of the Lion grade placing a censer on an altar, echoing the image of Sol-Mithras offering incense on the Köln pot (Fig. 6.3:A). The figure is small compared to the others on the relief, suggesting that he is a mortal among heavenly beings, and his rather formally curled hair may be an indication of a lion mask (Vermaseren 1956/1960, no. 1275; Schwertheim 1974, Taf. 36, no. 138).

The distribution of the censers with pierced-rims coincides with an area where a number of tauroctony reliefs show a variation from the usual arrangement. While the snake normally leaps up with the hound to drink the bull's blood, on these reliefs it is placed in the foreground with the additional images of a crater and a lion, a triad which recalls the pots themselves with their lion and snake mounts. The symbolism of the crater and the snake was complex and closely linked (Gordon 1998, 248–258), but on one level at least the lion introduces a rather different aspect. Water, which the crater is usually understood to represent, was inimical to the fiery Lions and Porphyry writes that their hands and tongues had to be purified with honey instead (*De antro nympharum*, 15). Perhaps in this area of Germany the Lion grade had attained a particular prominence or influence, which might account for the presence of lions on the reliefs (Huld-Zetsche 1989). It might also be suggested that the craters on at least some of these reliefs – and perhaps even on other images such as the Santa Prisca processions – would have been understood to contain a substance more appropriate to them: honey, or even incense.[5]

While the contents of most crater images cannot be identified, that on the tauroctony from *mithraeum* III at Heddernheim is clearly filled with a granular substance which would best be interpreted as incense (Fig. 6.3:B) (Vermaseren 1956/1960, no. 1118; Schwertheim 1974, no. 61, a; Huld-Zetsche 1986, no. 28; Huld-Zetsche 1994, Abbn 88a and 88b); this is also the *mithraeum* which yielded the two reliefs of the lions carrying altar-shovels, perhaps indicating a particular emphasis on fire and incense ritual. On the analogy of this crater, Ingeborg Huld-Zetsche suggests that the ritual pot from the Ballplatz *mithraeum* in Mainz, which is decorated with seven barbotine figures and has a snake and a raven, and perhaps originally a lion, on the rim, may have been used to store incense (Huld-Zetsche 2004, 220).[6] The crater on the tauroctony from Heidelberg-Neuenheim also shows unusual features: it is handleless, apparently the only image of a crater to be so, and very similar in shape to the tazza type of incense-burner (Fig. 6.3:C) (Vermaseren 1956/1960, no. 1283; Schwertheim 1974, Taf. 40, no. 141, a). A further find which may be relevant is a samian jar from the *mithraeum* at Mühlthal, where a tauroctony scene is shown which includes the lion, snake and crater (Fig. 6.3:D). Here the crater has two globular objects on its rim, perhaps an attempt to indicate grains of incense in the difficult barbotine technique (Garbsch 1985, 398–401, Abbn 8 and 9, Taf. C; Wamser 2000, 407, Katalog 180, b; Bird 2001, 306). Comparison with the German tauroctonies shows that the small figure and its altar on the Ladenburg relief occupy the same position relative to the snake and crater as the actual lion on these reliefs, confirming its likely identity as a Lion offering incense; the separate 'real' lion at the top left of the scene may be reinforcing the grade connection.

One further distinctive type of incense that is attested from *mithraea* came from the large cones of the Mediterranean Stone Pine, *Pinus pinea*. The pine-cone, appearing dry

Fig. 6.3. A: snake and crater with what may be a member of the Lion grade placing an offering on an altar, from the Ladenburg / Mannheim tauroctony (after Schwertheim 1974). B: lion, snake and crater from the Heddernheim III tauroctony (after Huld-Zetsche 1986; 1994). C: lion, snake and crater from the Heidelberg-Neuenheim tauroctony (after Schwertheim 1974). D: lion, snake and crater from a samian beaker, Mühlthal (after Garbsch 1985).

and dead but carrying its seeds within it, was a symbol of rebirth in a number of mystery religions, and cones or images of cones appear regularly in funerary contexts. They burn with a pungent and invigorating scent, and their use in sacrifice is recorded in several Egyptian papyri of the 2nd and 3rd centuries AD (Richmond and Gillam 1951, 6–7, especially note 2). The connection between cones and incense is demonstrated by a series of votive pottery lamp stands made at Cnidus in Asia Minor, which often include a small incense burner standing on a pine-cone (Bailey 1983), while a lamp in the form of a pine-cone was found in the *mithraeum* at Linz (Karnitsch 1956, no. 229; Schatzmann 1997, 35, note 156). The cones would have been imported into the northern provinces for use as incense and for the culinary value of their seeds, and both cones and branches, complete with needles, were found among the mixed cargo of a mid-1st century BC wreck at La Madrague, near Toulon (Tchernia, Pomey and Hesnard 1978, 117–118, pl. 6, nos 1–3). An incised text added to an inscription from Potoci in Dalmatia apparently records the gift by one Rumanus Marcianus of two pine-trees and ten fig-trees to a *mithraeum,* probably to provide cones for incense and fruit and nuts for the ritual meals (Vermaseren 1956/1960, no. 1891/1892; Clauss 2000, 141, fig. 35).

A large pine-cone is shown in the left hand of Cautes on a tauroctony from Tîrgşor in Moesia Inferior (Fig. 6.4:A) (Vermaseren 1956/1960, no. 2306) and two further, more damaged, Dacian reliefs, from Apulum and probably from Constantia, may also show cones, in the hands of Cautes and Cautopates respectively (Vermaseren 1956/1960, nos 1973 and 2302). However, although there are occasional finds of stone and marble models of cones from *mithraea,* including a group of four from *mithraeum* IV at Aquincum (Vermaseren 1956/1960, no. 1772) and single examples from Lambaesis (Clauss 2000, 126) and from the Santa Prisca and *Castra Peregrinorum mithraea* in Rome (Vermaseren and van Essen 1965, 343 no. 25, pl. 78, no. 3; Clauss 2000, 126), real cones of *P. pinea* have rarely been recorded. A partially burnt one was found on the first floor of the Walbrook mithraeum in London (Shepherd 1998, 155, 161), but the best evidence comes from the mithraeum at Carrawburgh. Here in the first shrine a complete cone was found against the back wall, and there was also a stone bunker in the nave which contained a charcoal made from pine-cones and hazel-wood. The shrine was later extended, and from Phase IIB came two complete cones, placed on the heather matting inside the entrance to the cult niche, and, on the west bench, the altar-shovel noted above with its remains of pine-cone charcoal. In the 4th century three altars were placed at the niche end, and the votive deposit beneath them included a beaker containing two large pieces of the cone charcoal and some chicken bones (Richmond and Gillam 1951, 6–8, 20, 35–36, 86–87, figs 2, 4, pls. 2B, 3A, 15B).

A statue from the port of Rusicade in Numidia shows a member of the Lion grade wearing a lion mask and carrying a key; he has a large pine-cone beside each foot, showing that the grade was responsible for this type of incense too (Fig. 6.4:B) (Vermaseren 1956/1960, no. 25). The image of Mithras' rock-birth from the San Clemente *mithraeum* in Rome has the rock in the shape of a pine-cone (Vermaseren 1956/1960, no. 344; Clauss 2000, fig. 92), and there are others where the rock is worked in a way that is perhaps intended to suggest the scales of a cone, such as those from Köln *mithraeum* II (Clauss 2000, fig. 23) and Heddernheim *mithraeum* I (Vermaseren 1956/1960, no. 1088; Huld-Zetsche 1986, no. 4), while a panel from the cult-relief at Heddernheim I shows Mithras apparently emerging from a pine-tree (Vermaseren 1956/1960, no. 1083.1; Huld-Zetsche 1986, no. 1, Abb. 10; Clauss 2000, fig. 33). Mithras most frequently appears from the rock holding one or two torches, but the rock itself is occasionally shown as fiery, as on a fresco from Dura Europos (Vermaseren 1956/1960, no. 42.5) and on a cult-relief panel from Moesia Superior (Vermaseren 1956/1960, no. 2237; Clauss 2000, fig. 97); a snake-entwined rock from Rusicade is pierced with holes to show the light from a lamp in a niche at the back (Vermaseren 1956/1960, no. 127; Clauss 2000, fig. 96). The medical writer Dioscorides recommended the burning of pine-cones to ease childbirth (*De materia medica,* 1.69.1), and perhaps the burning of cones in *mithraea* was part of a specific ritual connected with the birth of the god. The cones also recall the landscape in which the cult scenes take place; coniferous trees resembling cypress or pine appear regularly in the background of tauroctony reliefs, as well as on the painted censer from Mainz discussed above. This complex imagery and its cosmic significance may be reflected on a small jar decorated in brown barbotine with pine-trees and stars, from the probable *mithraeum* on Zeughausstrasse, Köln (Ristow 1974, no. 15, Taf. 17, Abb. 20).

Incense clearly played a significant role in Mithraic ritual, and the evidence for its use comes from a wide range of finds: from substantial items such as sculptures, mosaics

Fig. 6.4 A: Cautes holding a pine-cone, from the Tîrgşor tauroctony (after Vermaseren 1960). B: masked Lion with pine-cones, from Rusicade (after Vermaseren 1956).

and wall-paintings to more humble objects such as pottery censers, iron altar-shovels and pine-cones. Many of these also appear to emphasise the role of the Lion grade in the relevant rituals. In the confined space of a *mithraeum* the combination of incense with the resinous pitch from the fires would have produced a rich and intoxicating atmosphere, enhancing the spiritual experience of the initiates. The analysis undertaken on the Tienen pottery to identify traces of food-stuffs or other substances left on the surface shows how much can now be learned from such examination (Martens 2004a, 32, 34). It would be of great interest if burnt residues on censers and altars and any surviving charcoal deposits in *mithraea* could be analysed, to determine which of the many scented gums, oils and spices which made up incense in the ancient world were used by the worshippers of Mithras, and whether any particular aromatics were preferred.

Acknowledgements

I would like to thank David Bird, who has read and commented on the text, and Brenda Dickinson, Richard Gordon and Ingeborg Huld-Zetsche, who have given me a number of helpful suggestions and references. I am indebted for photographs to Ingeborg Huld-Zetsche, to Michael Klein (Mittelrheinisches Landesmuseum Mainz), to Marcus Marquart (Museen der Stadt Aschaffenburg) and to Cornelius Ulbert. I am also grateful to Marleen Martens and her colleagues for their generous permission to reprint the Tienen paper here.

Notes

1. The original publication of this paper was in a volume on Mithraic studies that followed a conference at Tienen in Belgium in 2001. The need to rearrange the notes to fit the format of the present volume has provided an opportunity to make a few additions, notably the inclusion of the Rome censer-lampstands described by Lucia Saguì in the Tienen volume and some updating of notes 4 and 6.
2. Examples of the form are illustrated by Gose (1950), types 443–448. Miniature versions of it appear as small censers on other cult pottery, such as the three alternating with snake-entwined handles on a jar from Pocking in Bavaria (Ulbert 1963, Abb. 1; Wamser 2000, 406, Katalog 180c) and the vessel composed of a tazza and three small jars on a ring-base from London (Merrifield 1995, pl. 7).
3. Ogawa (1978) suggests that this was a crater for honey, but he seems not to have been aware of its close similarity to incense-burners; nor are there any motifs among the decoration to indicate a specific link with the two Mithraic grades, the Lion and the Persian, which according to Porphyry (*De antro nympharum*, 15) were purified with honey.
4. It seems probable that significant sherds of cult pottery were deliberately separated and deposited, and the Mainz rim mounts may be an example of this, as may the seven snakes and two ravens found at the Ballplatz mithraeum in Mainz (Huld-Zetsche 2004, 222–223). At Bornheim-Sechtem individual sherds of a large lead-glazed crater, respectively showing a lion, a snake and the torchbearer Cautes, were recovered from three separate ritual deposits dating to two different phases (Wulfmeier 2004, 91–93). The finds from Mainz and from Bornheim-Sechtem are discussed further in Ulbert, Wulfmeier and Huld-Zetsche 2004. At Tienen the terra sigillata lion and snake sherds, the soot-stained lid decorated with lion, snake and crater, and other pottery, including sherds of a lead-glazed crater with a head of Mithras and an apparently unique spouted vessel, were all found in a group of contemporary pits probably filled after a feast celebrating the summer solstice (Martens 2004a, 30–45; 2004b).
5. A smaller group of tauroctonies from Dacia (for example Vermaseren 1956/1960, nos 1935, 1958, 1972, all from Apulum) have the snake in its usual position with the hound, while the lion and crater are placed at one side, behind Cautes and, on Vermaseren 1956/1960, 1958, outside the cave altogether. Whether they would have been 'read' in the same way as the German reliefs is impossible to say.
6. A rim and handle fragment of a samian jar from mithraeum IV at Aquincum carries a hand-modelled lion, with large head and disproportionately small body and tail. The rim diameter is 20 cm, and the shape of the rim and the angle of the handle indicate a wide-bodied jar similar to the Ballplatz pot (Vermaseren 1956/1960, no. 1772; Nagy 1943, 550, Abb. 26, where it was originally identified as a dog; photographs and information courtesy of Ingeborg Huld-Zetsche). A further vessel of similar size and shape to the Ballplatz pot comes from the probable mithraeum on Zeughausstrasse, Köln, and may have served the same purpose. It has a frilled rim and an elaborately incised and painted crested snake on each handle (Ristow 1974, no. 13, Tafn 14–15, Abbn 15–17).

Bibliography

Atchley, E.G.C.F., 1909. *A history of the use of incense in divine worship*. Alcuin Club Collections, 13, London.
Bailey, D.M., 1983. A Cnidian relief ware sherd from London. *Antiquaries Journal*, 63.2, 374–376.
Becatti, G., 1954. *Scavi di Ostia, II: i mitrei*. Rome.
Behrens, G., 1952. Römische Kult-gefässe, *Germania*, 30, 111–112.
Binsfeld, W., 1960–61. Neue Mithraskultgefässe aus Köln, *Kölner Jahrbuch für Vor- und Frühgeschichte*, 5, 67–72.

Bird, J., 2001. Censers, incense and donors in the cult of Mithras. In Higham, N.J. (ed.), *Archaeology in the Roman Empire: a tribute to the life and works of Professor Barri Jones.* British Archaeological Reports International Series 940, Oxford, 303–310.

Bird, J., 2004. Incense in Mithraic ritual: the evidence of the finds. In Martens and de Boe 2004, 191–199.

Bloom, J., and Blair, S., 1997. *Islamic arts.* London.

British Museum, 1921. *A guide to the early Christian and Byzantine antiquities.* second edition, London.

Campbell, M., 1987. Metalwork in England, *c.* 1200–1400, and entries in Catalogue. In Alexander J. and Binski P. (eds), *Age of chivalry. Art in Plantagenet England 1200-1400.* London, 162–168, 193–540.

Clauss, M., 2000. *The Roman cult of Mithras.* translated R. Gordon, Edinburgh.

Detienne M., 1977. *The gardens of Adonis*, translated J. Lloyd, Hassocks.

Garbsch, J., 1985. Das Mithraeum von Pons Aeni. *Bayerische Vorgeschichtsblätter*, 50, 355–462.

Gillam, J.P., and Macivor, I., 1954. The temple of Mithras at Rudchester. *Archaeologia Aeliana* fourth series 32, 176–219.

Gordon, R. L., 1998. Viewing Mithraic art: the altar from Burginatium (Kalkar), Germania Inferior. *Antigüedad: Religiones y Sociedades*, 1, 227–258.

Gose, E., 1950. *Gefässtypen der römischen Keramik im Rheinland.* Beihefte der Bonner Jahrbücher 1, Bonn.

Henig, M., 1984. *Religion in Roman Britain.* London.

Horn, H.G., 1994. Das Mainzer Mithrasgefäss. *Mainzer Archäologische Zeitschrift*, 1, 21–66.

Huld-Zetsche, I., 1984. *Der römische Fasanenkrug aus Mainz. Zur figürlichen Bemalung der Wetterauer Ware.* Archäologische Berichte aus Rheinhessen und dem Kreis Bad Kreuznach 2, Mainz.

Huld-Zetsche, I., 1986. *Mithras in Nida-Heddernheim.* Archäologische Reihe 6, Frankfurt am Main.

Huld-Zetsche, I., 1989. *Neues zum Mithraskult in Nida.* Unpublished lecture text. Deutscher Kongress für Archäologie, Frankfurt am Main.

Huld-Zetsche, I., 1994. *Nida – eine römische Stadt in Frankfurt am Main.* Schriften des Limesmuseums Aalen, 48, Stuttgart.

Huld-Zetsche, I., 2004. Der Mainzer Krater mit den sieben Figuren. In: Martens and De Boe 2004, 213–227.

Karnitsch, P., 1956. Der heilige Bezirk von Lentia. *Historisches Jahrbuch der Stadt Linz* 8, 189–285.

Loeschcke, S., 1909. Antike Laternen und Lichthäuschen. *Bonner Jahrbücher*, 118, 370–430.

Lowther, A.W.G., 1976. Romano-British chimney-pots and finials. *Antiquaries Journal*, 56.1, 35–48.

Martens, M., 2004a. The mithraeum in Tienen (Belgium): small finds and what they can tell us. In Martens and De Boe 2004, 25–56.

Martens, M., 2004b. The ritual deposits of the temple of Mithras at Tienen. *Journal of Roman Archaeology* 17, 333–353.

Martens, M., and De Boe, G., (eds) 2004. *Roman Mithraism: the evidence of the small finds.* Archeologie in Vlaanderen Monographie, 4, Brussels.

Merrifield, R., 1995. Roman metalwork from the Walbrook – rubbish, ritual or redundancy? *Transactions of the London and Middlesex Archaeological Society*, 46, 27–44.

Miller, J.I., 1998. *The spice trade of the Roman Empire*, Oxford.

Nagy, T., 1943. Bericht des Archäologischen Instituts von Budapest über die Forschungen der Jahre 1938–1942, *Budapest Régiségei* 13, 537–558.

Ogawa, H., 1978. Mithraic ladder symbols and the Friedberg crater. In De Boer, M. and Edridge, T.A. (eds), *Hommages à M.J. Vermaseren. Receuil d'études offert par les auteurs de la* série *Études Préliminaires aux Religions Orientales dans l'Empire Romain à Maarten J. Vermaseren à l'occasion de son soixantième anniversaire le 7 avril 1978*, Études Préliminaires aux Religions Orientales dans l'Empire Romain 68.2, Leiden, 854–873.

Pétry, F., and Kern, E., 1978. Un mithraeum à Biesheim (Haut-Rhin). Rapport préliminaire. *Cahiers Alsaciens d'Archeologie, d'Art et d'Histoire*, 21, 5–32.

Richmond, I.A., and Gillam, J.P., 1951. The temple of Mithras at Carrawburgh. *Archaeologia Aeliana* fourth series, 29, 1–92.

Ristow, G., 1974. *Mithras im römischen Köln*. Études Préliminaires aux Religions Orientales dans l'Empire Romain 42, Leiden.

Saguì, L., 2004, Il mitreo della Crypta Balbi e i suoi reperti. In Martens and De Boe 2004, 167–178.

Schatzmann, A., 1997. *Archäologie and mithräischer Kultalltag. Zur Problematik funktioneller Bereiche im Innern von Mithrasheiligtümern*. Unpublished seminar paper, Abteilung für Ur- und Frühgeschichte, Universität Zurich.

Schatzmann, A., 2004. Möglichkeiten und Grenzen einer funktionellen Topographie von Mithrasheiligtümern. In Martens and De Boe 2004, 11–21.

Schleiermacher, L., 1928. Das zweite Mithräum in Stockstadt am Main. *Germania*, 12, 46–56.

Schwertheim, E., 1974. *Die Denkmäler orientalischer Gottheiten im römischen Deutschland*. Études Préliminaires aux Religions Orientales dans l'Empire Romain 40. Leiden.

Shepherd, J.D., 1998. *The temple of Mithras, London. Excavations by W F Grimes and A Williams at the Walbrook*. English Heritage Archaeological Report 12, London.

Tchernia, A., Pomey, P. and Hesnard, A., 1978. *L'épave romaine de La Madrague de Giens (Var)*. Gallia Supplement, 34.

Thomas, M., 2004. Kultgefässe in Terra Sigillata aus Rheinzabern. In Martens and De Boe 2004, 201–212.

Ulbert, C., Wulfmeier, J.-C. and Huld-Zetsche, I., 2004. Ritual deposits of Mithraic cult-vessels: new evidence from Sechtem and Mainz. *Journal of Roman Archaeology*, 17, 354–370.

Ulbert, T. 1963. Römische Gefässe mit Schlangen- und Eidechsenauflagen aus Bayern. *Bayerische Vorgeschichtsblätter*, 28, 57–66.

Vermaseren, M.J., 1956/1960. *Corpus inscriptionum et monumentorum religionis Mithriacae*, two volumes. The Hague.

Vermaseren, M.J., and Van Essen, C.C., 1965. *The excavations in the mithraeum of the church of Santa Prisca in Rome*. Leiden.

Von Pfeffer, W., 1960. Kultgefäss mit aufgemalter Mithrasdarstellung. *Germania*, 38, 145–148.

Wamser, L., (ed.) with Flügel, C., and Ziegaus, B., 2000. *Die Römer zwischen Alpen und Nordmeer. Zivilisatorischen Erbe einer europäiscben Militärmacht*, Mainz.

Wulfmeier, J.-C., 2004. Ton, Steine, Scherben – Skulpturen und Reliefkeramiken aus dem Mithraeum von Bornheim-Sechtem. In Martens and De Boe 2004, 89–94.

Zabehlicky-Scheffenegger, S., 1985. Töpfe mit gelochtem Einsatz vom Magdalensberg. In *Pro Arte Antiqua. Festschrift für Hedwig Kenner, Sonderschriften des Österreichischen Archäologischen Institutes in Wien*, 18.2, Vienna/Berlin, 361–366.

Chapter 7: Incense and the Port of Adulis

David Peacock and Lucy Blue

Adulis, now in Eritrea, was by any standards one of the great ports of the ancient world. It lay on the Red Sea route to India and was a major stopping place for provisioning and trade (Fig. 7.1). It was connected by an inland route to the Ethiopian Highlands, including

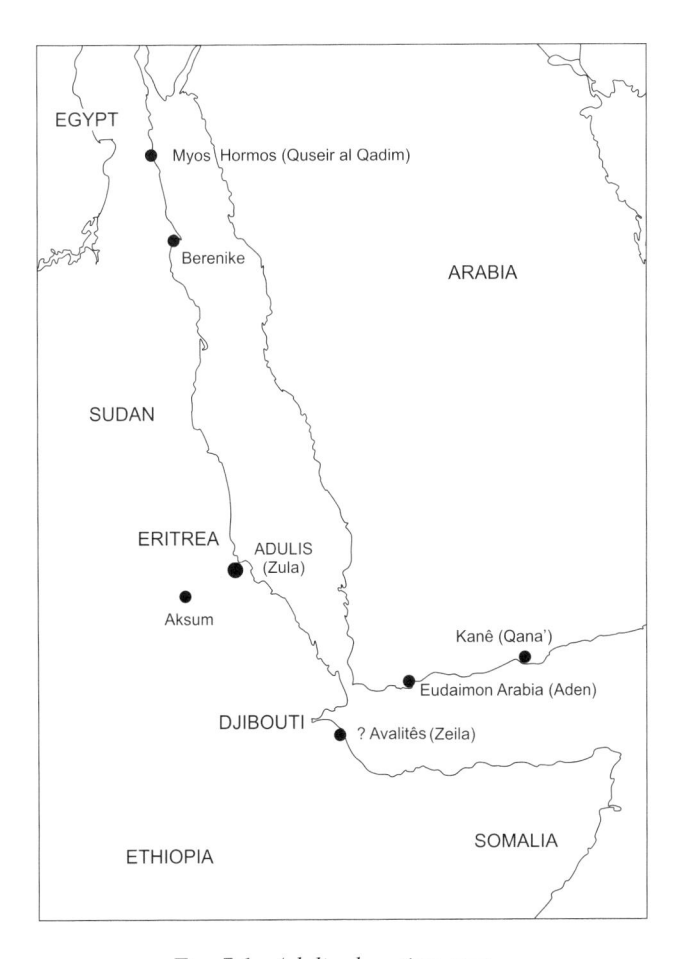

Fig. 7.1. Adulis: location map.

the Aksumite capital, Aksum, from whence came the finest luxuries Africa had to offer. As incense was grown in neighbouring lands if not Eritrea itself, the port would presumably have played a pivotal role in the distribution network. The object of this note is to examine the evidence, both literary and archaeological for this possibility.

The origins of Adulis are hard to establish. Paribeni (1907) found pre-Aksumite pottery which he thought represented archaic activity, although recent radiocarbon dates on associated shell suggest that this may belong, at least in part, to the Roman period (Peacock and Blue forthcoming). However, the *Monumentum Adulitanum* inscriptions recorded in the 6th Century AD by *Cosmas Indicopleustes,* but now lost, indicate that the site was operational by the time of Ptolemy III (247–222 BC). We do not know what form it took, but the erection of stele bearing Greek inscriptions hints at monumentality which in turn points to a sophisticated town rather than a beaching place.

However, it is in the Roman period that Adulis first fully emerges as an important port of trade. The *Periplus of the Erythrean Sea*, a mid-first century AD sailors' log, gives details of its location and of the goods which could be traded there.

> *...20 stades from the sea is Adulis a fair-sized village. From Adulis it is a journey of three days to Koloê, an inland city that is the first trading post for ivory, and from there another five days from the metropolis itself, which is called Axômitês; into it is brought all the ivory from beyond the Nile through what is called Kyêneion, and from there down to Adulis. The mass of elephants and rhinoceroses that are slaughtered all inhabit the upland regions, although on rare occasions they are also seen along the shore around Adulis itself. In front of the port of trade, that is, towards the open sea, on the right are a number of other islands, small and sandy, called Alalaiu; these furnish tortoise shell that is brought to the port of trade by the Ichthyophagoi*

(Casson 1989, 53)

It is thought that Koloê would equate with Qohaito in the Eritrean Highlands, Axômitês would of course be Aksum and the Alalaiu must be the Dahlak islands. There is some debate about the location of Kyêneion (Casson 1989, 107). The curious thing is that Adulis is referred to elsewhere as 'a legally limited port of trade' and yet it is 20 stades (3.3 km) from the sea. The *Periplus* tells us that ships used to moor off Diodorus Island, but because the island was connected to the land by a causeway it was overrun by barbarians and was thereafter moved to an offshore island called Oreinê (hilly). This can be none other than Dese, the only hilly island in the area.

As a result of recent field work we now know that there was a Roman period harbour on Dese, and Diodorus Island seems to have been a small skerry some 6.5 km south-east of Adulis near the Galala hills (Peacock and Blue forthcoming). This has been ascertained through archaeological field walking and sedimentological survey. Not only has the identification of 1st century AD ceramics and in the case of Dese Island, 1st century building remains, confirmed the existence of activities in these areas, but sedimentological analysis has also determined the location and nature of the coast during this period. It is abundantly clear from the *Periplus* that these were major ports of call on the long haul down the Red Sea and across the Indian Ocean to India, presumably to take on water as well as to trade. The main centre of habitation was located inland for reasons that are unclear, however, this situation is far from unique: the location of harbours at some distance from the main settlement had been practiced for centuries prior to the Roman period (Raban 1985) and continued to be observed through the Roman period as Ostia and Portus the great harbours of Rome, to provide but one example, demonstrate.

Adulis is mentioned in Pliny's *Natural History* (VI, 29), dating to 1st century AD and the *Geography* of Claudius Ptolemy (IV, 7.8; viii, 16.11), written in the 2nd century AD. Thereafter, the sources are silent until the late Antique era. Procopius of Caesarea, who wrote *History of the Wars* in the 6th century, refers to Adulis as a major port of arrival for journeys across the Red Sea (I, xix, 17–22). It appears therefore that there was a strong link with the incense growing lands of Arabia and it would be surprising if the port was not involved in the traffic of incense to some extent.

The port of Adulis in the later period was known as Gabaza. It may have been a substantial affair because a Geez document *The Martyrdom of St Arethas* relates that King Kaleb amassed a fleet of 70 ships here (Pereira 1899). 15 came from Ayla (Aqaba), 20 from Clysma (Suez), 7 from Iotabe (?Tyran), 2 from Berenike, 7 from Farasan, and 9 from India, while 10 were made at Adulis itself. The list is interesting because it suggests that despite the distance, the predominant connections were with Suez and Aqaba during the 6th century. The site of Gabaza was originally identified by Sundström (1907) because quantities of Aksumite pottery, like that from Adulis, were found near the Galala hills (although he mistakenly called them 'Gamez', the name of the next range of hills to the west). Recent survey has confirmed the identification of the 6th century AD harbour of Gabaza and also located the earlier 1st century AD Roman mooring on a small skerry at the seaward extent of the rocky outcrop. Sedimentological analysis of the low-lying, prograding alluvial sediments to the east of the Galala hills has confirmed that this region was in fact inundated with seawater during antiquity. Specific analysis of the sediments has yet to be undertaken to confirm the exact date of inundation and the subsequent process of sedimentation, but the identification of 1st century AD ceramic remains on the most south-westerly of the Galala hills, indicates that this area was utilised as an anchorage during this period. The fact that this outcrop was connected to the mainland by a causeway also concurs to the description of the Roman mooring presented in the *Periplus*. Shelter along this essentially barren and exposed coastline, would thus have been provided in the lee of the Galala hills.

The most important source for the 6th century is an anonymous Egyptian monk known as *Cosmas Indicopleustes* (the Indian voyager) who wrote a treatise called *Christian Topography*, essentially to prove that the world was flat rather than spherical. In a previous life he had been a trader engaged in commerce with India and so he knew the ports, including Adulis, intimately. Amongst other things he included the first regional map of the Adulis area (Fig. 7.2) showing the town in relation to Aksum and two coastal places Samidi and the 'customs of Gabaza', certainly the port. He naturally comments on incense and spices which were clearly an important object of trade.

The region which produces frankincense is situated at the projecting parts of Ethiopia, and lies inland, but is washed by the ocean on the other side. Hence the inhabitants of Barbaria, being near to hand, go up into the interior and, engaging in traffic with the natives, bring

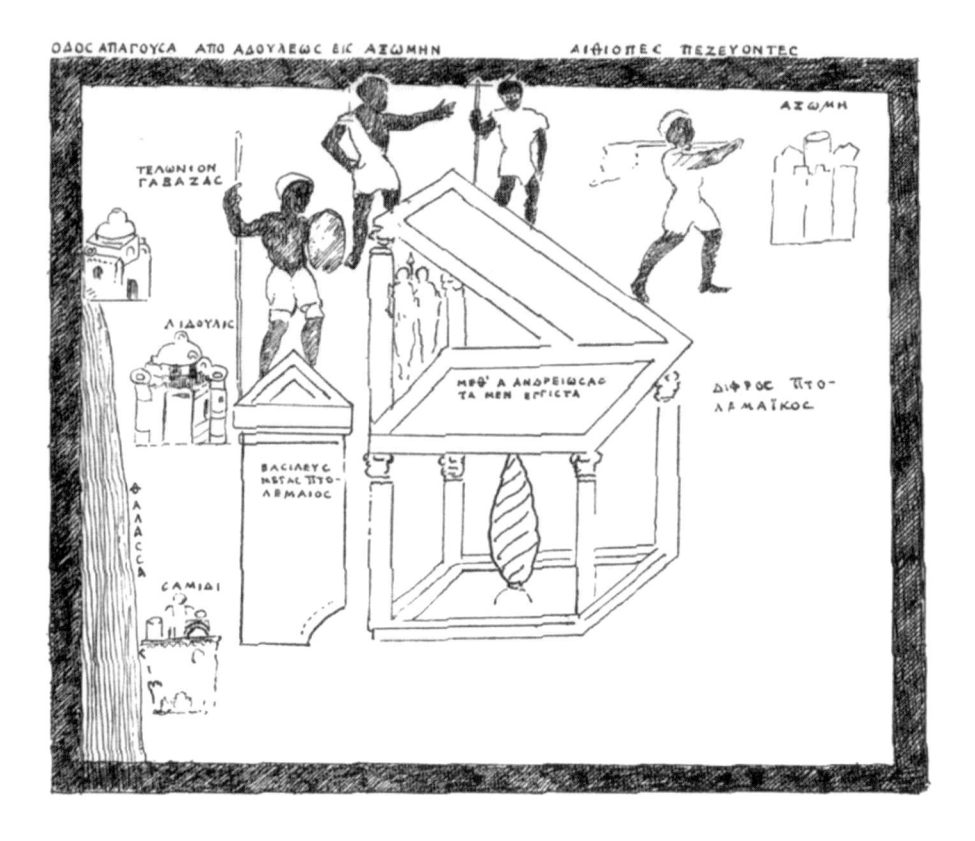

Fig. 7.2. Cosmas Indicopleustes' map of the Adulis area. From Wolska-Conus 1968.

back from them many kinds of spices, frankincense, cassia, calamus, and many other articles of merchandise, which they afterwards send by sea to Adulê, to the country of the Homerites, to Further India and Persia

(McCrindle 1897; Wolska-Conus 1968, 356)

The country of the Homerites would be Yemen, and the production region must be the highlands of what is now known as Somaliland. It is of particular interest that Cosmas mentions this area, but not the main production region of southern Arabia. It is possible that by this period Arabian incense went across the desert once again, along the traditional route to Gaza, and Cosmas knew only of the seaborne trade, or it may be that at this period Somaliland had overtaken southern Arabia in importance. This latter view is supported to some extent by the evidence from Qani' which suggests that in this period the port was a shadow of its former self, although clearly still in existence (chapters 3 and 4 above). The other commodities are of interest. Cassia (*Cinnamomum cassia*) is sometimes known as False Cinnamon and it is a bark similar in appearance and taste to true Cinnamon, which originated in China. It is a spice which is often used as a flavouring, but also has medicinal attributes as a tonic, carminative or stimulant and in the treatment of nausea and diarrhoea. It grows in hot wet climates. Calamus (*Acorus calamus* or Sweet Flag) is a grass with a root, which when ingested, has hallucinogenic properties. It is a hardy semi-aquatic plant growing almost anywhere in the northern hemisphere where there is ample water and sunshine. Both Calamus and Cassia were known in Biblical times as key ingredients of 'holy anointing oil' (Exodus 30, 22–25).

The export of these commodities to Adulis is of particular interest. Calamus as well as frankincense could be needed in church liturgy and this would have been why Cosmas was interested in them. Adulis was certainly well endowed with churches: three have been excavated, two by Paribeni (1907) and one by the British Museum in 1868 (Munro-Hay 1989). However, above all Adulis was a trade centre, and it is probable that much of the incense would merely have been in transit elsewhere. This is confirmed by Cosmas who states that

> *On the coast of Ethiopia, two miles off from the shore, is a town called Adulê, which forms the port of the Axômites and is much frequented by traders who come from Alexandria and the Elanitic Gulf.*

(McCrindle 1897; Wolska-Conus 1968, 364)

The latter is the Gulf of Aqaba at the head of the Red Sea. We have yet to find traces of Alexandrian traders, but the maritime connection with Suez, referred to above may well have been on the route to Alexandria. The canal connecting the Red Sea and the Nile was operational at this period and from about AD170 it would have been possible to sail between Alexandria and Clysma (Jackson 2002, 76). However the traders from Aqaba are well represented in the archaeological material. The surface of the site is littered with pottery, the bulk of which are 6th – 7th century amphorae, costrels and coarse ware from the kilns at Aqaba (Melkawi, 'Amr and Whitcomb 1994; Tomber 2004). It seems probable that incense traded through Adulis would have found its way to Aqaba, thence to the region of modern Jordan and Israel.

Evidence of Roman trade with Adulis is hard to find, but two fragments of obsidian from Quseir al-Qadim seem, on the basis of chemical analysis, to come from Eritrea and may well have been obtained via Adulis (Chapter 3 above). There is no proof that Somaliland incense was being taken to Quseir, but it is a possibility. Interestingly, the Tiberian encyclopaedist Celsus, called it Calamus Alexandrinus, suggesting that at this period Alexandria was a main distribution centre (Miller 1969, 94).

The evidence is scant and largely inferential, but clearly in the 6th century Adulis was involved in the Somali incense trade. The remaining problem is the extent of this involvement, but here we must await new evidence.

Incense from Arabia and possibly Somaliland, not only travelled northwards but also eastwards towards China, although Roman period works such as the Hou Han Shu and the Weilue (Hill 2003; 2004) do not single out Da Qin (Rome) as a special source. To the Chinese 'all the perfumes of Arabia' would have been the 'perfumes of Da Qin' or later 'the perfumes of Po-ssu' (Leslie and Gardiner 1996, 204–5). There are particular indications that frankinsence and storax were imported to China. The latter was brought by an embassy of AD 519 from Fu-nan, a large state occupying parts of Cambodia and Thailand, but was clearly known earlier, according to Leslie and Gardiner (1996, 204). Liang-Shu writing in the seventh century suggests that the Romans prepared storax by mixing the juice of various fragrant trees (including the storax tree) and squeezing out a balsam. The dregs were sold on to other countries and when it arrived in China it was not so very fragrant (Hill 2004).

Bibliography

Casson, L., 1989. *The Periplus Maris Erythraei*. Princeton.
Hill, J.E., 2003. *The Western Regions According to the* Hou Han shu. http://www.depts.washington.edu/uwch/silkroad/index.html.
Hill, J.E., 2004. *The Peoples of the West from the* Weilue *by Yu Huan*. http://www.depts.washington.edu/uwch/silkroad/index.html.
Jackson, R.B., 2002. *At Empire's Edge. Exploring Rome's Egyptian Frontier*. Yale.
Leslie, D.D., and Gardiner, K.H.J., 1996. *The Roman Empire in Chinese Sources*. Rome.
Melkawi, A., 'Amr, K., and Whitcomb, D., 1994. The excavation of two seventh century pottery kilns at Aqaba. *Annals Department of Antiquities Jordan*, 37, 447–68.
McCrindle, J.W.,1897. *The Christian Topography of Cosmas an Egyptian Monk*. London Haklyut Society.
Miller, J.I., 1969. *The Spice Trade of the Roman Empire*. Oxford.
Munro-Hay, S., 1989. The British Museum excavations at Adulis, 1868. *Antiquaries Journal*, 69, 43–52.
Paribeni, R., 1907. Richerche nel luogo dell'antica Adulis. *Monumenti Antichi*, 18.
Peacock, D.P.S. and Blue, L.K., Forthcoming. *The Eritro-British expedition to Adulis*.
Pereira, F.M.E., 1899. *Historia dos Martyres de Nagran. Versão Ethiopica*. Lisbon.
Raban, A., 1985. The ancient harbours of Israel in Biblical times. In Raban, A., (ed.) *Harbour Archaeology*. Proceedings of the First International Workshop on Ancient Mediterranean Harbours. Caesarea Maritima 24 – 28.6.1983. BAR International Series, 257, 11–14. Oxford.
Tomber, R., 2004. Amphorae from the Red Sea and their contribution to the interpretation of Late Roman trade beyond the Empire. In Eiring, J., and Lund, J., *Transport Amphorae and Trade in the Eastern Mediterranean*. Mon. Danish Inst. Athens, 5, 393–402.
Sundström, R., 1907. Report on an expedition to Adulis. *Zeitschrift für Assyriologie*, 20, 171–82.
Wolska-Conus, W., 1968. *La Topographie chrétienne. Sources chrétienne III*. Paris.

Chapter 8: Frankincense and Myrrh Today

Myra Shackley

Introduction

Frankincense trees have specific environmental requirements; they grow in only a few regions within southern Arabia and the Horn of Africa, preferring arid climates with moisture provided by morning mists. The trees require limestone-rich soils, and most are found growing on steep hillsides, cliffs or dried up riverbeds in the valleys beneath. The main source of contemporary frankincense is *Boswellia sacra carterii (Boswellia thurifera)* harvested in the Dhofar region of southern Oman and part of Yemen, with lesser quantities of resin from *Boswellia frereana,* mainly sourced from Somalia. This restriction in growth areas has meant that the contemporary harvest and trade in frankincense resin has extremely close parallels with the ancient trade. Indeed, the same could be said of the uses to which the resin is put in the modern world, confirming the view that the trade in frankincense has remained essentially unchanged for 5000 years. Different areas produce different resin quality; the trade seems agreed that at present the best quality frankincense comes from Dhofar. Estimating the world's annual production is difficult since much resin is harvested and exported illegally to avoid taxation, with the trade being increasingly dominated by powerful cartels in the United Arab Emirates. However, a figure of 5000 tonnes/year is probably about right, although it is probable that ten times this amount is harvested locally and used domestically throughout the Middle East. In the modern world frankincense has three major uses:

- Burnt as an major component of church incense. (Incense is still used in many different kinds of religious services, especially in Eastern Orthodox Christian rites).
- Distilled to produce an essential oil for the perfume, cosmetics and aromatherapy trade (the essential oil distilled from frankincense resin is used as an ingredient in perfume, soaps, cosmetic and hair-care products).
- In traditional medicine and as a fumigant. (Frankincense is used domestically in Middle Eastern households for fumigation and perfuming clothing and utensils. The raw gum is chewed for teeth and also used as a traditional remedy for many complaints, with frankincense smoke being especially favoured for coughs and bronchial infections).

Interest in frankincense and its role in the ancient world has also generated a cultural tourism industry based around sites associated with the ancient trade, combined with an opportunity to watch the modern harvest and buy its products. These topics are considered in more detail below.

Contemporary Frankincense – Trade and Harvest

Southern Oman

The contemporary harvest of frankincense is concentrated in two main areas, the Dhofar region of southern Oman centring on the town of Salalah, and eastern Somalia. In Dhofar, the frankincense trees cluster the fringes of the Nejd desert and the dry lower reaches of the *jebels* of the Dhofar region. The trees are harvested either by local villagers or by imported Somali labourers working under contract. Resin is stored in 40 kg sacks and transported to Salalah by jeep or camel for processing and subsequent export. Much of the trade goes unreported, including substantial quantities of resin that are produced and exported without the benefit of any official records. In this region trees may be the property of specific tribal groups or families (mainly the Bayt Kathir and al-Mahra tribes in whose territories the best trees grow) but some resin trade cartels also seem to be operating. In Oman, the freshly harvested gum resin is sorted into four principal varieties according to colour and quality. Light pastel shades are the most popular, and a particularly desirable variety is never sold commercially but reserved for the exclusive use of the Omani ruling family. The exact quantity exported is unknown, though unlikely to be more than a few hundred tonnes/year. In Oman collection begins in winter, peaks in spring and ends with the summer monsoon. Small ovals of bark are shaved from the *Boswellia sacra* using a small putty-knife shaped tool called a *minquaf* (spellings vary) and the resin oozes slowly from the wounds into tear-like drops which gradually harden and are scraped off the trees. Yields can vary from 1–3 kg/tree with the best being obtained in a rainy year or from trees which are not regularly tapped, hence the universal practice of 'resting' frankincense trees for a year every 5–6 years. The first and second scrapings which are made at 2 week intervals produce only low-quality resin, with the third scraping producing the best quality, light and clear in colour. The raw resin is sometimes referred to as '*al luban*'(from the Arabic for milk) a word which has been anglicised to *olibanum,* another name for frankincense (Wahab *et al.* 1987). Any visitor to southern Oman is struck by the large number of frankincense trees, many apparently unused. Local people estimate that at least ten times the amount of resin could be produced if there was a market, although there is a problem with overgrazing of frankincense trees by goats and camels. At present most Omani incense is exported via Muscat.

Somalia

Resin is produced in Somalia by much the same methods, with around 80% of top grade Somali frankincense being exported to Saudi Arabia, Egypt and Yemen with a smaller amount going through to the Emirates where it is transhipped to Europe or the Far East. Somalia incense is generally shipped directly to major gum trading centres at Riyadh and Jeddah where the raw product is cleaned and sorted for resale to local outlets in Saudi Arabia where it is sold for domestic use by the gram or kilo. Consumption peaks during the *haj*. Frankincense of lesser quality is mainly exported via the UAE to Europe for processing for use in the perfumery trade, with some going to China (again via the UAE) for incorporation in traditional medicines. Although most Somali resin comes from *Boswellia sacra (sn. Certerii)* (and is known locally as *beyo*), some (called *maydi*) comes from *Boswellia frereana* and is considered by Somalis to be of better quality; its major market is as a chewing gum in Saudi Arabia (Chiavari *et al.* 1991). Both varieties come from trees native to northern Somalia, found on steep coastal escarpments up to 750m above sea level from the Gulf of Berbera in Somaliland to around the Horn in Puntland. Gum collectors harvest and store ungraded resin in dry caves before shipping it to coastal merchants, just as in Oman. Subsequent sorting and packing takes place for eventual export, usually via Gulf merchants who control demand and price. Considerable disruption to the trade has resulted from political uncertainty in Somalia, with a result that the frankincense export trade is thought to be operating at only a fraction of its former volume (Farah 1988). As in Oman it is probable that there is extensive illicit trade in gum, to avoid taxation and gain better exchange rates. No reliable estimates exist for current production but it is unlikely to exceed 2000 metric tonnes. However, actual production is very much higher as most Somali families have a tree or trees used for their personal consumption. There are 7 grades of *maydi*, which must be stored at intermediate altitudes since the gum melts under hot Red Sea coastal conditions and gets too hard if left at high altitude. *Beyo* and *maydi* produce different oils which have to be distilled separately, with the latter being favoured by some manufacturers of aromatherapy oils since it has a very intense pure aroma. Somali producers have problems with the perceived erratic nature of their production and poor quality control. They also lack direct access to international and Saudi markets making them heavily dependant on Gulf transhipment, especially through the UAE (Coulter 1987; Chaudhry 1993).

Other production areas

Yemen was traditionally the main frankincense production centre of the ancient world until the First World War, and Aden was the main trading centre for frankincense gums from Somalia, as well as for the export of Yemeni frankincense. This trade has all but died out, with Somali exporters using Omani and UAE ports. Although domestic Yemeni resin harvesting still continues, very little is exported. Attempts to introduce the trees to Kenya and elsewhere in Africa have met with little success, nor can the tree be grown commercially. Smaller quantities of frankincense from *Boswellia papyrifera (Del.) Hochst* are harvested in Ethiopia, Eritrea and Sudan mainly for domestic use. *Boswellia serra Roxb.* grows in dry regions of northwest India and other *Boswellia* varieties elsewhere but have no role in the commercial trade (Demissew 1993). In global terms it is thought that European demand for frankincense remains roughly steady while that of the People's Republic of China has increased. Germany is apparently now importing significant amounts of Ethiopian incense gum with the direct trade between Somalia and Saudi Arabia continuing to flourish. Best estimates suggest a global export trade of anywhere between 3–5000 tonnes / year, but because of the illegal nature of much of the frankincense trade, it is possible that this figure could be very inaccurate.

Processing the resin

A number of European companies are also involved in the import and processing of frankincense, generally those which produce a wide range of other flavourings, fragrances and essential oils. Processing companies either import and process raw materials themselves or arrange for processing via a network of contractors, then manufacturing a wide range of aromatic products. This process is separate from the manufacture of liturgical incense which is usually carried out by relatively small-scale producers who supply church suppliers and church requisite shops directly. In the UK, for example, much of the church incense used by all Christian denominations is prepared by the Benedictine monks of Prinknash Abbey who import frankincense and then combine it with other ingredients including fragrances in different proportions, package and market the product under impressive church sounding names such as 'basilica' or 'cathedral'. Prices vary with the percentage of frankincense used in the mixture.

Commercial processors are more usually concerned with the production of essential oils and will usually work with a large variety of basic ingredients. Within Europe there are less than a dozen such manufacturers involved in the distillation of frankincense oil, and it is estimated that the total world market for frankincense oil is around 30–50 tonnes / year. Assuming a 10% yield from the resin (seldom achieved) this suggests a global demand of 300–500 tonnes of raw material for oil production. However, this represents only a fraction of the total world market for the gum which is dominated by its domestic use in the Middle East for chewing, aromatic and medicinal purposes and the liturgical incense trade. In practice commercial manufacturers only expect a 6% yield of oil from resin, unless the material is especially high quality. Frankincense oil is expensive to manufacture compared with other essential oils and some European processors have relocated this operation to India where the process is far cheaper (£65–70 / kg compared with £90–100 in the UK). Thus, much European frankincense is now imported from the Middle East via India where it is processed. By far the majority of essential oils distilled in Europe are produced in Grasse in the south of France, the centre of the perfume industry, using a two-stage distillation process involving solvent extraction and water distillation. Some processors use gas-cooled mass spectroscopy to ensure quality control. This is much more complex than the procedure used for other essential oils. Not all contract distillers will deal in frankincense as the process is so sticky and the equipment requires extra cleaning, maintenance and renewal of vital parts. One UK distiller noted that at present the quality of imported resin from Oman produced 150–200kg of oil from a shipment of just over 2 tonnes. Overall reduction in international freight charges has changed the shape of the export routes from Oman as importation from the Middle East (even via India) adds only a few pence to the price of the finished oil making it more cost effective to process in Asia. Compared with other essentials of the aromatics/perfume industry (such as aloe vera) frankincense is expensive to buy and expensive to process. Manufacturers put pressure on suppliers to deliver a high quality product, which requires not only good quality resin but also resin free from twigs and bits, shipped reliably at a competitive price. When produced the oil has a very good shelf life so that it can be stored for a long time, meaning that manufacturers can be choosy about their suppliers, which is not the case with, for example, fresh flower essences which require instant processing. Some commercial distilling operations are currently using more myrrh than frankincense – the resin is more expensive but the oil is easier to produce.

Frankincense in Worship

Church incense is made of frankincense blended with other substances in different proportions to produce a pleasantly-scented and combustible incense of slightly different odours, which is burnt on charcoal in a censer. Incense is used only occasionally in the liturgies of the Anglican and Roman Catholic Churches, but is used for every divine liturgy in the Eastern Catholic churches. The smoke of incense traditionally signified the prayers of the faithful rising towards God; its burning symbolised the zeal of the faithful and the cloud of incense became a symbol for the unseen reality of God. Today, incense is usually contained within a censer (thurible) which is swung on chains in the direction of the congregation, gospel book, altar and clergy at different times according to the appropriate rite. Grains of frankincense are also traditionally inserted into the Pascal candle and may be put into consecrated altars. Frankincense also appears in the traditional oils used for anointing and embalming. The use of incense for liturgical purposes was common in Jewish ritual where it was used in connection with offerings of oil, fruits, wine or animal sacrifices. It is not easy to say when its use was introduced into the Christian church but this does not seem to have happened until at least AD 400, although its use in the Temple and references to it in the New Testament (*e.g.* Luke 1:10) mean that early Christians would have been familiar with its use. The earliest authentic reference to its use in the services of the church is found in Pseudo-Dionysius and in the 5th century liturgies of Sts James and Mark. In the Roman church incensation of the gospel at Mass was common from the 11th century, and in connexion with the elevation and benediction of the Blessed Sacrament from at least the 14th century. Today, incense is used at Solemn Mass, solemn blessing, specific functions and processions, some choral offices and absolutions of the dead in Roman Catholic rites, but is usually confined to High Mass and Benediction within the Anglican Communion.

In the last twenty years the use of incense has declined in Roman Catholic churches, partly as a result of liturgical revisions following the second Vatican Council (Sullivan 1918). Within the Anglican Communion in the UK its use is restricted to 'high' church worship (most cathedrals and some churches which belong to the more catholic wing of the Anglican Communion) and until recently incense use has been out of favour as evangelical Anglicans outnumbered catholic Anglicans, at least within the Church of England. However, there is some evidence that its use is now increasing as part of a revival of interest in ancient liturgical practices and in the use of sensory aids such as aromatics to facilitate prayer and contemplation. Some Methodist churches have even begun to use incense – a practice unheard of a decade ago. Church incense is tested for purity by a number of agencies including the International Fragrance Association created in 1973 in Brussels, but despite this there have been several recent health scares about its potential toxicity if too much smoke is been inhaled. A doctor in the Irish government warned that the health of altar boys and girls might be put at risk by excessive incense use on the grounds that incense smoke contributes unacceptable levels of polyaromatic hydrocarbons into poorly ventilated churches. The pro-incense Catholic faction says that this is rubbish and notes the existence of a 'protestant cough' used by members of the congregation to protest when a more catholic rite involving incense is being used. It is curious to note that there is a prevailing belief that liturgical incense is bad for those with chest complaints, when in fact frankincense was traditionally used to treat exactly those conditions.

Perfumes Cosmetics and Medicines

Perfume oils and unguents have been used for thousands of years, and in the Middle East extensive use has always been made of myrrh and frankincense in their production, often combined with flower essences. On the walls of the temple at Edfu a 2000 year old Egyptian formula dedicated to Hathor includes frankincense in a perfume recipe, and the Song of Solomon reports the Queen of Saba (Sheba) as being 'perfumed with myrrh and frankincense'. It is often suggested that the art of perfumery was developed systematically within the Arab world, especially during the reign of the Umayyad and Abbasid caliphates, and that a taste for perfumes was brought back to Europe by the Crusaders (Groom 1981). Eventually the skills of commercial perfume production were transmitted from Arab Spain to southern France, with the town of Grasse coming to dominate the industry until the present day. Perfume is big business; the global perfume industry is estimated to have a value of over 1 billion dollars. Today's perfume industry uses a huge variety of natural and synthetic substances either singly or in combination, to produce scents perfumes, cosmetics, body creams and lotions, hair preparations and air fresheners. Mass production of perfumes began in the 19th century as a direct result of improvements in organic chemistry which enabled certain synthetic perfume products to be used in place of expensive or hard to find natural commodities. Today, about 2600 chemicals are used to make perfume of which 95% are synthetic compounds derived from petroleum. The rest are natural plant oils and flower essences. Frankincense and myrrh produce the heaviest and longest lasting fragrances of any essential oil. However, part of the intrinsic value of frankincense to the perfume and aromatic business is that so far it has proved impossible to replicate artificially to any satisfactory level. The balance of ingredients controls not only the signature of the fragrance but also the time that it will last on the skin. Perfumes with a high proportion of 'oriental' essential oils such as frankincense as their base notes are extremely long lasting with the user only requiring a very small amount (Verghese 1988).

By contrast 'natural' perfumes are made without synthetic ingredients using up to 25% of essential oils, diluted in carrier oils (often jojoba oil) as well as alcohol or water. In the western world natural perfumes are typically produced in small quantities by specialist companies, but in the Middle East they are still made locally from local ingredients to produce products whose recipes have remained unchanged for thousands of years. In the perfume *suq* of Salalah in Oman, for example, perfume blenders utilise locally-harvested frankincense as the base for a wide variety of natural perfumes, many of which are created to match the personal taste of the wearer. Other ingredients might include sandalwood, attar, rosewater, myrrh and many other aromatic oils and resins blended together. Raw frankincense is also 'cooked' with sugar to produce a solid block called *bokhur*, from which pieces are broken to be burnt in small clay domestic incense burners to perfume and fumigate clothes and rooms – a practice widespread in the Middle East. Oman also produces a commercial frankincense perfume billed as the most expensive fragrance in the world. 'Amouage' was developed to capitalise and promote Oman's frankincense trade and its reputation for craftsmanship in metalworking. The perfume is developed from oils derived from the best quality frankincense from Dhofar and contains 140 ingredients including tuberose, rose, jasmine, lily of the valley, some fruit essence, patchouli, sandalwood, ambergris and musk. It is sold in flasks designed by Asprey's of London which are produced locally by traditional silversmiths. Often billed as the most expensive perfume in the world, large (120 ml) flasks retail for more than $5000. In 1995 to celebrate Oman's Silver Jubilee year the company producing 'Amouage' brought out a new frankincense-based fragranced called 'Ubar' after the semi-mythical frankincense trading city of southern Oman.

Aromatic essences from plants are increasingly being used in aromatherapy where their specific smells are supposedly related to specific physical and psychological affects. Frankincense oils are also sold with the essential oil blended with other substances, often Jojoba oil, in small quantities to burn or use in the bath. In Somalia the chewing of low-grade frankincense resin is common to help teeth, gums and breath, with frankincense also being added to night fires to deter snakes and insects. Tears of good quality resin are utilised in Africa to treat backache, cough, polio and chest problems and also used as an incense in mosques. Frankincense and myrrh have long been used as painkillers as they apparently affect the brains opiod receptors. The ingredients sesquiterpenes-furano-eudesma-1, 3–diene and curazene produce an analgesic effect, but in the west this has now been replaced by commercially patented drugs (Tucker 1986). However, traditional medicines are making a comeback and there is increased interest in the use of frankincense and myrrh as antimicrobial agents for infections, coughs and worm infestations (Watts and Sellar 1996). Frankincense is also used in traditional medicine as an anti-inflammatory for urinary, respiratory and digestive problems. Boswellic acid, a by-product of the extraction of the distilled resin, is being used to treat arthritis.

Frankincense Tourism

Several Middle Eastern countries, notably Oman, Egypt and Yemen, actively promote tourism to sites associated with their ancient frankincense trade. Others, including some of the Gulf States such as Dubai and Abu Dhabi, include visits to the *suq* (market) where frankincense is still sold, as major attractions (Gabr 2000). Jordan and Saudi Arabia both include major cultural heritage sites (Petra and Med'ain Salah) associated with the frankincense trade, although the former is not usually marketed on that basis and the latter is seldom visited by international tourists because of visa restrictions. Although Somalia (plus Eritrea, Djibouti, Sudan and part of North Kenya) were also significant in the ancient trade and still produce substantial amounts of resin today, no archaeological sites associated with the trade are promoted for visitors since tourism access to the country is extremely limited. Both the ancient and modern trade in frankincense involved major European cities including Rome and Athens, as well as trading ports such as Alexandria, Gaza and Istanbul (Fig. 8.1). All these cities include major cultural heritage attractions but none are specific to the frankincense trade. Frankincense tourism, therefore, is really a Middle Eastern phenomenon.

It is possible to envisage how these different elements of frankincense tourism could be packaged together. Highlights of a modern tour following the ancient itinerary (Fig. 8.2) could include the Deir el Bahri temple near Luxor (Egypt), and the Sinai desert including the spectacular 6th century fortified monastery of St. Katherine at the foot of Mount Sinai which is the region's major cultural attraction (Shackley 1998). Sinai was crossed by ancient frankincense caravan routes from Gaza to Petra, and possibly by a coastal Ra's Mohammed-Aqaba route heading towards Petra (Fig. 8.1). In Oman visitors could see the contemporary frankincense harvest in Dhofar, the site of Shisr, claimed as the lost frankincense-trading city of Ubud (Fiennes 1992), and the impressive ruins of the 3rd millennium frankincense port of Khor Rori (now a World Heritage Site) and Marbat castle (Kashoob 1999). The restored castle of Nizwa is the centre of the cultural tourism trade, with nearby Bahla Fort with its 15 gates and 132 watchtowers now closed for restoration. Dhows, similar to those used in the ancient trade, are still being built at Sur harbour. Saudi Arabia has many attractions relevant to frankincense, including the Asir region in the south west, target of a campaign in 25BC by the Roman General Aelius Gallus who was sent to conquer the incense-producing regions. Najrān is close to the current Yemeni border and has a 4000 year history as a trading centre; it was the last important stop on the frankincense route before the caravans branched east or west. The most spectacular archaeological site in Saudi Arabia, Med'ain Saleh, was the model for Petra and is just beginning to appear on tourist itineraries. Yemen is currently receiving EC assistance with the development of its cultural tourism, with particular effort being targeted at combating a negative media image, improving staff training and tour guiding. The World Heritage cities of Shibam, Ṣana'ā' and Zabid were all associated with the frankincense trade and the country is marketed as a 'cross-roads of the spice, incense, myrrh and gold routes and the meeting point of the Far East and Mediterranean'. Highlights include Mārib, the capital of the kingdom of Saba which controlled Yemen for 800 years, where visitors can see the remains of the oldest dam in the world. The prosperity of Saba derived from the incense trade, and visitors can still trace the ancient route through Wadi Ḥaḍramawt and the desert city of Shibam and Shabwa, the latter being an important centre for caravans of incense which had to pay 1/10 of its loads as gifts for priests of temples. Bi'r 'Alī, now a coastal village, was once the major port through which frankincense was exported with roads leading from there to all the northern and eastern routes. However, although it is undeniable that southern Arabia already has many destinations and tourism products associated with the ancient frankincense trade, there is almost no intra-regional co-operation and a surprisingly low growth rate for international tourism, partly because of political instability (Hazbun 2000). Although frankincense tourism does exist, the routes which it follows are fragmented by political borders, and at present no initiatives exist to overcome these restrictions and emulate the precedents set by the WTO Silk Road initiative (UNESCO 1998; 2000).

Conclusion

Part of the interest in frankincense as a commodity in the 21st century comes from the fact that everything from its harvesting to utilisation seems to have changed so little over such an immense period of time. The distribution areas of the trees has not changed, nor has the method of harvesting. However, there has undeniably been a dramatic reduction in the volume of resin harvested and a significant shift in the use to which the resin is put.

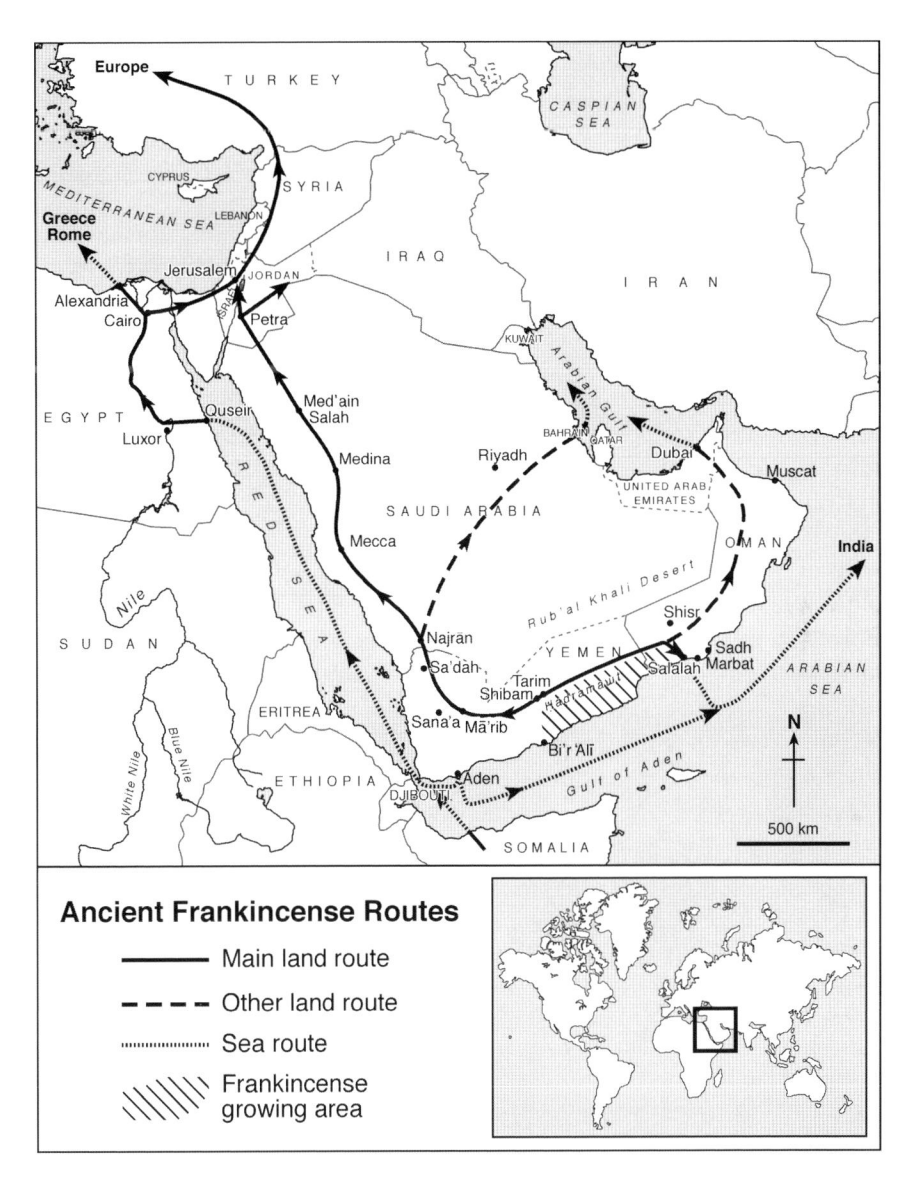

Fig. 8.1. Ancient frankincense routes.

Probably 50% of today's harvest goes towards the perfume, aromatic and medicine trade, whereas this would have been negligible in classical times. However, today's liturgical use of incense is only a fraction of that used in the classical and pre-classical worlds. Part of the fascination of frankincense comes from its exclusivity; the trees only grow in a restricted area, cannot be grown commercially and the oil cannot be artificially replicated with any degree of success. Frankincense is always associated in people's minds with the gifts of the three Kings to an infant Jesus, and thus with wealth and exclusivity. It is an intensely romantic commodity – easy to envisage camel caravans of precious resins crossing the deserts of southern Arabia under the control of Nabatean traders.

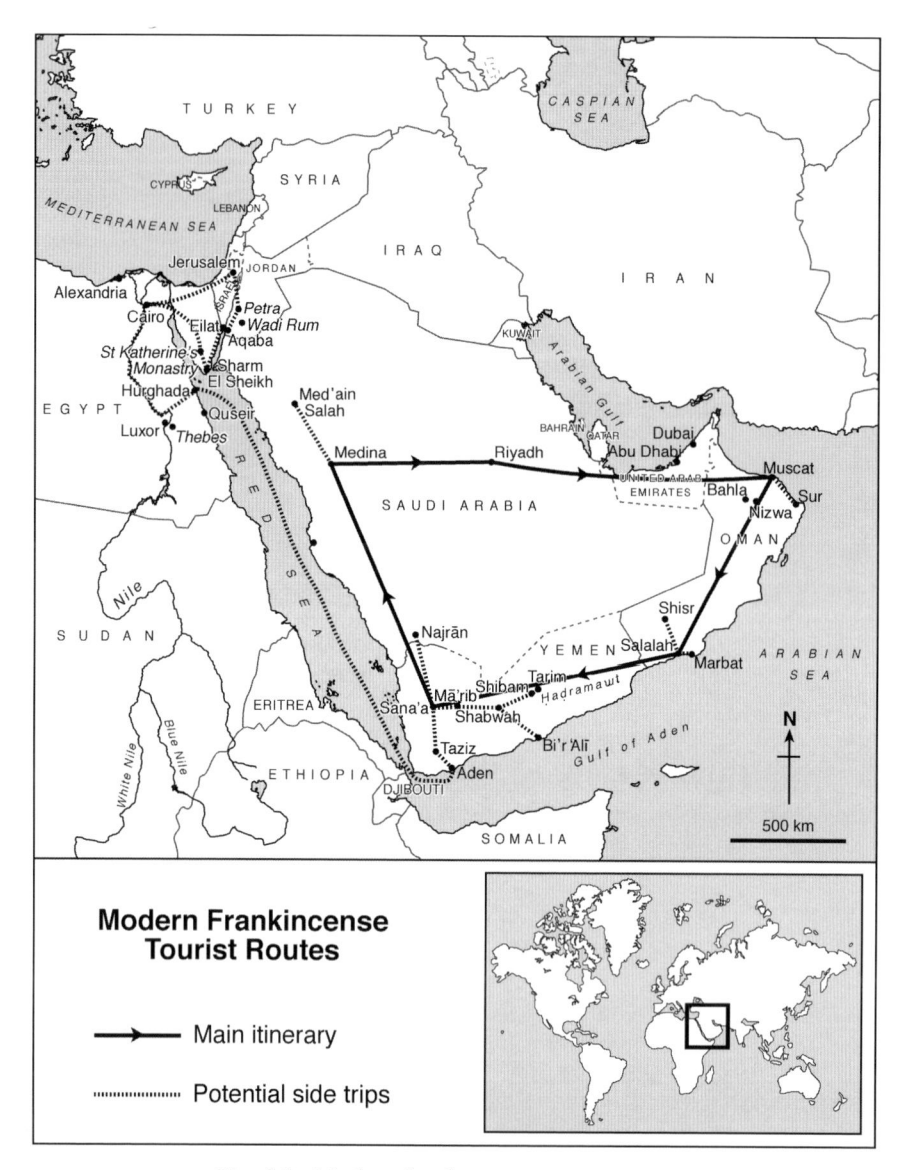

Fig. 8.2. Modern frankincense tourist routes.

This romanticism underpins the idea of frankincense tourism, offering the visitor the opportunity to explore the material remains of cities associated with that most glamorous of natural commodities. It seems unlikely that this level of interest will diminish in the future and increasingly possible that new medicinal uses will be found for frankincense resin at a time when many are turning again to traditional remedies. The frankincense trade is still big business, although now controlled by powerful cartels in the UAE, and the fact that so much of it is illegal only adds to the attraction – reinforcing an image of the fascinating and the mysterious.

Bibliography

Chiavari, G., Galletti, G.C., Piccaglia, R., and Mohamud, M.A., 1991. Differentiation between resins from *Boswellia carterii* and *Boswellia Frereana* (frankincense) of Somali origin. *Journal of Essential Oil Research,* 3 (3) 185–186.

Chaudhry, K.A., 1993. The myths of the market and the common history of late developers. *Politics and Society,* 21 (3) 245–274.

Coulter, J., 1987. *Market study for frankincense and myrrh from Somalia.* Unpublished study undertaken for the European Association for Cooperation. Chatham, UK; Natural Resources Institute.

Demissew, S., 1993. A description of some essential oil bearing plants in Ethiopia and their indigenous uses. *Journal of Essential Oil Research,* 5 (5), 465–479.

Farah, A.Y., 1988. *The milk of the Boswellia forests: frankincense production among the pastoral Somali.* Thesis, London School of Economics and Political Science, University of London UK.

Fiennes, R., 1992. *Atlantis of the Sands.* London.

Gabr, H., 2000. Heritage and architectural preservation for tourist development; reflections on the historic Bastakia distct in Dubai. In Robinson, M. Evans, N., Long, P., Sharpley, R., and Swarbrooke J. (eds). *Tourism and Heritage Relationships: global, national and local perspectives.* Gateside.197–211.

Groom, N., 1981. *Frankincense and Myrrh. A Study of the Arabian Incense Trade.* London.

Hazbun, W., 2000. Enclave orientalism; the state, tourism, and the politics of post-national development in the Arab World. In Robinson, M. Evans, N., Long, P., Sharpley, R., and Swarbrooke J. (eds) *Management, Marketing and the Political Economy of Travel and Tourism.* Gateside. 191–207.

Kashoob, A., 1999. *Towards a solution for the seasonality problem in Dhofar* unpublished MSc Thesis, School of Management Studies for the Service Sector, University of Surrey.

Sullivan, J.F., 1918. *The externals of the catholic church.* New York.

Tucker, A.O., 1986. Frankincense and myrrh. *Economic Botany,* 40(4), 425–433.

UNESCO 1998. http://www.unesco.org/culture/silkroads/html_eng/exhibition.htm.

UNESCO 2000. http://www.unesco.org/whc/reporting/arab.

Verghese, J., 1988. *Olibanum* in focus. *Perfumer and Flavorist,* 13 (1), 1–12.

Wahab, S.M.A., Aboutabl, E.A., El-Zalabani, S.M., Fouad, H.A. de Pooter, H. L. and El-Fallaha, B., 1987. The essential oil of *olibanum. Planta Medica,* 53 (4), 382–384.

Watt, M. and Sellar, W., 1996. *Frankincense and Myrrh.* Saffron Walden.